Minicomputers
and Large Scale Computations

Peter Lykos, EDITOR

Illinois Institute of Technology

A symposium sponsored by the
ACS Division of Computers in
Chemistry at the Second Joint
Conference of the Chemical Institute
of Canada and the American Chemical
Society, Montreal, Canada,
June 1, 1977.

ACS SYMPOSIUM SERIES **57**

AMERICAN CHEMICAL SOCIETY

WASHINGTON, D. C.   1977

Library of Congress CIP Data

Minicomputers and large scale computations.
(ACS symposium series; 57 ISSN 0097-6156)

Includes bibliographical references and index.

1. Chemistry—Data processing—Congresses. 2. Minicomputers—Congresses.
I. Lykos, Peter George, 1927–   . II. American Chemical Society. Division of Computers in Chemistry. III.
Joint Conference of the Chemical Institute of Canada and
the American Chemical Society, 2nd, Montreal, Quebec,
1977. IV. Series: American Chemical Society. ACS symposium series; 57.

QD39.3.E46M56	542'.8	77-15932
ISBN 0-8412-0387-3	ACSMC8 57	1–239

ACS Symposium Series

Robert F. Gould, *Editor*

FOREWORD

The ACS Symposium Series was founded in 1974 to provide a medium for publishing symposia quickly in book form. The format of the Series parallels that of the continuing Advances in Chemistry Series except that in order to save time the papers are not typeset but are reproduced as they are submitted by the authors in camera-ready form. As a further means of saving time, the papers are not edited or reviewed except by the symposium chairman, who becomes editor of the book. Papers published in the ACS Symposium Series are original contributions not published elsewhere in whole or major part and include reports of research as well as reviews since symposia may embrace both types of presentation.

CONTENTS

vii

PREFACE

This symposium on "Minicomputers and Large Scale Computations" brings together a representative set of reports of concrete experiences, including cost analyses, in which computer users have turned to so-called minicomputers to handle computational problems which just a few years ago could have been handled by only large scale scientific computers.

This book should be viewed as a snapshot of a dynamic situation changing fairly rapidly in time. The chapters have been arranged in sequence starting with the smallest instrument (a hand-held programmable calculator) to the largest (a dual large scale, or super, minicomputer). Several superposed trends are operating, and it is important to sort them out so that one can intelligently analyze how to best approach a particular set of computational needs.

In its first manifestation with widespread use (the DEC PDP-8) the minicomputer was physically small (made to fit in a standard instrument rack), slow in cycle time, and small in main memory size; it had a short list of machine instructions, a short word length, minimal software support, and virtually no peripherals except a teletypewriter. Its target users were experimenters interested in automated data collection and reduction and those concerned with real-time control applications, somtimes in nonfriendly physical environments. Gradually the minicomputer evolved in several directions including toward the large scale or "super" minicomputer typified by the last four chapters (13–16). The super minicomputer class includes machines with 16-, 24-, and 32-bit word-based architectures, fast floating-point arithmetic (achieved in different ways), virtual memories, a full range of peripheral devices (mass storage, printers, card readers, etc.), and sophisticated multi-user supporting operating systems, compilers, interpreters, and data-base management systems. Indeed the PRIME 400 even has a super-speed small (or cache) component of the main fast memory similar to the IBM 370/195. Thus the full power of the superscientific computer of 10 years ago is now available for an order of magnitude less the costs of purchase, maintenance, and operation. In addition, the space and air conditioning requirements have been reduced to that of an ordinary small research laboratory.

Even the modern laboratory minicomputer, similar in many respects to the venerable PDP-8, is being pressed into service as a scientific calculator. Chapters 2, 3, 6, 7, 8, 10, and 11 present examples in which the computer program was reorganized compared with the way in which it would have been done for a large scale scientific computer. The small main memory forced the users to (a) make more, and more clever, use of disk storage where available, (b) search for non-conventional algorithms, in some cases more specifically problem-oriented, and (c) in two cases minimize the need for floating-point operations by scaling, and by table searching and interpolation. Of special concern here, because of the long (wall clock) running times, is the finite probability of machine failure.

Chapters 4, 5, 6, and 16 explore the trade-offs involved in using minicomputers for portions of the calculations and conventional large scale computers for the remainder. Indeed Chapter 4 introduces APL (a mathematically oriented language not so widely used by chemists as the ubiquitous FORTRAN) and also a feature of the IBM 5100 APL processor which permits the unsophisticated (i.e., higher level language) programmer to build in details of communication protocol easily where optimal distribution of computing tasks among several processors is sought.

Another trend is toward the design of special-purpose processors intended to be enslaved to conventional processors. The array processor AP-120B, as an add-on to the Harris 6024/4 at the National Astronomy and Ionosphere Center, has handled highly organized floating-point operations at 12.4 megaflops (millions of floating-point operations per second) which has been compared with the 5-megaflop CDC 7600 and the 15-megaflop ILLIAC IV (*see* Wolin, L., "Procedure Evaluates Computers for Scientific Applications," *Computer Design* (1976) **15**, 93 for a more detailed comparison of minicomputers and current large scale scientific systems). Chapters 5, 8, 10, and 12 use specialized hardware to hardware-tailor a computer system to the requirements of a specific class of problems.

The quantum of computational power is shrinking in physical size and cost to the point where the choice, as well as the computer, is in the hands of the individual user. The microprocessor has burst upon the scene. The mushrooming of over 400 retail computer hobby outlets has been sparked by the large scale integrated circuit (LSI) computer-on-a-chip and the growing personal computing market. The hand-held electronic calculator has decreased in physical size to the limit that conventional computer input–output can tolerate—namely the resolving power of the human eye and the physical size of human fingers. Chapter 1 illustrates attache-case-portable programmable computers with off-line storage and built-in printer capability. However, a parallel limiting process also becomes evident, i.e., the decreasing level of software support and the need for programs in machine language. For the conventional computer (the serial processor) the increasing sophistication of LSI chip circuitry and the decreasing cost per bit of corresponding large scale non-electromechanical mass memory makes it more and more likely that the large-scale conventional computer system of today will be replaced by a small inexpensive package that can support today's complex software (*see* Turn, Rein, "Computers in the 1980's," Columbia University Press, 1974). But by the time that happens, who will want it?

Because of the decreasing size and cost of individual processors, computer designers can contemplate highly concurrent multiprocessor devices. However, such devices with so many degrees of freedom available in their design must be problem-oriented. In addition, the algorithms developed to solve problems on conventional serial processors are no longer optimal for more complex computer systems. The recent symposium on High Speed Computer and Algorithm Organization (proceedings to be published by Academic Press, late 1977) revealed that the surface has hardly been scratched in that regard. Furthermore, the computer designer is severely restricted because historically the user has accepted the designer's product passively and adapted his problems and algorithms to the computer rather than vice versa.

Perhaps the most important trend of all is that the awesome computer mystique is gradually being supplanted by a more healthy attitude on the part of a computer-acculturated and increasingly demanding community of users who are discovering the Golden Rule, namely, "He who has the gold . . . rules."

Chicago, Illinois
September 1977

PETER LYKOS

Microcomputer Plus Saul'yev Method Solves Simultaneous Partial Differential Equations of the Diffusion Type with Highly Nonlinear Boundary Conditions

R. KENNETH WOLFE, DAVID C. COLONY and RONALD D. EATON

University of Toledo, Toledo, OH 43606

Important today is the ability to answer rapidly and inexpensively the complex questions posed by an increasingly complex society. Mathematics has played an important role in scientific problem solving. Practical solutions today rely heavily on computerized numerical approaches.

This paper extends for use with the Hewlett-Packard 67/97 a numerical method due to Saul'yev (1,2). His method is very similar to the popular method of Schmidt (3) used in graphical, numerical and computer computations to study transient heat conduction problems. This paper will illustrate the use of a small minicomputer (microprocessor) to apply the Saul'yev approach to a simple case and also to a more complex case. The complex case is that of a hot solid slab bounded on one side by a cooler semi-infinite solid and exposed at the hot surface to solar radiation, cloud cover and forced or free convective heat losses to air.

A Simple Case

Consider a solid cylinder with faces fixed at two different temperatures. The sides of the cylinder are insulated. Temperature and time are then related through the extension of Fourier's law to the parabolic partial differential equation:

1)
$$\alpha \frac{\partial^2 T}{\partial x^2} = \frac{\partial T}{\partial t}$$

$T = T(x,t)$ = temperature at a point x and a time t.
x = distance, in feet
t = time in hours
α = k/pc = thermal diffusivity
k = thermal conductivity, BTU/hrft °F/ft
ρ = density, lb_m/ft^3
C = heat capacity, BTU/lb_m°F

Equation 1) is the diffusivity equation which applies to heat transfer as well as to the transport of matter. Assume that the cylinder has an initial constant temperature of T_1 and that at time zero one face is instantaneously brought to a temperature T_s. The time-temperature relationship can then be determined analytically by any of several methods to be:

2) $T(x,t) = (T_1-T_s)erf(x/\sqrt{2\alpha t}) + T_s$

   erf(z) = error function

   $$= \frac{2}{\sqrt{\pi}} \int_0^z e^{-\S^2} d\S$$

   $$= 1 - \frac{exp(-z^2)}{\sqrt{\pi}} (\frac{1}{z} - \frac{1}{2z^3} + \frac{1 \cdot 3}{2^2 z^5} - \frac{1 \cdot 3 \cdot 5}{2^3 z^7} + \cdots).$$

Equation 2) is developed in most heat transfer texts. Two good references which treat this problem are Chapman (4) and Carslaw and Jaeger (5). But direct application of this analytical treatment is not often feasible. Other methods of solution are required. Approximations of the error function are given in Abramowitz and Stegun (6) which are highly accurate and very fast on computers.

Schmidt's Numerical Method Consider, as shown in Figure 1, a cylinder that is divided into hypothetical elements which are frequently called nodes in heat transfer literature. To develop Schmidt's numerical method, an energy balance around an element i is written:

[Heat flow from i-1] + [Heat flow from i+1]= Heat accumulation in i

3) $\dfrac{kA(T_{i-1} - T_i)}{\Delta x} + \dfrac{kA(T_{i+1} - T_i)}{\Delta x} = \dfrac{\rho CA\Delta x(T'_i - T_i)}{\Delta t}$

   A = area perpendicular to flow, ft^2
   Δx = element length, ft
   Δt = small increment of time, hours
   T'_i = temperature of element i at time t+ t
   T_i = temperature of element i at time t.

Rearranging equation 3) gives:

   $\dfrac{k\Delta t}{\rho C\Delta x^2} [(T_{i-1} - T_i) + (T_{i+1} - T_i)] = T'_i - T_i$

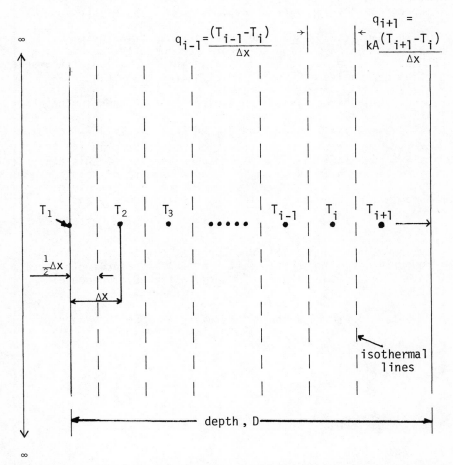

Figure 1. *Imaginary division of slab with finite depth and large surface dimensions in relation to the depth*

4) $\alpha N T_{i-1} + (1-2\alpha N)T_i + \alpha N T_{i+1} = T_i'$,

$$\alpha = \text{thermal diffusivity,}$$
$$N = \Delta t / \Delta x^2$$

For numerical stability, the coefficients of all temperature variables must be non-negative. This means as far as equation 4) is concerned that N must be selected such that $\alpha N \leq 1/2$.

The Saul'yev Method   The Saul'yev method was originally created to conserve computer memory for computerized numerical methods. The method is based upon an interpretation of the second partial derivative $\frac{\partial^2 T}{\partial x^2}$ which results from evaluating the finite partial derivatives first in one direction and then in the other. This process is called alternating direction. The alternating direction process is made clearer, perhaps, by the following:

5) $\dfrac{\partial^2 T}{\partial x^2} = \dfrac{\partial (\frac{\partial T}{\partial x})}{\partial x}$

$$\frac{(\frac{\partial T}{\partial x})_{x,t} - (\frac{\partial T}{\partial x})_{x-\Delta x, t+\Delta t}}{\Delta x} \quad \text{Forward Difference}$$

$$\frac{(\frac{\partial T}{\partial x})_{x,t+2\Delta t} - (\frac{\partial T}{\partial x})_{x-\Delta x, t+\Delta t}}{\Delta x} \quad \begin{array}{l}\text{Backward}\\ \text{Difference}\end{array}$$

Returning to equation 4) and using the Saul'yev concept:

Forward Difference

6) $\alpha N \Delta x \left\{ \left(\dfrac{T_{i-1}' - T_i'}{\Delta x} \right)_{t+\Delta t} + \left(\dfrac{T_{i+1} - T_i}{\Delta x} \right)_t \right\} = T_{i,t+\Delta t}' - T_{i,t}$

Backward Difference

7) $\alpha N \Delta x \left\{ \left(\dfrac{T_{i-1} - T_i}{\Delta x} \right)_{t+\Delta t} + \left(\dfrac{T_{i+1}' - T_i'}{\Delta x} \right)_{t+2\Delta t} \right\}$

$$= T_{i,t+2\Delta t}' - T_{i,t+\Delta t}$$

Algebraically manipulating 6) and 7) to solve for $T_i^!$ gives:

Forward Difference

8) $\alpha N(T_{i-1}^! + T_{i+1}) + (1-\alpha N)T_i = (1+\alpha N)T_i^!$

Backward Difference

9) $\alpha N(T_{i-1} + T_{i+1}^!) + (1-\alpha N)T_i = (1+\alpha N)T_i^!$

Equations 8) and 9) are unconditionally stable with no restrictions for stability on the numerical values of αN.

As an illustration, consider a semi-infinite solid with a temperature of 100°F. At time zero, the face is brought instantaneously to 300°F. Assume that we desire the temperature of the face at t = one hour. The solid has the following thermophysical properties:

    k = 2
    ρ = 100
    C = .25
    α = .08

Equations 8) and 9) can be used to compute a table of temperatures at different times. For these computations, use the following parameters:

    Δt = 5 min. = 1/12 hr.
    Δx = 2 inches = 1/6 ft.
     α = .08
    αN = $(.08 \times 1/12)/(1/6)^2$ = 0.240

The total depth is 24 inches and the total number of nodes is made equal to 13.

Table I gives the computed results. For this computation, the temperature at 24 inches is considered constant at 100°F. This assumption is confirmed by comparing the computed results with the analytical solution.

The analytical results are also shown in Table I. The maximum difference between the analytical and the numerical results is 2°F at t=1.0 hr. This difference seems in itself to represent a quite acceptable approximation, but it should be noted that its magnitude is exaggerated by rounding off to the nearest degree.

The rows of numerical results are labeled by $n\Delta t=t$. For odd values of n, equation 8) is used while for even values, equation 9) is required. The numbers (temperatures) in each row correspond to the memory registers in the HP 67/97 computer. By examining equations 8) and 9), it can be seen that new registers are not required to store new results. This is one major advantage of the

Table I. Numerical Time–Temperature Results for Saul'yev Method on HP 67/97 Compared with Analytical Results

x (inches)	0	2	4	6	8	10	12	14	16	18	20	21	22	24
i (node #)	0	1	2	3	4	5	6	7	8	9	10	11	12	13
t=0 T°F	300	100	100	100	100	100	100	100	100	100	100	100	100	100
Numerical Results (Equations 8 and 9), table entries are in °F														
t=1Δt	300	139	107	101	100	100	100	100	100	100	100	100	100	100
t=2Δt	300	165	113	102	100	100	100	100	100	100	100	100	100	100
t=3Δt	300	181	124	106	102	100	100	100	100	100	100	100	100	100
t=4Δt	300	194	132	109	102	101	100	100	100	100	100	100	100	100
t=5Δt	300	203	141	114	104	101	100	100	100	100	100	100	100	100
t=6Δt	300	211	419	118	106	102	100	100	100	100	100	100	100	100
t=7Δt	300	216	156	123	108	103	101	100	100	100	100	100	100	100
t=8Δt	300	222	162	127	110	103	101	100	100	100	100	100	100	100
t=9Δt	300	225	167	131	113	105	102	101	100	100	100	100	100	100
t=10Δt	300	230	172	135	115	106	102	101	100	100	100	100	100	100
t=11Δt	300	232	177	139	118	107	103	101	100	100	100	100	100	100
t=12Δt = 1 hr	300	235	181	143	120	109	103	101	100	100	100	100	100	100
Analytical Results (Equation 2), °F														
t=1 hr	300	235	181	142	119	107	102	101	100	100	100	100	100	100

Saul'yev method. Other methods, such as Schmidt's, require the use of new registers for this purpose.

It can be stated that the agreement between the analytical results and the numerical results is excellent.

Since the Saul'yev method is an alternating direction method, an even number of rows is required for accurate results. Each pair of rows is called a pass; the total number of passes, P, is equal to $t/(2\Delta t)$.

Programming the HP 67/97 to obtain the results in Table I, with printout of intermediate results, required 56 program steps out of 224 available. Two memory registers were used to store αN and to maintain a count of the number of rows computed.

A More Complex Problem

In this section we examine a more complex case and develop some extended formulas. Figure 2 shows a recent situation where the authors (7) needed to provide a method for field engineers to predict time-temperature cooling curves for hot asphaltic surfaces placed during highway construction, in order to support decisions on whether or not to allow paving work during marginal weather conditions.

Figure 2 also shows the various factors which influence the heat transfer and the temperature-time history of a hot pavement layer. The mathematical model which is applicable to this situation is summarized below:

Governing Equation for Hot Layer

10)
$$\alpha_1 \frac{\partial^2 T}{\partial x^2} = \frac{\partial T}{\partial t}$$

Governing Equation for Cold Base

11)
$$\alpha_2 \frac{\partial^2 U}{\partial x^2} = \frac{\partial U}{\partial x}$$

Surface Energy Balance

12)
$$k_1 \frac{\partial T(0,t)}{\partial x} = - aMH + .65v^{.8}(T(0,t) - T_{air})$$
$$+ \varepsilon\sigma(T(0,t) + 460)^4$$

Hot Layer - Cold Layer Interface

13) $T(\ell,t) = U(\ell,t)$ contact condition

14) $k_1 \frac{\partial T(\ell,t)}{\partial x} = k_2 \frac{\partial U(\ell,t)}{\partial x}$ energy balance condition at medium A to medium B interface

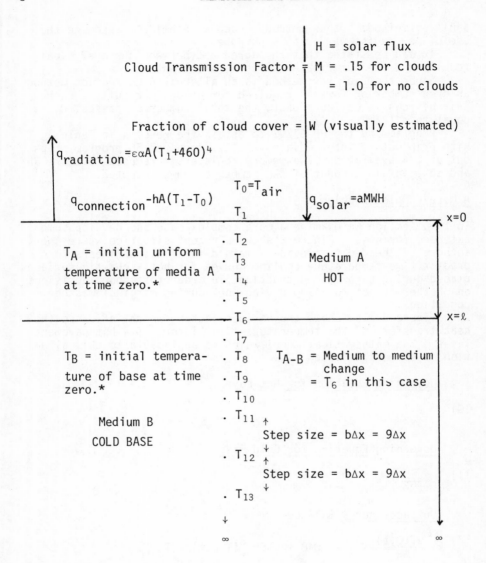

* Temperatures T_i are specified at all node points at time zero.

Figure 2.   *Hot slab on cold semi-infinite base with surface radiation, convection, and insolation*

Initial Conditions

15) $T(x,0) = T_0 \qquad 0 \le x \le \ell$

16) $U(x,0) = U_0 \qquad \ell \le x \le \infty$

The above set of equations must be considered simultaneously. Analytical solution of such a set is impossible. Among other reasons, analytical solution is rendered impossible by the presence of the T^4 radiation term. To obtain results useful in practical application, more manageable methods are mandatory.

Numerical methods exist for the above set of equations based upon Schmidt's conditionally stable, explicit method. In order to utilize an HP 67/97 computer, the Saul'yev method is the method of choice. To apply the Saul'yev approach, his method must be extended to handle the interface conditions 13) and 14), and the surface energy balance 12). Also, a way to extend the total depth is required.

Generalized Change   This section develops the equation to describe a change in Δx, a change in medium, or a change in both conditions.

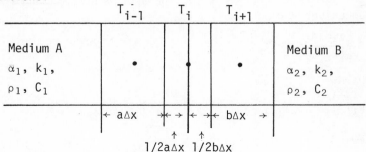

The above diagram depicts the generalized change interface.   The energy balance equation is:

17) $\dfrac{k_1 A(T_{i-1} - T_i)}{a\Delta x} + \dfrac{k_2 A(T_{i+1} - T_i)}{b\Delta x}$

$$= \left(\frac{(a\rho_1 C_1 + b\rho_2 C_2)A\Delta x}{2}\right)\left(\frac{T_i' - T_i}{\Delta t}\right)$$

18) $F\left(\dfrac{k_1}{a}(T_{i-1} - T_i) + \dfrac{k_2}{b}(T_{i+1} - T_i)\right) + T_i = T_i'$

  (Forward)   (Backward)

19) $F = \dfrac{2\alpha_1\alpha_2\ N}{a\alpha_2 k_1 + b\alpha_1 k_2}$, $N = \dfrac{\Delta t}{\Delta x^2}$

Now give 18) a backward and forward interpretation:

Forward

20) $F(\dfrac{k_1}{a}\ T'_{i-1} + \dfrac{k_2}{b}\ T_{i+1}) + (1 - Fk_2/b)T_i = (1 + Fk_1/a)\ T'_i$

Backward

21) $F(\dfrac{k_1}{a}\ T_{i-1} + \dfrac{k_2}{b}\ T'_{i+1}) + (1 - Fk_1/a)T_i = (1 + Fk_2/b)\ T'_i$.

When medium A and medium B are identical and a=b, equations 20) and 21) reduce to equations 6) and 7).

Medium to Medium Change   Equations 20) and 21) can be specialized for the case where there is a change in the media but the step size, Δt, is maintained identical on both sides of the interface. For this case a=b=1 and the appropriate backward-forward equations are:

22) $F = \dfrac{2\alpha_1\alpha_2 N}{\alpha_1 k_2 + \alpha_2 k_1}$

Forward

23) $F(k_1 T'_{i-1} + k_2 T_{i+1}) + (1-Fk_2)T_i = (1+Fk_1)T'_i$

Backward

24) $F(k_1 T_{i-1} + k_2 T'_{i+1}) + (1-Fk_1)T_i = (1+Fk_2)T'_i$

Change in Step Size Δx To improve accuracy of the computation, the step size and the time increment Δt can be made smaller. Where there is a rapid change in the temperature, it is wise to use small values of Δt and Δx. In cases where there is a relatively mild change in temperature, the step size Δx can be made larger. In cases where the problem includes both rapid changes and mild changes it is appropriate to change the step size. For the problem depicted in Figure 2, the change in Δx will occur in the colder medium with $\alpha_1 = \alpha_2$ and $k_1 = k_2$. For this situation, equations 20) and 21) become:

Forward

25) $\dfrac{2N\alpha}{1+b}$ $(T_{i-1} + \dfrac{T_{i+1}}{b}) + (1 - \dfrac{2\alpha N}{b(1+b)})T_i = (1 + \dfrac{2\alpha N}{(1+b)})\,T_i'$

Backward

26) $\dfrac{2N\alpha}{1+b}$ $(T_{i-1} + \dfrac{T_{i+1}'}{b}) + (1 - \dfrac{2\alpha N}{(1+b)})\,T_i = (1 + \dfrac{2\alpha N}{b(1+b)})\,T_i'$

b = the step size multiplier, $\Delta x_{new} = b\ \Delta x_{old}$

Interface Temperature When a hot solid and a cold surface are placed together at time zero, an interface temperature must be assigned. The literature on this subject generally recommends an arithmetic average. This value is obviously incorrect and a better assignment is required.

The literature (4,5) contains the mathematical solution for this case, which is:

28) $T(x,t) = U_1 + \dfrac{T_1 - U_1}{1+r}\ (1 + r\ \mathrm{erf}(z))$

$T(x,t)$ = temperature at x and t of solid 1
T_1 = initial temperature of solid 1
U_1 = initial temperature of solid 2
$r = \dfrac{k_2}{k_1}\ (\dfrac{a_1}{a_2})^{1/2}$, subscripts 1 and 2 refer to

solids 1 and 2

$z = \dfrac{x}{2(\alpha,t)^{1/2}}$

$\mathrm{erf}(z)$ = see equation 2
x = 0 at the solid to solid interface
as $t \rightarrow 0$, $T(0, t \rightarrow 0)$
$T(x,t) = \dfrac{T_1 + rU_1}{1+r}$

When the two media have the same thermophysical properties, r=1 and

$T(0,0) = \dfrac{T_1 + U_1}{1+1} = 1/2(T_1 + U_1)$

It is clear from the foregoing equation that the arithmetic average correctly represents the interface temperature only when the thermophysical properties of the hot and cold media are equal.

Surface Equations The surface of a hot laid asphaltic concrete pavement layer is acted upon by several environmental
influences. These influences include solar radiation (insolation)
and cloud cover along with air velocity and turbulence. Solar
radiation varies in intensity with time of day and the season of
the year, while wind conditions are even more variable. Solar
radiation can be measured with a pyrheliometer, but in practice,
the equations and tables in the ASHRAE Handbook of Fundamentals
(8) can be used to accurately determine the solar flux.
    The effect of cloud cover is perhaps more difficult to eval-
uate since height, thickness, water droplet size and percentage of
cloud cover all influence the transmission of solar energy.
    For the present purposes, the cloud cover is assumed either to
exist or not to exist. If it exists, solar radiation is reduced by
85% in all computations.
    The following diagram depicts the surface element and node
construction appropriate to the problem under discussion:

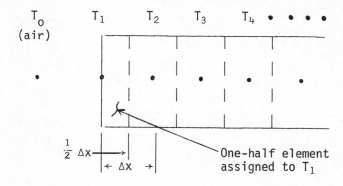

The energy balance at the surface element yields:

- radiation loss + solar gain + gain from T_2 - connective loss
                    = energy gain/loss in T_1 element

29) $-\varepsilon\sigma A(T_1+460)^4 + aMAH + \dfrac{kA(T_2-T_1)}{\Delta x} - hA(T_1-T_{air})$

$$= 1/2A\Delta x\rho C\dfrac{(T_1'-T_1)}{\Delta x}$$

Rearranging terms gives:

30) $\dfrac{2h\alpha N\Delta x}{k}(T_0-T_1) + 2\,N(T_2-T_1)$

$+ \dfrac{2a\alpha NM\Delta xH}{k} - \dfrac{2\varepsilon\sigma\alpha N\Delta x}{k}(T_1+460)^4 + T_1$

$=T_1'$

Forward and backward interpretations of the above are:

Forward

31) $\dfrac{2\alpha N\Delta x}{k}$ $(hT_0' + aMH - \varepsilon\sigma(T_1+460)^4)$

$$+ 2\alpha N(T_2-T_1) + T_1 = (1 + \frac{2h\alpha N\Delta x}{k}) T_1'$$

Backward

32) $\dfrac{2\alpha N\Delta x}{k}$ $(hT_0 + aMH - \varepsilon\sigma(T_1+460)^4)$

$$+ (1 - \frac{2\alpha N\Delta\ h}{k}) T_1 + 2\alpha NT_2' = (1+2\alpha N)T_1'$$

In equations 31) and 32) the radiation term, $(T_1+460)^4$, has not been applied in a forward and backward sense, since the solution for T_1' would otherwise be unduly complicated. Tests show this omission to yield negligible errors. The largest discrepancy occurs in T_1 only during the early minutes after time zero.

Solution of Problem in Figure 2   The above equations provide a means for solving the problem depicted in Figure 2. To further illustrate this problem, the following data are hypothesized:

Environmental conditions

Solar radiation H = 200 BTU/hr (obtained from ASHRAE
   Handbook of Fundamental Tables (8).
M = 1 or .15, assume cloud cover with M=.15
Air velocity = 10 MPH
Air Temp. = 80°F
h = convection coefficient
α = .65v·^{8}= .65(10)·^{8}= 4.10
Air temperature = 70°F
Surface radiation = $\varepsilon\sigma(T+460)^4$ = .95 x 1.731·$10^{-9}(T+460)^4$
   = 1.644·10^{-9} $(T+460)^4$

Hot Solid	Cold Solid

Hot Solid

Absorptivity a for solar flux
   = .85
Emissivity   for solar
   radiation = .95
Initial temperature = 300°F
k = 1.5 ρ = 150
C = .25 α = 0.04
Δx= 0.5" = $\dfrac{1}{30}$ ft.
Elapsed time = 15 minutes
Δt =

Cold Solid

Initial temperature = 70°F
k = 3
C = .25
ρ = 150
α = 0.08
Δx from node 5 to node 10 = .5 in
   Δx from node 10 to node 13
      = 9 x .4 = 3.6 inches

Total depth of base = 1.6 + 10.8 = 12.4 inches.
    Table II gives the results of computations using the HP 67/97
at one minute increments up to 15 minutes. These results have
been compared with highly accurate results from an IBM 360 and
they agree within 2°F at all points.

Program

The program to obtain the results in Table II took 223 steps out
of an available 224 steps. The authors have made several hundred
computations using the HP67 or HP97. To these authors, the
results are extremely satisfactory. The computations are convenient and the method is generally superior to other approaches.
The programs are appended to this paper. Current purchase price
of an HP67 computer is $400 and that of an HP97 is $750. No
hardware other than one of the foregoing was needed to perform
the complex heat transfer calculations which have been described.
Monthly maintenance cost of these instruments can be considered
negigible.

Conclusion

Examples have been presented which demonstrate the usefulness of
a small, handheld computer for performing numerical solutions of
simultaneous partial differential equations of the diffusion type.
Some mathematical development, or extension, of a standard
numerical solution method was required to adapt the method to a
small computer. But the results obtained compare very closely to
those yielded by an IBM 360 computer; and the use of a small
computer makes possible rational decisions on the site in real
time by a construction project engineer. It has not been possible,
hitherto, to support "go - no go" decisions at a paving site with
such detailed analysis of environmental data.

Acknowledgements

The authors wish to thank Mr. Leon Talbert and Mr. Willis Gibboney
of the Department of Transportation, State of Ohio, for their
assistance and encouragement.
    The research reported in this paper was supported in part by
the Department of Transportation, State of Ohio, and the U.S.
Department of Transportation, Federal Highway Administration.

Table II. Temperature Profile of Problem in Figure 2 as a Function of Time

Inches from Surface

Interface

t/x	0.0"	0.4"	0.8"	1.2"	1.6"	2.0"	2.4"	2.8"	3.2"	3.6"	7.2"	10.8"	14.4"
0	300	300	300	300	300	165	70	70	70	70	70	70	70
1min	275	293	296	288	250	156	111	85	76	72	70	70	70
2min	264	283	286	271	228	158	124	99	84	76	71	70	70
3	256	274	275	256	216	157	131	108	91	80	73	70	70
4	247	263	263	245	208	159	135	113	97	84	75	70	70
5	238	254	253	235	201	159	137	117	101	88	77	70	70
6	230	244	243	226	196	158	139	120	104	91	80	70	70
7	222	235	234	219	192	157	140	122	107	93	82	70	70
8	214	227	226	212	188	157	140	124	109	96	84	71	70
9	207	219	219	207	184	155	140	125	111	98	87	71	70
10	200	212	212	201	180	154	140	126	112	100	89	71	70
11	193	205	205	195	177	153	140	126	113	101	91	71	70
12	188	199	199	190	174	152	139	127	114	103	93	72	70
13	183	193	194	186	171	150	139	127	115	104	95	72	70
14	177	187	189	182	168	149	138	127	116	106	96	72	70
15	172	182	184	178	165	147	138	127	117	107	98	73	70

Time in Minutes

APPENDIX A
User Instructions

STEP	INSTRUCTIONS	INPUT DATA/UNITS	KEYS		OUTPUT DATA/UNITS
1.	Input side 1 and side 2				
2.	Enter problem data and constants:	10		A	10
	Time span (seconds)	t		R/S	11
	Medium 1 thermal diffusivity(ft^2/hr)	α_1		R/S	12
	Medium 1 thermal conductivity (BTU/ft-hr-°F)	k_1		R/S	13
	Medium 2 thermal diffusivity	α_2		R/S	14
	Medium 2 thermal conductivity	k_2		R/S	15
	Step size (inches)	Δx		R/S	16
	Node number of medium to medium change + 10			R/S	17
	Air velocity (MPH)	v		R/S	18
	Solar flux times cloud factor (BTU/hr-ft^2)	MH		R/S	19
	Number of back-and-forth passes	P		R/S	20
	Temperature of air(°F)	$T_0=T_{air}$		R/S	21
	Temperature of asphalt (°F)	T_{asp}		R/S	22
	Temperature of base (°F)	T_{base}		R/S	23
3.	Set F2 if h=0.53 $v^{0.8}$, default h=0.65 $v^{0.8}$		f	STF	
			2		
4.	Calculate parameters required for Saul'yev			B	
	program				
5.	Allocate temperatures to R10 to R23			C	
6.	Change to Saul'yev program.				
7.	Input side 1 and side 2 after using Saul'yev				
	program				
8.	Determine average temperature of Medium A layer			E	T_{avg}
9.	Print T_0, T_1, T_2, ..., T_{13}, printing stops			D	
	with error displayed.				

STEP	KEY ENTRY	KEY CODE	COMMENTS	STEP	KEY ENTRY	KEY CODE	COMMENTS
001	*LBLA	21 11	SEQUENTIAL DATA	057	RCL2	36 02	
002	STOi	35 45	ENTRY-enter R#,	058	x	-35	
003	XᵢI	16-41	press A, R# dis-	059	+	-55	
004	RCLi	36 45	played, enter data	060	÷	-24	
005	R/S	51	into Rx, press R/S,	061	ISZI	16 26 46	$\frac{2\alpha_1\alpha_2 N}{\alpha_1 k_2 + \alpha_2 k_1} = F$
006	STOi	35 45	next R# displayed,	062	STOi	35 45	
007	*LBLa	21 16 11	continue.	063	RCL6	36 06	
008	ISZI	16 26 46		064	ISZI	16 26 46	(node # + 10) of
009	9	09		065	STOi	35 45	solid-solid inter-
010	CHS	-22		066	ISZI	16 26 46	face
011	XᵢI	16-41		067	1	01	
012	GTOi	22 45		068	.	-62	
013	*LBLB	21 12	COMPUTE CONSTANTS	069	3	03	
014	FᵢS	16-51	FOR SAUL'YEV PROGRAM	070	5	05	
015	RCL0	36 00		071	STOi	35 45	h = 1.35
016	RCL5	36 05		072	3	03	
017	XᵢY	53		073	RCL7	36 07	OR
018	÷	-24		074	X>Y?	16-34	
019	RCL9	36 09		075	GSB6	23 06	h = 0.65 v$^{0.8}$
020	÷	-24		076	RCL8	36 08	
021	5	05		077	ISZI	16 26 46	
022	0	00		078	STOi	35 45	NH (as entered)
023	÷	-24		079	RCLi	36 01	
024	STOE	35 15	$N = \dfrac{\Delta t}{\Delta x^2}$	080	RCL5	36 05	N = cloud cover
025	1	01		081	x	-35	factor = 1.0 or
026	0	00	$= \dfrac{t}{2P\Delta x^2} \quad \dfrac{Hr}{ft^2}$	082	RCLE	36 15	0.15
027	STOi	35 45		083	x	-35	
028	RCL9	36 09		084	RCL2	36 02	
029	STOi	35 45	P = # of passes	085	÷	-24	
030	RCLE	36 15		086	0	06	
031	RCLi	36 01		087	÷	-24	
032	x	-35		088	ISZI	16 26 46	$\dfrac{2\alpha_1\Delta t}{k_1\Delta x} = R$
033	ISZI	16 26 46		089	STOi	35 45	
034	STOi	35 45	$\alpha_1 N$	090	RCLi	36 01	
035	RCL2	36 02		091	RCL3	36 03	
036	ISZI	16 26 46		092	÷	-24	
037	STOi	35 45	k_1	093	√x	54	
038	RCLE	36 15		094	RCL4	36 04	
039	RCL3	36 03		095	RCL2	36 02	
040	x	-35		096	÷	-24	
041	ISZI	16 26 46		097	x	-35	
042	STOi	35 45	$\alpha_2 N$	098	STOE	35 15	r
043	RCL4	36 04		099	RCL0	36 13	
044	ISZI	16 26 46		100	x	-35	
045	STOi	35 45	k_2	101	RCLE	36 12	
046	RCLE	36 15		102	+	-55	
047	RCL1	36 01		103	RCLE	36 15	
048	RCL3	36 03		104	ENT1	-21	
049	x	-35		105	1	01	
050	x	-35		106	+	-55	
051	2	02		107	÷	-24	
052	x	-35		108	STOD	35 14	$T_{interface}$
053	RCLi	36 01		109	FᵢS	16-51	
054	RCL4	36 04		110	RTN	24	
055	x	-35		111	*LBL6	21 06	
056	RCL3	36 03		112	.	-62	

REGISTERS									
0 P	1 $\alpha_1 N$	2 k_1	3 $\alpha_2 N$	4 k_2	5 F	6 NODE$_{int}$	7 h	8 MH	9 R
S0 t	S1 α_1	S2 k_1	S3 α_2	S4 k_2	S5 x	S6 Node$_{int}$	S7 v	S8 MH	S9 P
A T_{air}	B $T_{asphalt}$	C T_{base}	D used	E used	I used				

Program Listing

STEP	KEY ENTRY	KEY CODE	COMMENTS	STEP	KEY ENTRY	KEY CODE	COMMENTS
113	8	08		169	X≠I	16-41	
114	Yˣ	31		170	RCLi	36 45	
115	.	-62		171	1	01	
116	6	06	$h = 0.65v^{0.8}$	172	0	00	
117	5	05		173	-	-45	
118	ENT↑	-21	OR	174	PSE	16 51	Display node number
119	.	-62	IF F2 ON	175	RCLi	36 45	
120	5	05	$h = 0.53v^{0.8}$	176	PRTX	-14	
121	3	03		177	*LBL0	21 00	
122	F2?	16 23 02		178	ISZI	16 26 46	
123	X≷Y	-41		179	*LBL1	21 01	
124	R↓	-31		180	1	01	
125	×	-35		181	5	05	
126	STOi	35 45		182	CHS	-22	
127	RTN	24		183	X≠I	16-41	
128	*LBLC	21 13	TEMPERATURES	184	GTOi	22 45	
129	1	01	DISTRIBUTED	185	*LBLE	21 15	COMPUTE AVERAGE
130	0	00	FROM R10 to R23	186	1	01	TEMPERATURE OF
131	STOI	35 46		187	1	01	LAYER 1 USING
132	RCLA	36 11		188	STOI	35 46	TRAPEZOIDAL RULE
133	STOi	35 45		189	RCLi	36 45	
134	RCLI	36 46		190	RCL6	36 06	
135	X≠I	16-41		191	STOI	35 46	
136	RCLB	36 12		192	R↓	-31	
137	ISZI	16 26 46		193	RCLi	36 45	
138	STOi	35 45		194	+	-55	
139	RCLI	36 46		195	2	02	
140	RCL6	36 06		196	÷	-24	
141	1	01		197	DSZI	16 25 46	
142	-	-45		198	R↑	16-31	
143	X=Y?	16-33		199	*LBL7	21 07	
144	GTO8	22 08		200	CLX	-51	
145	1	01		201	RCLi	36 45	
146	4	04		202	+	-55	
147	CHS	-22		203	DSZI	16 25 46	
148	X≠I	16-41		204	RCLI	36 46	
149	GTOi	22 45		205	1	01	
150	*LBL8	21 08		206	1	01	
151	RCLD	36 14		207	-	-45	
152	ISZI	16 26 46		208	X≠0?	16-42	
153	STOi	35 45		209	GTO7	22 07	
154	ISZI	16 26 46		210	R↓	-31	
155	*LBL9	21 09		211	RCL6	36 06	
156	RCLC	36 13		212	1	01	
157	STOi	35 45		213	1	01	
158	ISZI	16 26 46		214	-	-45	
159	RCLI	36 46		215	÷	-24	
160	2	02		216	RTN	24	
161	4	04		217	R/S	51	
162	X=Y?	16-33					
163	RTN	24					
164	GTO9	22 09		220			
165	*LBLD	21 14	PRINT TERMPERATURES				
166	1	01	FROM R10 to R23				
167	0	00					
168	STOI	35 46					

	LABELS				FLAGS		SET STATUS		
A Date input	B Compute T's	C Allocate	D Print/out	E T_avg	0				
a input bypass	b	c	d	e	1		FLAGS	TRIG	DISP
0 used	1 used	2	3	4	2		ON OFF		
5	6 $h=cv^{0.8}$	7 used	8 used	9 used	3		0 ☐ ☐	DEG ☐	FIX ☐

FLAGS: 0 ☐ ☐ | 1 ☐ ☐ | 2 ☐ ☐ | 3 ☐ ☐
TRIG: DEG ☐ | GRAD ☐ | RAD ☐
DISP: FIX ☐ | SCI ☐ | ENG ☐ | n ____

APPENDIX B

User Instructions

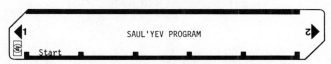

SAUL'YEV PROGRAM

Start

STEP	INSTRUCTIONS	INPUT DATA/UNITS	KEYS		OUTPUT DATA/UNITS
1	Put in data with Saul'yev input/output program				
2	Read Saul'yev program				
3	Output from Saul'yev input/output program				

STEP	KEY ENTRY	KEY CODE	COMMENTS	STEP	KEY ENTRY	KEY CODE	COMMENTS
001	*LBLA	21 11	START	057	RTH	24	END!!
002	GSBB	23 12	Calc. T_1	058	GTOA	22 11	Start next pass.
003	*LBLa	21 16 11	MAIN PROGRAM	059	*LBL3	21 03	Routine to keep
004	1	01		060	RCLI	36 46	RI negative if
005	RCLi	36 01		061	F0?	16 23 00	F0 on.
006	-	-45		062	CHS	-22	
007	STxi	35-35 45		063	STOI	35 46	
008	DSZI	16 25 46		064	ISZI	16 26 46	
009	RCLi	36 45		065	GTOa	22 16 11	
010	ISZI	16 26 46		066	*LBLB	21 12	SURFACE TEMPERA-
011	ISZI	16 26 46		067	1	01	TURE.
012	RCLi	36 45		068	0	00	
013	+	-55		069	STOI	35 46	
014	RCLi	36 01		070	RCLi	36 46	
015	x	-35		071	RCL7	36 07	
016	DSZI	16 25 46		072	x	-35	
017	ST+i	35-55 45		073	ISZI	16 26 46	
018	1	01		074	RCLi	36 45	
019	RCLi	36 01		075	4	04	
020	+	-55		076	6	06	
021	ST÷i	35-24 45		077	0	00	
022	ISZI	16 26 46	Next T_i	078	+	-55	
023	RCL6	36 06		079	4	04	
024	RCLI	36 46		080	Y^X	31	$\epsilon\sigma=1.644\cdot10^{-9}$
025	ABS	16 31		081	1	01	
026	X=Y?	16-33	$T_{interface}$?	082	.	-62	
027	GTOC	22 13		083	6	06	
028	2	02		084	4	04	
029	1	01	Step size change?	085	4	04	
030	X=Y?	16-33		086	EEX	-23	
031	GTOD	22 14		087	9	09	
032	2	02		088	CHS	-22	
033	3	03		089	x	-35	
034	RCLI	36 46	T_{13}?	090	-	-45	
035	X=Y?	16-33		091	RCL8	36 08	
036	GTO1	22 01		092	.	-62	
037	1	01		093	8	08	Solar absorptive
038	1	01		094	5	05	= 0.85
039	CHS	-22	Surface T_1?	095	x	-35	
040	X=Y?	16-33		096	+	-55	
041	GTO2	22 02		097	RCL9	36 09	
042	GTOa	22 16 11		098	x	-35	
043	*LBL1	21 01	Prepare for backward	099	RCLi	36 45	
044	SF0	16 21 00	pass, set flag 0.	100	+	-55	
045	2	02		101	RCL1	36 01	
046	2	02		102	2	02	
047	CHS	-22		103	x	-35	
048	STDI	35 46	Set RI to negative	104	ISZI	16 26 46	
049	GTOa	22 16 11	values.	105	RCLi	36 45	
050	*LBL2	21 02	END OF BACKWARD PASS	106	DSZI	16 25 46	
051	GSBB	23 12		107	F0?	16 23 00	
052	CF0	16 22 00		108	GTOb	22 16 12	
053	1	01	Reduce # of passes	109	RCLi	36 45	
054	ST-0	35-45 00	left by one.	110	-	-45	
055	RCL0	36 00		111	*LBLb	21 16 12	
056	X=0?	16-43		112	x	-35	

REGISTERS

0 P	1 $\alpha_1 N$	2 k_1	3 $\alpha_2 N$	4 k_2	5 F	6 Node$_{int}$	7 h	8 MH	9 R
S0 $T_0=T_{air}$	S1 $T_1=T_{surf}$	S2 T_2	S3 T_3	S4 T_4	S5 T_5	S6 T_6	S7 T_7	S8 T_8	S9 T_9
A T_{10}	B T_{11}	C T_{12}	D T_{13}	E used		I used			

Program Listing

STEP	KEY ENTRY	KEY CODE	COMMENTS	STEP	KEY ENTRY	KEY CODE	COMMENTS
113	+	-55		169	RCL3	36 03	
114	RCL9	36 09		170	x	-35	
115	RCL7	36 07		171	1	01	
116	x	-35		172	+	-55	
117	F0?	16 23 00		173	ST÷i	35-24 45	
118	GSB0	23 00		174	GTO3	22 03	
119	1	01		175	*LBLD	21 14	STEP SIZE CHANGE
120	+	-55		176	STO1	35 46	
121	÷	-24		177	8	08	$b^2=81$
122	STOi	35 45		178	1	01	
123	ISZi	16 26 46		179	F0?	16 23 00	
124	RTN	24		180	STx1	35-35 01	
125	*LBL0	21 00		181	9	09	b=step size
126	RCLi	36 45		182	F0?	16 23 00	multiplier=9
127	x	-35		183	1	01	
128	-	-45		184	1/x	52	
129	RCL1	36 01		185	RCL1	36 01	b+1=10
130	2	02		186	2	02	
131	x	-35		187	x	-35	
132	RTN	24		188	1	01	
133	*LBLC	21 13	MEDIUM TO MEDIUM	189	0	00	
134	STO1	35 46	TEMPERATURE	190	-	-24	
135	RCL1	36 01		191	STOE	35 15	
136	RCL3	36 03		192	x	-35	
137	STO1	35 01		193	CHS	-22	
138	X≷Y	-41		194	1	01	
139	STO3	35 03		195	+	-55	
140	1	01		196	STxi	35-35 45	
141	RCL4	36 04		197	DSZi	16 25 46	
142	RCL2	36 02		198	RCLi	36 45	
143	F0?	16 23 00		199	ISZi	16 26 46	
144	X≷Y	-41		200	ISZi	16 26 46	
145	R↓	-31		201	RCLi	36 45	
146	RCL5	36 05		202	9	09	
147	x	-35		203	÷	-24	
148	-	-45		204	+	-55	
149	STxi	35-35 45		205	RCLE	36 15	
150	DSZi	16 25 46		206	x	-35	
151	RCLi	36 45		207	DSZi	16 25 46	
152	RCL2	36 02		208	ST+i	35-55 45	
153	x	-35		209	1	01	
154	ISZi	16 26 46		210	F0?	16 23 00	
155	ISZi	16 26 46		211	9	09	
156	RCLi	36 45		212	1/x	52	
157	RCL4	36 04		213	RCLE	36 15	
158	x	-35		214	x	-35	
159	+	-55		215	1	01	
160	RCL5	36 05		216	+	-55	
161	x	-35		217	ST÷i	35-24 45	
162	DSZi	16 25 46		218	8	08	
163	ST+i	35-55 45		219	1	01	
164	RCL2	36 02		220	ST÷i	35-24 45	
165	RCL4	36 04		221	F0?	16 23 00	
166	F0?	16 23 00		222	STx1	35-35 01	
167	X≷Y	-41		223	GTO3	22 03	
168	R↓	-31		224	R/S	51	

	LABELS				FLAGS		SET STATUS		
A START	B SURFACE	C INTERFACE	D STEP SIZE	E	0		FLAGS	TRIG	DISP
a	b	c	d	e	1		ON OFF	DEG ☐	FIX ☐
0	1 SFO	2 End?	3 RI sign?	4	2		0 ☐ ☐	GRAD ☐	SCI ☐
5	6	7	8	9	^		1 ☐ ☐	RAD ☐	ENG ☐
							2 ☐ ☐		n ___
							3 ☐ ☐		

Notation

a = solar absorptivity, dimensionless

A = area, ft^2

a, b = multiplier used to change Δx step size, $\Delta x_{new} = b\Delta x_{old}$

C_ρ, C = heat capacity, BTU/lbm - °F

D = depth of hot slab, inches or feet

$F = 2\alpha_{asphalt} \alpha_{base} \; N/(\alpha_{asphalt} k_{base} + \alpha_{base} k_{asphalt})$

h = convective heat transfer coefficient between hot surface and air, BTU/ft^2 - hr - °F

H = solar heat flux, BTU/hr - ft^2

k = thermal conductivity, BTU/ft^2 - hr - (°F/ft)

k_a = thermal conductivity of hot asphalt mat, BTU/ft^2-hr-(°F/ft)

k_{base} = thermal conductivity of base upon which hot layer is placed, BTU/ft^2 - hr - (°F/ft)

L = length of a side of a square, ft

M = cloud cover factor = 1.0 with no clouds = 0.15 with clouds.

$N = \Delta t/\Delta x^2$, sec/in^2 = hr/ft^2, used in finite difference equations

P = number of backward and forward passes used in Saul'yev method (one forward computation plus one backward computation equal <u>one</u> pass)

q = rate of heat flow, BTU/hr - ft^2

$r = k_{base}/k_{asphalt} \; \overline{\alpha_{asphalt}/\alpha_{base}}$

t = time, hrs., or seconds

T = temperature, °F or °R

T_i = temperature at node i, °F

T_i' = temperature at node i at time t = t + Δt, °F

T_0 = temperature of air, °F

T_1 = temperature at hot surface or the initial hot layer temperature, °F

T_{a-b} = temperature at interface of medijm A and medium B, °F

T_s = temperature of surface, °F

U_1 = initial temperature of base, a semi

v = velocity of wind, miles per hour

W = percentage of cloud cover

x = distance (usually from asphalt surface), inches or feet

z = $x/\sqrt{\alpha t}$, dimensionless, used in analytical equations

α = thermal diffusivity = $k/\rho c$, ft^2/hr

α_a = thermal diffusivity of hot layer, ft^2/hr

α_b = thermal diffusivity of cold base, ft^2/hr

ϵ = emissivity, dimensionless

σ = Stefan-Boltzman constant = 1.713×10^{-9}, $BTU/hr - ft^2 - °R^4$
(theoretical) = $1.731.10^{-9}$ $BTU/hr - ft^2 - °R^4$ (experimental)

ρ = density, lbm/ft^3

Literature Cited

1. Saul'yev, V. K., "Integration of Equations by the Method of Nets," Macmillan Company, 1964.
2. Carnahan, Brice; Luther, H. A.; Wilkes, James O., "Applied Numerical Methods, John Wiley & Sons, Inc., 1969.
3. Dusinberre, G. M., "Numerical Analysis in Heat Flow," McGraw Hill Book Company, Inc., New York, 1961.
4. Chapman, Alan J., "Heat Transfer," Macmillan Company, New York, 1967.
5. Carslaw, H. S.; and Jaeger, J. C., "Conduction of Heat in Solids," Clarendon Press, Oxford, 1959.
6. Abramowitz, Milton and Stegun, Irene A., "Handbook of Mathematical Functions," National Bureau of Standards, Dover Publications, Inc., New York, 1972.
7. Wolfe, R. K. and Colony, D. C., "Final Report, Asphalt Cooling Rates: A Computer Simulation Study, Project 2844," for Ohio Department of Transportation and U.S. Department of Transportation, Federal Highway Administration, 1976.
8. ASHRAE, "ASHRAE Handbook of Fundamentals," American Society of Heating, Refrigeration and Air-Conditioning Engineers, Inc., 1972.

2

Conjugate Gradient Methods for Solving Algebraic Eigenproblems

J. C. NASH
Research Division, Economics Branch, Agriculture Canada, Ottawa K1A 0C5, Canada

S. G. NASH
Mathematics Department, University of Alberta, Edmonton, Alberta, Canada

The problem which is addressed in this paper is that of finding eigensolutions $(e, \underline{x})$ which satisfy

$$A \underline{x} = e B \underline{x} \qquad (1)$$

where A and B are real symmetric matrices and B is positive definite. The particular case where B is the identity is also of interest. This study will focus on methods using the conjugate gradient algorithm because this is very frugal of storage when used to solve linear equations [1] or function minimization problems [2]. The algorithm can be used in either fashion to solve the eigenproblem (1):

1) By solution of the equations

$$(A - kB) \underline{y}_i = B \underline{x}_i \qquad (2)$$

with

$$\underline{x}_{i+1} = \underline{y}_i / \| \underline{y}_i \| \qquad (3)$$

where the double vertical lines mean "the norm of", it is possible to find the eigenvector $\underline{x}$ (or $\underline{y}$) having eigenvalue e closest to the shift k. This is the process of inverse iteration [3,4].

2) By minimization of the Rayleigh quotient

$$R = \underline{x}^T A \underline{x} / \underline{x}^T B \underline{x} \qquad (4)$$

with respect to $\underline{x}$, where the ^{T} denotes transposition, the eigenvector $\underline{x}$ corresponding to the most negative eigenvalue e is found [5]. R takes on the value e at its minimum. Note that if B is the identity, minimization of

$$R' = \underline{x}^T (A - kI)^2 \underline{x} / \underline{x}^T \underline{x} \qquad (5)$$

24

gives the eigenvector corresponding to the eigenvalue which is closest to the shift k. Alternatively, root-shifting or ortho-gonalization as discussed by Shavitt et al. [6] may be used to find some of the higher eigensolutions.

The approaches above suggest ways of finding one eigenvalue and vector at a time. No deflation or orthogonalization technique is needed for problems with distinct eigenvalues. Only a few vectors of storage are required and the programs we have written run in very small memories and could be used on very small mach-ines such as the programmable desk top calculators.

The aim of the work reported here was to find a reliable yet simple method for solving the symmetric matrix eigenproblem when the matrices involved would not necessarily fit in main memory in the computing device. In this regard, the methods of Nesbet [7] and Shavitt [6] had proved unreliable, while that of Davidson [8] was too complicated for the target machines.

Conjugate Gradients

Beale [9] has given a short but lucid derivation of the conjugate gradients (cg) family of algorithms. The fundamental idea is to generate a set of linearly independent search direct-ions by means of a recurrence relationship. That is, given a function $S(\underline{x})$ and its gradient $\underline{g}(\underline{x})$ together with the j'th search direction $\underline{t}_j$, the next search direction is defined as

$$\underline{t}_{j+1} = \alpha \, \underline{t}_j - \underline{g} \tag{6}$$

where α is some parameter, the formula for which determines the method. Once search directions exist, provision of a mechanism for actually performing a line search completes the specification of an algorithm except for start or restart conditions. Within this work we chose always to set

$$\underline{t}_0 = -\,\underline{g} \tag{7}$$

and if the algorithm had not converged in n steps, where n is the order of the problem, to restart in the same way from the current point or vector $\underline{x}$.

Minimization of the particular function

$$S(\underline{x}) = \underline{x}^T \, C \, \underline{x} \; + 2 \, \underline{x}^T \, \underline{w} + \text{(any scalar)} \tag{8}$$

where C is a given positive definite symmetric matrix and $\underline{w}$ is a given vector solves the linear equations

$$C \, \underline{x} = -\,\underline{w} \tag{9}$$

Moreover, in this case it can be shown that the algorithm should converge in no more than n steps, while the line search simplifies to the computation of the step length

$$h_j = g^T g / t_j^T C t_j \tag{10}$$

Similar simplifications exist for the Rayleigh quotient (4). These are dealt with below.

Both the specialized and general-purpose cg minimization algorithms are notoriously sensitive to implementation details which bedevil any comparisons. These details are discussed at greater length in [10] where the algorithms are presented in step-description form. Chapter 19 of [10] is partly founded on the present study.

Direct Rayleigh Quotient Minimization

As a result of other research, a conjugate gradients program for general function minimization was available [11] and our initial hope was to apply this directly to the minimization of (4) or (5). The major difficulty this reveals is that both these functions are homogeneous of degree zero, implying that the scale or normalization of x is arbitrary. This causes the matrix of second partial derivatives, or Hessian, of the function $R(x)$ to be only positive semidefinite, violating some to the assumptions which underly the cg algorithm. Bradbury and Fletcher [5] adopted a strategy which restricts x to lie on a convex surface, thus removing the troublesome degree of freedom at the expense of some extra work within the program. One could also fix one of the elements of x and allow all the others to vary, except that the chosen component should perhaps be very small compared to the rest, resulting in very large alterations in these at each step of the algorithm. Rather than employ specific constraints, we tried various penalty functions to impose a normalization on x. These are summarized in Table I. Unfortunately we must report that none of these techniques can be considered generally useful due to the slow convergence to the minimum of the function. Our tests were primarily made using the biharmonic matrix defined by Ruhe [12] with B the identity.

Primarily the general minimization is inefficient because the line search is inexact. For the Rayleigh quotient without any penalty function to maintain normalization this can be corrected since the gradient of (4) is

$$g = 2 (A x - R B x)/ x^T B x \tag{11}$$

so that the one dimensional minimization of $R(x + h t)$ with respect to the step length h is accomplished by the solution of a quadratic equation. This is straightforward, though not to be underestimated (see Acton [13]).

Apart from the search, the Rayleigh quotient minimization can be organized so the recurrence (6) generates search directions which are conjugate with respect ot the local Hessian matrix. This avoids search directions which cause large growth in the elements of $\underline{x}$. The approach is due to Geradin [14]. However, he does not specify the details of his implementation. That which we have adopted is given in full by Nash [10].

Inverse Iteration by Conjugate Gradients

Except by the use of orthogonalization or projection techniques Rayleigh quotient minimization cannot find other than the extreme eigensolutions of (1). However, inverse iteration can find an eigensolution with eigenvalue closest to any prescribed shift k provided a starting vector not totally deficient in the required eigenvector is given. (In some cases this is a non-trivial provision. Furthermore, for multiple eigenvalues we can only find one eigenvector from the relevant subspace unless some orthogonalization scheme is employed.)

Comparing equations (2) and (9) shows that to use the cg method we should make the identification

$$C = (A - kB) \; ; \quad \underline{w} = -B\,\underline{x}_i \; ; \quad \underline{x} = \underline{y}_i \tag{12}$$

However, C was supposed to be positive definite, which is now impossible if k is greater than the smallest (most negative) eigenvalue of our problem (1). Then one may try to solve the least squares problem

$$(A - kB)^T (A - kB)\,\underline{y}_i = (A - kB)^T B\,\underline{x}_i \tag{13}$$

which does have a positive semidefinite coefficient matrix but which increases the amount of work and worsens the numerical condition of the equation system. Following Ruhe and Wiberg [4] we have opted to ignore the requirement that C be positive definite, thereby discarding the convergence results which have been proven for the cg algorithm applied to linear equations. To compensate for this, we must check that the step length computed in (10) is not too large, since this would imply that the shift k is too close to an eigenvalue. This poses the dilemma:

1) For rapid convergence of inverse iteration it is desirable to have k as close to an eigenvalue as possible.

2) For the cg algorithm to work without overflow, k should not be too close to an eigenvalue.

Ruhe and Wiberg [4] nevertheless used cg-inverse iteration to refine eigenvectors, using shifts very close to the eigenvalue, afterwards refining the eigenvalue itself by means of the Rayleigh quotient. We have applied their method to the more difficult case where the starting vector may contain only a small component of the desired eigenvector and only a crude estimate of the eigenvalue may be available. In the case where the step length (10) exceeds some tolerance (the reciprocal of the square root of the machine precision) our program halts, since we have yet to be convinced that a suitable automatic shifting procedure can be devised.

As a control on the progress of the inverse iteration we compute the residuals

$$r = (A - sB) \underline{x} \tag{14}$$

where s is the current estimate of the eigenvalue. The sum of squares $r^T r$ provides a convenient convergence test. Unfortunately different normalizations arise in the implementations of this algorithm and that of Geradin, so that the convergence criteria are not directly comparable. We have so far chosen not to perform the extra computation needed to make the convergence criteria identical.

Hybrid Algorithms

Having now several programs at our disposal, it is tempting to consider, say, combining a function minimization with inverse iteration to refine the vector. Early though quite extensive trials with the general minimization algorithm using function D of Table I followed by inverse iteration as in the previous section showed that this combination could be more effective than function minimization alone. However, if only the extreme eigensolutions are desired, the Geradin algorithm can in our experience supply an accurate solution more efficiently than any combination method, including Geradin with inverse iteration.

Discussion and Examples

Table II lists the programs either developed or used for comparison purposes within this study. We tentatively recommend the algorithms which underly those called GER and INVIT. The reader is advised that this can be no more than a tentative recommendation since work is still going on in this area. For instance, the authors understand that Prof. G.W.Stewart of the University of Maryland has been developing algorithms for the sparse eigenproblem. His bibliography [16] provides a wealth of possible directions for research. At the time of writing, we are still investigating the cg methods of Fried [17].

There remain to be settled the questions of (1) convergence criteria and (2) starting values for the shift and the initial vector. For the program GER convergence is assumed when the gradient norm squared $g^T g$ falls below some tolerance. With INVIT the residual sum of squares $r^T r$ is used, as mentioned above. In addition to this a usually different tolerance is used to decide when the gradient in the linear equations sub-problem is small enough to presume that the equations have been solved.

For an initial vector we suggest simply a column of ones.

Table I: Functions which may be minimized to solve the
eigenproblem $A \underline{x} = e \underline{x}$.

	Function	Comments
A)	$\underline{x}^T A\underline{x}/\underline{x}^T\underline{x}$	Smallest eigenvalue only. Prone to produce large vector elements since no normalization imposed.
B)	$\underline{x}^T A\underline{x}/\underline{x}^T\underline{x} + z(\underline{x}^T\underline{x} - 1)^2$ for $z > 0$	Usually finds smallest eigenvalue and normalized vector.
C)	$\underline{x}^T(A-kI)^2\underline{x} + (\underline{x}^T\underline{x}-1)^2$	Least squares. This is not a Rayleigh quotient. Difficulties in finding certain solutions unless starting vector "good".
D)	$\underline{x}^T(A-kI)^2\underline{x}/\underline{x}^T\underline{x} + (\underline{x}^T\underline{x}-1)^2$	Extremely slow when eigenvalues poorly separated.
E)	$\underline{x}^T\underline{x}/(\underline{x}^T(A-kI)^2\underline{x}) + (\underline{x}^T\underline{x}-1)^2$	An unsuccessful attempt to separate close eigenvalues. Slow convergence.

Table II: Programs appearing in the study.

GER   The Geradin algorithm [14] as implemented in [10].

INVIT   Inverse iteration using conjugate gradients for solution of the linear equations (2).

TQL   A BASIC version of TQL1 in [15] for the eigenvalues only of a symmetric tridiagonal matrix.

SSE   Eigenvalues only of a symmetric tridiagonal matrix using Sturm sequences [3].

NES   Nesbet's algorithm [7].

MOR   Method of optimal relaxation [6].

CGT(B)   General conjugate gradients function minimizer using penalized Rayleigh quotient (B) of Table I with $z = 1$.

(This is not normalized.) However, in some cases this vector is lacking a component in the direction of the desired eigenvector, especially in cases where there are symmetries in the matrices (other than that about the principal diagonal) or the matrix elements are integers. In such cases we have used a pseudo-random number generator to produce elements in the interval (-0.5,0.5) if the vector of ones seemed inappropriate.

The algorithms have been tested in BASIC in a 6000 byte partition of a Data General NOVA operating in 23 bit binary floating point arithmetic. This corresponds quite closely to some of the small desk top computers in size of memory. Some of the programs - GER, INVIT, and CGT( ) - were also tested on an IBM 370/168 and/or Amdahl V6 in single precision (six hexadecimal digits).

GER and INVIT are quite short, being approximately 100 to 150 lines of BASIC depending on the code for initialization, normalization and printing of results. GER was implemented and tested once in less than two hours from a step-description recipe. That is, less than two hours elapsed from the moment the first line of BASIC was written until the computer printed correct results for a test problem. INVIT is slightly longer in lines of program, but requires only 1918 bytes of storage compared to 2022 for GER. Moreover, it needs only 6 instead of 7 working vectors, so that the order 100 problem reported in Table III took 4962 bytes to run with GER but only 4426 with INVIT. Both programs require sub-programs to compute the results of the multiplications

$$\underline{v} = A\underline{x} \; ; \quad \underline{c} = B\underline{x} \tag{15}$$

By way of illustration, consider the tridiagonal matrix defined by

$$A_{ii} = -2 + 1/[(n+1)^2 + i^2] \text{ for } i=1,2,\dots,n.$$
$$A_{i,i+1} = A_{i+1,i} = 1 \text{ for } i=1,2,\dots,n-1. \tag{16}$$

which we call the Froberg matrix. B will be set to the identity. On the NOVA we computed the smallest eigensolution of this matrix for orders n = 4, 10, 50, and 100. The results, with comparable values forother programs, are given in Table III. Very similar results were found on the IBM 370. They illustrate what we have observed in all cases to date, that is, that when only the smallest (or largest) eigenvalue is desired the program GER is the most efficient yet produces accurate solutions. Using this program with the matrix

$$(A - k I)^2 \tag{17}$$

to obtain a solution with eigenvalue closest to k causes a very substantial slow-down in the rate of convergence. This is hardly surprising since we have squared the condition number of the matrix as well as doubling the work in each matrix-vector product step of the program. The general function minimizer CGT(B) performs reasonably well on these matrices but uses roughly five times as much effort. Inverse iteration (INVIT) is almost as tedious. However, the rate of convergence here is governed by the ratio

$$p = (e_1 - k)/(e_2 - k) \qquad\qquad (18)$$

where e_1 is the eigenvalue closest to k and e_2 the next closest. INVIT in its major iteration converges as fast as powers of p tend to zero. Fortunately, as the eigenvector begins to dominate

Table III: Minimal eigensolution of Froberg's matrix.

Program	Order	Eigenvalue	Rayleigh quotient	Matrix products
GER	4		0.350144	5
INVIT	4	0.350142	0.350144	27 (7)
TQL	4	0.350145		
SSE	4	0.350144		
CGT(B)	4		0.350144	36
NES	4		0.350144	10
MOR	4		0.350505	>1000
GER	10		7.44406E-2	11
INVIT	10	7.44379E-2	7.44407E-2	43 (6)
TQL	10	7.44434E-2		
SSE	10	7.44405E-2		
CGT(B)	10		7.44407E-2	57
NES	10		failed	
MOR	10		7.48813E-2	>1000
GER	50		3.48733E-3	26
INVIT	50	3.48618E-3	#.4873E-3	147 (5)
TQL	50	3.49247E-3		
SSE	50	3.48753E-3		
CGT(B)	50		3.48748E-3	123
GER	100		8.89216E-4	51
INVIT	100	8.86582E-4	8.89202E-4	242 (4)
TQL	100	9.64072E-4		
SSE	100	8.89313E-4		

The figure in parentheses after the number of matrix products is the number of inverse iterations. In all cases the shift k=0.

x_i, the cg linear equations solution is usually accomplished in many fewer than n matrix-vector products. This has also been observed by Ruhe and Wiberg [4]. The number of inverse iterations, starting form a shift k=0, has been included in parentheses behind the number of matrix-vector products in Table III.

Acknowledgements

While this study used very minimal computing resources, we wish to acknowledge time provided on the Data General NOVA and IBM 370 (Datacrown Ltd.) at Agriculture Canada and the Amdahl V6 at the University of Alberta.

Literature Cited

[1] Hestenes M.R. and Stiefel E., J. Res. Nat. Bur. Standards Section B (1952) 49, 409-436.

[2] Fletcher R. and Reeves C.M., Computer Journal (1964) 7, 149-154.

[3] Wilkinson J.H.,"The algebraic eigenvalue problem",Clarendon Press, Oxford, 1965.

[4] Ruhe A. and Wiberg T., BIT (1972) 12, 543-554.

[5] Bradbury W.W. and Fletcher R., Numer. Math.(1966) 9,259-267.

[6] Shavitt I., Bender C.F., Pipano A., and Hosteny R.P., J. Computational Physics (1973) 11, 90-108.

[7] Nesbet R.K., J. Chem. Phys. (1965) 43, 311-312.

[8] Davidson E.R., J. Computational Physics (1975) 17, 87-94.

[9] Beale E.M.L., in Lootsma F.A., "Numerical methods for nonlinear optimization", 39-44, Academic Press, London, 1972.

[10] Nash J.C., "Compact numerical methods: linear algebra and function minimization", To be published, probably in 1978.

[11] Nash J.C., "Function minimization with small computers", submitted to ACM Trans. Math. Software, 1976.

[12] Ruhe A., in Collatz L.,"Eigenwerte Probleme", 97-115, Birkhäuser Verlag, Basel, 1974.

[13] Acton F.S., "Numerical methods that work", 58-59, Harper & Row, New York, 1970.

[14] Geradin M., J. Sound. Vib. (1971) 19, 319-331.

[15] Bowdler H., Martin R.S., Reinsch C., and Wilkinson J.H., Numer. Math. (1968) 11, 293-306.

[16] Stewart G.W., in Bunch J.R. and Rose D.J., "Sparse matrix computations", 113-130, Academic Press, New York, 1976.

[17] Fried I. J. Sound. Vib. (1972) 20, 333-342.

Large Scale Simulation with a Minicomputer

B. E. ROSS, PAULA JERKINS, and JAMES KENDALL

College of Engineering, University of South Florida, Tampa, FL 33620

This paper describes the alteration and development of an
Interdata 7/16 minicomputer to perform large-scale computations.
Substantial savings in cost and overall turnaround time resulted
from the act of performing the calculations with the minicomputer
instead of the previously used IBM 360.

Introduction

Since 1969, students and faculty of the College of Engineering at the University of South Florida have been developing a
co-ordinated set of digital computer models for environmental
simulation. Calculations of the hydrodynamical, chemical and
biological aspects of estuarine areas are included. Large-scale
physical areas are simulated over long real time periods and the
complexity of the interactions of the models result in large-
scale computations. A natural consequence of performing the
simulations with a general purpose IBM 360 are rapid execution
times but very delayed turnaround time due to system priorities
and other user demands.

The alternative of adapting and upgrading an existing Interdata computer was studied in detail. The developments in minicomputer technology in recent years have increased the obtainable
operating speed of the central processing units. Large-scale
main memories and large-scale auxiliary memories have become
available for economical minicomputer development.

The computer programs which are implemented with data and
become the simulation models are carefully co-ordinated into subroutines which lend themselves to overlay techniques. The principal numerical schemes involved are explicit so that core requirements and run time are flexible and interchangeable. The combination of subroutines and explicit solution greatly simplified the
transition of the programs from IBM to Interdata.

The Simulation Problem

The tasks to be performed by the computer involve the numerical solution of the vertically integrated equations of motion, continuity, and mass transport with chemical and biological interactions in two dimensions. The basic equations are as follows:

$$\frac{\partial U}{\partial t} + \frac{1}{D} U \frac{\partial U}{\partial x} + \frac{V}{D} \frac{\partial U}{\partial y} - \Omega V = -gD \frac{\partial H}{\partial x} - f \, QUD^{-2} - \frac{1}{\rho} D \frac{\partial P}{\partial x} \qquad (1)$$

$$\frac{\partial V}{\partial t} + \frac{U}{D} \frac{\partial V}{\partial x} + \frac{V}{D} \frac{\partial V}{\partial y} + \Omega U = -gD \frac{\partial H}{\partial y} - f \, QVD^{-2} - \frac{1}{\rho} D \frac{\partial P}{\partial y} \qquad (2)$$

$$\frac{\partial H}{\partial t} + \frac{\partial U}{\partial x} + \frac{\partial V}{\partial y} = 0 \qquad (3)$$

$$\frac{\partial C_i}{\partial t} + U \frac{\partial C_i}{\partial x} + V \frac{\partial C_i}{\partial y} + \frac{1}{D} \left[\frac{\partial}{\partial x} \left(DE_x \frac{\partial C_i}{\partial x} \right) \right] + \frac{1}{D}$$

$$\left[\frac{\partial}{\partial y} \left(DE_y \frac{\partial C_i}{\partial y} \right) \right] = \frac{M_i}{\rho} \qquad (4)$$

where

$$U = \int_{-d}^{H} u \, d_z \quad \text{Transport in the x direction}$$

$$V = \int_{-d}^{H} v \, d_z \quad \text{Transport in the y direction}$$

D = Local water depth
Ω = Coriolis parameter
H = Local water surface ela.
f = Local friction factor
$Q = [U^2 + V^2]^{\frac{1}{2}}$
P = Atmospheric pressure
C_i = Concentrations of water quality parameters or biota
M_i = Interaction process and sources or sinks
ρ = Mass density
Ex,Ey = Dispersion coefficients

For the solution scheme the equations are reduced to finite difference form and solved on a square grid matrix. An example of the application of the model to Hillsborough Bay, Florida, is shown in Figure One. Figure One shows the distribution of dissolved oxygen in the Bay resulting from the discharge of pollutants from industrial, municipal and natural sources, and the interaction of biota.

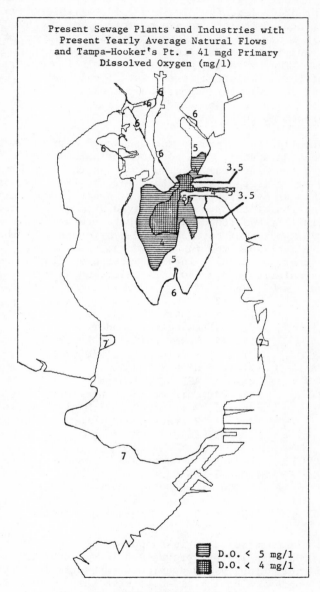

Figure 1.   Hillsborough Bay, Florida

The number of grid elements involved in the simulation are 90 X 36 or 3240 elements. There are 10 variables involved with each element. Calculations are performed for the hydraulic program in intervals of 90 seconds of real time for 24 hours. Numerous auxiliary calculations updating coefficients must be performed. The hydraulic portion (the solution of equations 1, 2, and 3) of this simulation is the set of calculations that were chosen for the computer comparison purposes.

The Interdata Computer

Basically the Interdata machine was a part of an experimental data reduction system. The cpu handles numbers at 16 bits, two bytes at a time internally. The word length is 32 bits so the roundoff error is the same as that for the IBM. The original machine had 8K bytes of memory and a magnetic tape unit. After an examination of the problem involved with overlay techniques, the possibility was found that adequate storage could be obtained by using 65K bytes of core and a 50 M byte disc. Both of these units were available for the Interdata.

The configuration of Interdata computer finally implemented for the simulation comparisons is described as follows:

Supplier	Unit		Price
	M71-012	7/16 CPU	3,700
	M71-101	Binary Display Panel	350
	M71-103	Automatic Loader	400
	M71-104	Power Fail/Auto Restart	400
	M71-105	Signed Multiply/Divide	950
INTERDATA	M71-106	High Speed ALU	5,000
	M46-004	ASR-33 Teletype	1,950
	M48-024	Current Loop Interface	400
	M46-500	9 Track 800 BPI Magtape Interface	2,950
	M46-501	9 Track 800 BPI Magtape Transport	6,000
	M47-102	RS-232 Interface	500
			$22,600
BALL COMPUTER	BD-50	50M Byte 3330 Type Disc Drive	7,000
MINI-COMPUTER	TDC-803	3330 Disc Interface	1,900
PUSHPA	PM9800	65K Byte Memory	4,000
			$35,500
HAZELTINE	2000	Video Terminal & Printer	4,000
			$39,500

The hardware selected is supported by a Disc Operating System (DOS) supplied by Interdata. This is not the most sophisticated operating system available but sufficient to meet the immediate needs. The installed version has capabilities as outlined below: D.O.S. (Disc Operating System)

I.   System Utility: A Copy Files
                             B Compress/Decompress
                             C Disc Backup

II.   Disc File   A Allocate Files
        Management: B Delete Files
                            C Protect Files
                            D List Files
                            E Position to a Subfile
III.   Software: A FORTRAN V Level 1
                            B Extended Basic
                            C OS Editor
                            D OS Library Loader
                            E OS Assembler
                            F OS Aids, Debugger

The language used in the simulation programs is FORTRAN V, level 1, which is a high level compiler supporting the requirements of ANSI standard FORTRAN and includes significant extension in both language and subroutine library to support process control applications and multi-tasking programs. Features of FORTRAN V, which may be of major importance to the FORTRAN programmer are:

(a) Mixed mode arithmetic is allowed
(b) Array initialization and implied - Do's in Data statements are provided for
(c) Multiple entries into FORTRAN subroutines are provided
(d) Hollerith constants may be declared using the apostrophe as a delimiter

Features which may be of interest to a FORTRAN programmer using FORTRAN V as a process control language are:

(a) The use of in-line assembly language is allowed
(b) Encode/decode statements are allowed
(c) Hexadecimal and character constants may appear as arguments in expressions as well as in Data statements and call parameter lists
(d) Analog input in a sequential order is allowed
(e) Analog input in any sequence is allowed
(f) Analog output in any sequence is allowed
(g) Logical functions intended to support the Instrument Society of America/Purdue Standards are available

FORTRAN V contains several features to simplify and expedite program debugging such as

(a) Over 60 compile-time diagnostics are provided
(b) 35 run-time error messages are provided
(c) Run-time trace capability is provided
(d) Optional compilation is provided which facilitates insertion of the programmer's diagnostics and allows these to be easily deleted from a program without physical removal.

Standard Operating Procedures with the Interdata

The main programs exist in source form on the 50 M Byte disc. These can be called by an operator. Basic input data are entered by the operator in an interactive mode. The program goes immediately to the compile and run modes. Intermediate

calculated data such as hydraulic velocities and water depths
are stored on the disc temporarily and printed on magnetic tape
at selected real time intervals. The total quantity of calculated data in this step is too great to be stored intact upon
the 50 M Byte disc.

Upon completion of the calculation of the hydraulics of a
bay, the water quality program is called. The water quality
program uses the hydraulic data from the magnetic tape to calculate chemical and biological results. Longer real time intervals are used in the water quality calculations, thus less data
are calculated. The calculated results are now stored upon disc
for printout, or reading onto another magnetic tape.

Comparisons of Costs and Time

The simulation calculations were alternately made by use of
an IBM 360, with 3 Megabyte active core and almost unlimited disc
space. However, this system is in a University and hosts many
languages and supports diverse users' needs so that much of the
capability is not available to a user. The IBM system is supported by the usual IBM operating system. The usual debugging
programs and some professional assistance is available by
appointment.

Comparisons are made for comparable computer environmental
simulations. Two times are important. These are cpu time and
turnaround time. Another parameter of interest is cost.

The results indicate that the test program utilized 4612.65
cpu seconds in the IBM machine. The machine elapsed time was 3
hours. The best turnaround for the simulation was 24 hours.
Usual turnaround times are on the order of 72 hours. The cost
of the test calculation on the IBM system was $303.43.

A comparable run was performed on the Interdata 7/16 before
hardware high speed floating point arithmetic unit was installed.
The cpu time was 74 hours which was also the turnaround time.
Costs of computation were based on the following factors:-

$34,300 amortized 4 years		$8,575
Interest 1st year		3,087
1/3 Technician time for general maintenance		4,000
Field repairs by Interdata per year		500
		$16,162
If computer used 50% time		$88.56/day
		or $ 3.69/hr.

Thus, based on 74 hours the cost of this long run was $273.06.

Analysis of the cpu usage during the long Interdata run
indicated that 85% of the time was spent in software operations
involving floating point arithmetic. A high speed floating
point arithmetic unit (HSALU) was investigated. Analysis showed
that if the same simulation was performed with HSALU the results

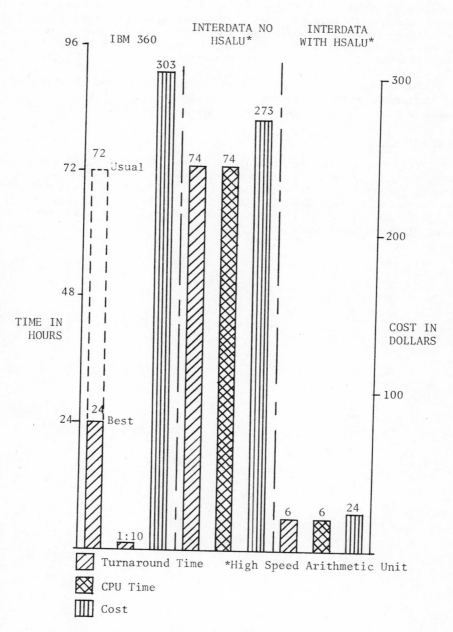

Figure 2.   Comparisons for runs yielding identical results

studied would indicate a cpu time of 5.69 hours which is also
the turnaround time. The costs are adjusted to reflect an
additional investment of $5,200 and the results indicate a cost
of $4.09/hour. The cost of this hypothetical run is $23.28.
Installation of the HSALU and subsequent simulation confirmed
the expected results.

Thus, the new run at highspeed saved $280.15 and 18 hours
of turnaround time. The results are summarized in Figure Two
where time and dollars have been rounded to the nearest integer.

Conclusions

The conclusions are that large-scale computations can be
accomplished on modern minicomputers with savings in time and
money. Accuracy is not sacrificed in 32 bit word machines and
maintenance and reliability appear to be realistic in cost.
Programs and numerical techniques must be compatible with the
size of the machine chosen.

APL Level Languages in Analysis

A Host-Microcomputer-Instrument Hierarchy in Light Scattering Spectroscopy

J. ADIN MANN, ROBERT V. EDWARDS, THOMAS GALL,
H. M. CHEUNG, F. COFFIELD, C. HAVENS, and P. WAGNER

Department of Chemical Engineering, Case Western Reserve University,
Cleveland, OH 44106

So far as we know this is the first report in the open
literature of a laboratory experiment instrumented totally
within the context of APL as the computer language driving each
level of a hierarchy. The significance of our report is the
demonstration that such a high level language improves by
orders of magnitude the effort required to implement
complicated experiments involving elements of control, data
acquisition, data processing, and modelling of complex
phenomena. It is especially easy to retain the degree of human
interaction required by the experiment. All of these
desirable results can be accomplished by persons with no
formal training in computer science.

Certainly other languages and combination of languages have
been used to write interactive systems for data collection and
analysis. We have had considerable experience with FORTRAN and
BASIC as well as assembly languages. Our experience with
operating systems for experimental work has been limited to the
DEC PDP 11/40 DOS and the DEC PDP11/45 RSX11D operating systems.
Unequivocally, APL and our hierarchy has proved to be an order
of magnitude more effective in reducing first concepts to
producing results with experimental equipment. The APL language
and the concepts of the APLSV or VSAPL implementations have
provided an integrity of design and ease of coding that from our
experience is far ahead of FORTRAN and BASIC oriented systems.
Certainly the human engineering that has gone into APL
implementations, e.g. the IBM 5100, is a factor in such a
significant improvement, but the major element is that the
structure of the language itself and the notation is much closer
to the mathematics involved in experimental work than any
computer language known to us.

The penalty one pays in using a high level language is that
of execution times for certain operations and, perhaps, cost of
the hardware. These disadvantages were more than balanced by
reduction in the time necessary to integrate the hierarchy into
the experiment. Should the measurements become routine, it may

be useful to have professional hardware and software technicians implement the APL algorithms in the appropriate assembly language. In that case, the APL functions serve as an unequivocal description of the "operating system" needed for the experiment.

We have chosen to describe our methods in the context of automating a specific experiment involving the determination of the diffusion coefficient of particles in a fluid by the analysis of fluctuations in scattered light. A description of the physics of the experiment is required in order to put the instrumental analysis in context.

The details of the interconnection of the hierarchy will be described and excerpts of code will be given to illustrate methods. Finally, performance will be outlined.

Light Scattering Spectroscopy: Particle Diffusion

Only a brief introduction will be given here to a class of experiments that involve the time series analysis of scattered light. Consult the books by Chu [1] and by Berne and Pecora [2] for details.

The object of the experiment is the study of the response of a system to small fluctuations over a large frequency range. When the frequency region is below perhaps 1MHz, the "response function" will yield measures of macroscopic constitutive coefficients such as diffusion coefficients, viscosity coefficients, elastic coefficients, rate constants and others. For frequencies larger than about 10GHz we observe relaxation effects associated with molecular distortions. We will specialize to the low frequency region below 1MHz and further outline only the problem of determining the diffusion coefficient of macroscopic particles in solution.

The diffusion coefficients of macroscopic particles ($10 \leq$ nm $d \leq 2000$ nm, d is the diameter of a particle) are of interest for a number of practical and theoretical reasons. Dispersions of particles are used by the medical profession, paint industry, the printing industry as well as analyzed in the context of environmental safety and in human medicine. The theory of colloid stability can be studied directly as can the implications of the theory of fluids [3].

Consider a suspension of small particles, d 200 nm, each particle will execute Brownian random motion that results from the very frequent collisions of the Brownian particle with the small molecules of the surrounding solvent. When the number density of the Brownian particle is small, the particles can be treated as individuals so that collisions between these large particles can be ignored. The desired information about diffusion can be calculated from the scattering function

$$F(q,\tau) = \int_o^\infty e^{-q^2 D\tau} p(D) \, dD$$

where p(D) is the distribution of diffusion coefficients, D
and q is the scattering vector. A complication due to the
variation of scattering cross-section with size is included as
part of the data analysis.

The intermediate scattering function is relatable to the
results of a light scattering measurement in the following way.
When the incident beam has an electric field $\vec{E}_o$ the scattered
beam, $\vec{E}_s$ will be modulated by the particle motion so that at
the detector the intensity will be i = $\beta |E_s|^2$ and the current
autocorrelation function produced by the detector will be

$$R_i(\mathcal{I}) = \langle i(\mathcal{I}) \, i(o) \rangle = A\delta(\mathcal{I}) + B \, F^2(q,\mathcal{I}) + C \quad (1A)$$

where A, B and C are constants for a given experiment.

Experimentally, $R_i(\mathcal{I})$ is computed from a time series produced
by the detector that is essentially the photocurrent as a
function of time. When the incident flux of the scattered
light is sufficiently high, the photocurrent is put through an
analog to digital conversion before the computation of the
correlation   function by the rule that

$$R_i(n\Delta\mathcal{I}) = \frac{1}{N} \sum_{j=1} i_j \, i_{j+n} \quad (1B)$$

When the incident flux is small, photon counting is done
directly but a similar formula holds with the definition that i_j
is the number of photoelectrons detected during a period $T \leq \Delta\mathcal{I}$
around jx$\Delta\mathcal{I}$. A computer is used for these calculations.

In practice, the relaxation times in R_i range between a few
tenths of microseconds to a few tens of milliseconds.
Relaxation times shorter than 1μsec require measurements of the
time series in the 10 to 100$m$sec range. The accuracy
requirement for $\{i_j\}$ is modest, eight bits is often sufficient,
but averaging must be done with respect to a large number of
time series. Even when direct memory access is fast enough the
memory of a conventional computer will be filled before a
large enough time series has been collected. We have been
using the SAICOR Mod 42 and 43 machines for preprocessing the
time series data.   While they are not programmable, control of
function can be done by a host computer. The result of a
determination of R_i is a set of 16 bit numbers, one for each
correlator   channel. As the device's memory is read, these
bits are available in two's complement code on 16 pins
mounted on the back panel of the correlator.

The analysis can take a number of forms and a convenient one
involves the computation of cumulants. Essentially,

$$\log F(q,\mathcal{I}) = C_o^{(M)} + \sum_{m=1}^{M} K_m^{(M)} \frac{(-\mathcal{I})^m}{m!} \quad (2A)$$

where the power series is truncated after the Mth term.   Then

$$K_1 = q^2 \int_0^\infty Dp(D)\,dD = q^2 \langle D \rangle \tag{2B}$$

$$K_2 = q^4 \langle (D - \langle D \rangle)^2 \rangle$$

. . .

Since for $\Upsilon > 0$

$$\log(R_i(\zeta) - C) = 2 \log F(q,\zeta) + \text{constant} \tag{3}$$

it is obvious that a polynomial must be fit to what amounts
to the log of the correlation function produced by the SAICOR
hardware. The coefficients of the polynomial can be interpreted
physically as the cumulants of the diffusion coefficient of
polydispersed particles.

The determination must be repeated often in the course of an
experiment. The sequence of events must be:

1. Computation of R_i goes on in real time for a
   selected period of time and may involve 10M
   bytes of information on the photocurrent.
2. The 100 to 400, 16 bit R_i vector must be sent
   to a computer and transformed to numbers from
   a two's compliment code.
3. The R_i vector must be subjected to a least
   squares analysis and the cumulants calculated.
4. The R_i vector must be archived with ID data
   and the cumulants made available for analysis.
5. Repeat this sequence many times for each
   experiment.
6. The data files for the experiment must be
   catalogued.
7. Repeat this entire sequence for many
   experiments by different users.

We have found that VSAPL or APLVS level of APL
implementations to be highly facile for handling these tasks
effectively. A hierarchy with an APL host was devised for
performing the data acquisition, computations and control
required. Before the details are described, a description of
APL is necessary.

APL   (A Programming Language)

APL is an array processing language for manipulating sets of
numbers or sets of characters of quite general shapes. The
formal syntax of APL is based on the mathematical concepts
of function and functions of functions or operators. Much of
the power of the language derives from the extensive set of

primitive functions and operators as well as the notation that represents their behavior.

Defined functions can be constructed simply by writing sequences of primitive functions that lead to the desired result. The defined function has the same syntax as the primitive functions.

Several examples will be sufficient to illustrate the use of the language. Suppose that the following double summation must be evaluated.

$$\sum_{ij} Y_i B_{ij} Y_j$$

In APL: $Y+.\times B+.\times Y$

The linear least–squares algorithm or one step in an iterative nonlinear least–squares algorithm would require the evaluation of the following matrix problem:

$$\underset{\sim}{K} = \left(\underset{\sim}{M}^{-1}\right) \cdot \underset{\sim}{C}$$

While FORTRAN requires DO looping and a call to a subroutine for computing the inverse matrix, APL does the entire operation as follows:

$K \leftarrow C \boxdot M$

It has been our experience that in general APL code is more compact by a factor of ten to 100 than the equivalent FORTRAN code and takes roughly a tenth of the time to produce and debug on a computer.

The large set of primitives as well as the syntax of the language allows for a surprisingly large redundancy in the ways one may code a particular calculation. This is an advantage for a number of reasons, not the least of which is that the language is very forgiving for the inexperienced programmer. A simple subset of the primitives is sufficient for handling most computations that an inexperienced programmer may want to do. As he gains experience, he will naturally take to exploring some of the sophisticated primitives allowed in the language. In our experience, APL has been far easier to teach to inexperienced programmers than any of the other languages commonly in use.

The APL language itself is indifferent to its implementation. The language has most often been implemented for time–sharing, but there is no reason to exclude a real–time implementation. Since about 1972, new APL systems based on the shared variable concept, have been written for the IBM 370 series computers. This approach allowed the APL processor to communicate to the external world easily. Since shared variables have exactly the same structure as any other variable in APL, defined functions could be written that use

data passed back and forth between the APL processor and
external processors easily. It is possible, therefore, to
consider an experimental apparatus as an external processor
that communicates with the APL processor through shared
variables.

The difference between implementations centers on whether or
not shared variables are used and whether or not certain
systems functions and systems variables are defined. In
practice, there is a degree of portability in user functions
that is beyond most other languages. The Appendix includes a table
of a number of APL systems that are supported on larger
machines. The list is probably not complete. We are of the
opinion that a small addition to the set of systems functions
and systems variables would provide all of the resources needed
for doing real time operation entirely within the context of an
APL machine. The implementation of such a proposal is beyond
the expertise that we have within the department. However, we
have found an attractive alternative to a full APL real-time
machine. A block diagram of the interfacing schemes that
have been used successfully in our laboratory for the last
year is shown and described in a later section as Figures 2 and 3.

The Hosts

The APL hierarchy is structured so that any machine running
with the equivalent of APLSV can be attached as an efficient
host. See table (1) in the Appendix. In particular, the IBM 5100
and the Xerox Sigma 7 machines have been used as hosts
extensively. The IBM 5100 with APLSV features was considerably
easier to use than the Xerox APL. However, the Xerox APL is
sufficient for the purpose even though awkward by modern
standards. The various IBM 370 machines running either VSAPL or
APLSV are entirely able to handle the host responsibilities.

The most effective interaction of the host with the hierarchy
does require communication rates above 300 baud. Since the IBM
5100 can transmit and then receive at rates programmable up to
9600 baud, it was a superior host. Although our experience is
limited, our trials show that the Hewlett Packard 3000 Series II
machines are also suitable as hosts. In fact, the terminal ports
for the HP 3000II can work to 2400 baud and the I/O bus to ca
300KBytes/sec or faster. Use of that I/O bus for the hierarchy
requires both hardware and software that does not exist.

The IBM 5100 architecture was described by Roberson [4] and
will not be repeated here. This APL system is small and portable
and includes a CRT display as well as a tape cartridge drive.
The cartridges have a capacity of about 220,000 bytes and the
system performs tape write and checking at about 900 bytes/sec
and tape read at about 2500 bytes/sec. Our work required a
printer as well as the auxiliary tape drive for efficiency. It

was necessary to use the maximum memory storage of 64K bytes which gives an actual workspace size of about 57K bytes. The serial I/O adapter was required in order to attach the IBM 5100 to the hierarchy. The cost of this system is about $23,000.

The IBM 5100 was physically attached to the hierarchy through its Serial I/O port. The APL processor allows the definition of shared variables that "appear" in both the APL workspace and the I/O interface. This is done by invoking an APL systems function for generating a shared variable offer, $\square$SVO, as in the expression 1 $\square$SVO ´ MICRO´ where the variable MICRO is now shared with the serial I/O processor so that assigning MICRO to another APL variable will cause information to be transferred from the I/O processor into the APL processor. Assigning to MICRO will cause information to be transferred from the APL processor to the I/O processor. One or more variables can be declared as "shared" by $\square$SVO.

The I/O processor must have some information about the data to be transferred and that is given by assigning literal strings of control information to the shared variable. Three classes of strings must be assigned to the shared variable before I/O communications occur. Firstly, when the literal string ´OUT 31001 TYPE=I´ is assigned to the shared variable, the serial I/O processor is put into command mode as designated by the ´device number´ 31001. If this is in fact done the vector 0 0 is assigned to the shared variable by the Serial I/O processor. A non-zero value implies an error and that condition can be checked by simple APL code. Similarly, ´IN 33001´ when assigned to the shared variable informs the I/O processor to prepare for input from device address 33 (input), file 001. Lastly, the assignment of ´OUT 32001 TYPE=I´ states that an output operation will occur for device 32, file 001 and the data type is specified.

After the command device is opened by assigning ´OUT 31001 TYPE=I´ to the shared variable, the next assignment to the shared variable is the specification of the device characteristics in the form of a character string. The input and output buffer sizes may be specified along with the data rate (0.5 baud steps). Such aspects as the prompting character, new-line character, end-of-buffer character, parity, number of stop bits and changes in the I/O translation tables can be specified at any time including during the execution of defined functions. The device characteristics that can be included are sufficient to handle any handshake protocol of the machines we have used. In fact, one may use 5, 6, 7 or 8 bit I/O code so that, for example, the IBM 5100 can be interfaced to EBCDIC or ASCII devices easily. It is convenient to define a small set of functions that handle the opening and closing of the Serial I/O "devices" automatically. The monadic function ∆COMMAND requires as a right argument the literal string of device specifications, ∆OUT outputs a literal string right argument, while ∆IN does not require an argument but can be used to assign whatever is in the input buffer to a variable. Each function checks the return code and reports error conditions in detail. The ease with which the details of the communication protocol could be built into defined functions was an important factor in producing code quickly.

The Device Control Processor

The microcomputer chosen for this study was the Motorola 6800 built up with the components listed on Figure 1. The microprocessing unit (MPU) was built up on one card with the MC 6800 as the processor. Off of the common address bus and data bus leading to the MPU were several types of I/O adapters. These chips provided I/O for two modes of terminal operation as well as interfacing to the APL host. The third mode of operation is that of asynchronous communications through a special chip called the MIKBUG ROM. This ROM provides an asynchronous program, a loader program, and a diagnostic program for use with the MPU. Two Kbytes of memory were built up from ICs on a memory card attached to the address bus and the data bus. Memory could be expanded simply by adding additional cards to the bus. Communications to the instruments required interfacing, part of which was organized on a channel card as shown in Figure 1. The peripheral interface adapter (PIA) was used for this purpose. The PIA allows eight bit bidirectional communication with the MPU and two bidirectional eight bit buses for interfacing to peripherals. Handshake control logic for input and output peripheral operation is also included in the chip. We used the two eight-bit buses together for the input of 16-bit parallel I/O from the lowest level of the hierarchy, the SAI 42 or 43 correlators (Honeywell – SAICOR).

The channel card of the DCP had a simple layout based on the Motorola PIA chip. We designed each channel to be of similar structure and only small adaptions, if any, had to be made in order to complete the interface. Our intent is to place all of the special interfacing in the instrument and keep the channel card as clean and ubiquitous as possible. The specification of six channels does not represent a design restriction, but reflects our estimate of what is needed for the laser light scattering experiment.

The boards and power supply of the DCP were built up by Hexagram, Inc., Cleveland, Ohio for a total cost of about $2,000 including labor. Software development for this particular version of our system was done by Hexagram, Inc. and brought the entire cost of the microcomputer to $4,000. Hexagram, Inc. produced a competent design and implementation for us and in the process taught us a fair amount of the technology needed for constructing the systems. We are planning to implement additional microcomputer systems in house at a savings.

Physically, a terminal and instruments are plugged into the various channels using conventional telecommunication connectors.

The host is connected into either the MIKBUG channel or the asynchronous communications interface adapter (ACIA) depending on whether the purpose is to load object code including the initialization of the program for the operating system. Once the operating system has been initialized, then the host is switched into an ACIA channel for the remainder of the session. Of course, the program for the operating system could be entered through other media but we very quickly learned that it was easy and fast to download a processing module as a hexadecimal character array. This was especially convenient to do with the IBM 5100 as the host since one could initiate a program load through assignment of the character vector to the shared variable. Transfer was accomplished at rates of 1200 baud and could be done considerably faster than that if desired.

The first operating system written for the device control processor was based on a set of commands for interacting with the correlator. The system was to be compatible with APL rules. This was easy to do once an APL function was written to emulate the behavior expected of the DCP. The))<COMMAND> is executed by the DCP while)<COMMAND> is executed by the APL processor. The following function defines the DCP.

```
DCPΔP;STR;CMNAME;CVAR
ΑEMULATION OF THE DEVICE CONTROL PROCESSOR OF FIG 1.
Α      NAMEΔP   IS A PROCESSOR
Α      NAMEΔF   IS A FUNCTION
Α               BLANKSΔF  STRIPS OFF BLANKS AND ' :',6ρ' '
Α      NAME     IS A VARIABLE OR LABEL
Α               CM IS SHORT FOR COMMAND
Α               CMARG IS THE ARGUMENT OF A COMMAND
Α      ⎕ REPRESENTS THE TERMINAL I/O TO THE DCP.
Α
L1: STR←BLANKSΔF ⎕,⎕←' :',6ρ' '
 →(∧/')')'=2↑STR)/MPU
 STR←APLΔP STR
 →(∧/')')'=2↑,STR)/MPU
 ⎕←⍕STR
 ' '
 →L1
MPU: CMNAME←TAKECMΔF STR←2↓STR
 →(~CHECKΔF CMNAME)/ERROR
 CMNAME DOCMΔF CMARG←(ρCMNAME)↓STR
 →L1
ERROR: ⎕←'IMPROPER COMMAND'
 →L1
```

The DCPΔP function, in the line labeled L1, simulates input
from a terminal connected to the appropriate ACIA port of the
DCP. The analysis for special control characters is performed in
the next line. If the)) pattern is found the branch to MPU is
made. The DCPΔP parses STR for a command and argument and then
executes that command in DOCMΔF, if possible. Errors are
detected and in case the instruction does not match a table of
instructions, that error is put out to the terminal. Control
then goes back to L1 and the terminal. If the system command
characters,)), are not detected in the string, then the
assumption is that the string contains an executable APL
statement. The function APLΔP then attempts to execute whatever
may be in the string and transmits back to the terminal the
result of the execution step. Should the host execute a function
that outputs leading)) characters, the DCPΔP recognizes that
it must execute a command. Again a branch to MPU occurs.

DCPΔP emulates exactly the operation of the DCP in the
hierarchy. The function APLΔP which is meant to emulate the
operation of the APL host does so through the   function.
However, APL systems commands cannot be executed in this way and
an APL error detected in execution will suspend DCPΔP as well as
APLΔP. The DCP microcomputer is distinct from the APL host so
that all functions execute properly in the real hierarchy.

The function DCPΔP assumes that the DCP is connected into the
host through a terminal port on the host. In that case the
terminal is connected into the DCP and the communication pathway
is from the terminal into the DCP and from there to the host
and back through the DCP for output from the host, see figure
(2).

This mode of operation in which the terminal and host
communicate with each other through the DCP is satisfactory for
communicating with large APL machines such as the Sigma 7 or the
IBM 370/145 that we have used on this project. The large
machines, though, have a disadvantage in that the size of their
input buffer and output buffer and the characters used to
signify the end of a line and the end of a buffer are not
subject to user control simply. We found that the Sigma 7 host,
though, could be interfaced through APL readily to the DCP with
the I/O going back and forth as "blind I/O". In this way the
Sigma 7 did not insert control characters into the software
character string sent across the telephone lines. This did mean
that a short and simple APL program had to be executing in the
host for the communications to work properly. This was easy to
do and not a hindrance in execution. There is no doubt that the
problem could be handled in the software of the DCP, should we
choose to do so.

We found that we needed to go more deeply into the
telecommunications protocol between computer systems than we had
really expected. And, in fact, in subsequent editions of our DCP

we will include all of the telecommunications protocol that is required for a particular host. It is most unfortunate that the computer industry does not have a well-defined set of standards for the handshake protocols used by computer systems. The RS 232C specification really only stipulates the hardware aspects of telecommunications and says nothing at all about the software protocol for establishing communications links.

We have found that the IBM 5100 is an easy host to use in our hierarchy. The communications link is very much simplified in that the IBM 5100 includes its own terminal input device. While we used a terminal hooked into the DCP in order to monitor the data transfer between various points on the hierarchy, in fact all of the commands as well as executing APL functions were initiated from the keyboard of the IBM 5100. It was possible to use the IBM 5100 as a terminal and operate with it as the principal host for the data acquisition and preliminary processing steps in performing the experiment, but then transfer the data set over to the larger host for somewhat longer calculations.

The hierarchy based on the DCP has worked exceedingly well for the light scattering experiment as will be documented later in this paper. The architecture including the software design can be generalized to a much more complicated experiment. The key was to recognize that the DCP was setting up implicit shared variables between the processors on the hierarchy. The shared variable concept has been exploited in the APLSV and VSAPL systems as developed and marketed by IBM for their 370 series computers. A paper by Lathwell [5] goes into the system formulation in some detail. We have developed the architecture for what we feel will be a hierarchy that exploits the shared variable extensively. Four levels will be used: HOST, SHARED VARIABLE PROCESSOR, DEVICE CONTROL PROCESSOR, and INSTRUMENTS.

The SVP and DCP will be plug compatible M6800 microcomputers but with quite different operating systems. The DCP will be a command based system with real time capabilities. The SVP will have commands, systems functions and systems variables as well as primitives necessary for handling the logic and array shaping required of data acquisition and control. In the end the SVP might have the APL capability of the IBM 5100 with about 10kbytes of memory. However the SVP must be able to link to several devices rather than just one. The shared variables protocol can be used directly with any number of serial I/O ports that fits the hardware limitations. We do anticipate the need for an interrupt structure now missing from APL implementations as well as some form of multi-tasking. These questions are under study.

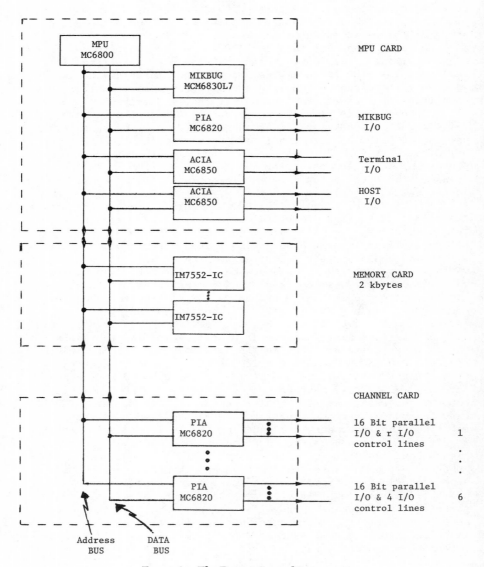

Figure 1.   The Device Control Processor

The Hierarchy

Two hierarchies were used extensively and are blocked out in Figures 2 and 3.

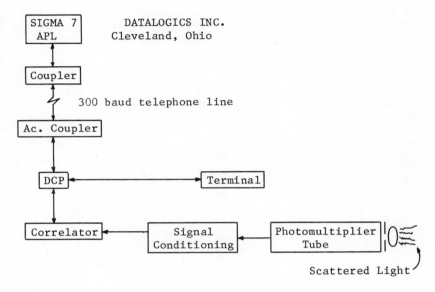

Figure 2

In general, the DCP accepts strings of characters from either the Sigma 7 host or terminal and passes them on to the target. The DCP is invisible to the user's dialog with the host.

Only when the characters '))' appear at the start of a string will the DCP look for an executable command to process. This operation is described in the previous section. Note that these commands can be organized for sequential transmission to the DCP as literal strings by APL functions resident in the host. The APL functions are initiated from the terminal while the APL system is in calculator mode. Timing can be introduced by an appropriate combination of a function that delays execution and comparison with what amounts to a time stamp variable. However, an interrupt structure was not available.

The data transmitted from the DCP buffer were taken into the Sigma 7 as quartets of hexadecimal characters followed by a blank all in a binary format. The dyadic ι function against the atomic vector gave the location of each character in the atomic vector. The decode function produced the desired set of numbers to a precision of 16 bits as transmitted by the correlator. In

fact, two data sets could be transmitted from the
correlator--one giving the most significant 16 bits of the 24 bit
correlator word and the second the least significant 16 bits. A
one-line APL function compared the common bits for register,
masked the common bits of the array having the least significant
bits of the correlator words and catinated the two arrays
producting a single array containing the entire dynamic range of
the correlator. While such precision is unnecessary in
conventional light scattering work, it was most interesting to
discover that bit level manipulations could be handled easily in
APL.

The 300 baud transmission rate was in fact uncomfortably slow
when more than 100 element data arrays (100 x 5 = 500
characters) had to be transferred to the host and processed.
The SAICOR Model 43 produces 400 element data arrays or 2000
characters. The delay was especially uncomfortable when the DCP
program for its operating system was down-loaded.   These
problems were eliminated by using the IBM 5100 as the host
computer.

The hierarchy that used the IBM 5100 has the following
configuration:

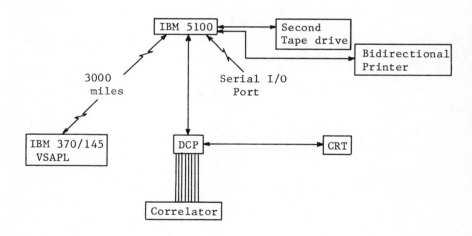

Figure 3

The IBM 5100 has a number of advantages in interfacing to the
DCP.   The size of the I/O buffers for the IBM 5100 can be
changed dynamically and easily under program control, the end of
line and end of buffer characters can be specified, and an
input prompt can be specified.   Incorporating this level of I/O
control into simple APL functions allows a direct dialog

between the correlator and the IBM 5100.   We have found it
easy to write APL functions that check for certain prompts that
are generated by the DCP (e.g., the MIKBUG prompts) so as to
detect completion of load conditions as well as operator errors.
Clearly the necessary programs could have been written in
assembler for the DCP but it was far easier to use the IBM 5100
shared variable processor through APL to accomplish the same
behavior. Since the IBM 5100 allows the transmission rate to be
set up to 9600 baud, transfer of data is no longer limiting in
collecting replicate runs. We presently run at 1200 baud and may
go to 3600 baud in the future. Further, the down-loading of
microcomputer code is rapid and is totally interactive.

      A second host arrangement was established between the IBM 5100
and an IBM 370/145 in order to handle larger least squares fitting.
A set of APL functions kindly provided by Gussin [6] was
extensively rewritten to include a command structure for
transmitting and fetching objects between the IBM 5100 and an
IBM 370/145. Data sets were transmitted back and forth so that
the data type and name of each array would be the same. Functions
were transformed into canonical representations ($\square$CR)
transmitted and fixed ($\square$FX) in the new environment
automatically without special conversion functions resident in
the host. Therefore, data sets could be read from magnetic tape
archives and transmitted to the large host for data processing
using functions sent over to the host. The DCP was programmed
to use ASCII code so that it could not serve as a three way
simultaneous interface between the IBM 370/145 (EBCDIC), the IBM
5100 (ASCII or EBCDIC) and the correlator. However, that mode of
operation is certainly possible with appropriate programming of
the DCP.

      We found that the IBM 5100 hierarchy was flexible but yet easy
to use and entirely reliable. The down time of the IBM 5100
amounted to a total of one day for six months. Adjustments to the
tape drive accounted for all of the down time. Further the
system was available at all times and did not depend on the
scheduling of a time sharing vendor.

An Operating System

      The attributes of the hardware, commands, and the high-level
language are integrated in a way that assists interactive
experimentation. This was done by writing a set of APL functions
that worked together as a processor. Based on previous
experience with a PDP 11/45 machine running under RSX 11D, we
estimated that such a processor would require at least eight
months to write and debug. Many of the subroutines would have
been written in assembly language. In contrast, one first year
graduate student (T. Gall) wrote and debugged the processor in
three months. This was his first serious   effort with APL so

that he also learned the language during that   period. We next
outline the operation of the processor and give an example of
APL functions that were written. Others will be sent upon request.
     The IBM 5100 serves four purposes in our experiments. It
gives instructions to the operator. It controls the
instrument. It archives the data and results on tape. It
calculates results from the data. The goal was to write an
operating system that could be used by technicians who did not
know the language.
     It was very easy to write APL functions that allow
interaction between the activity of the functions in controlling
the instrument and the experimentalist. A small set of
commands, thought of as niladic APL functions, was developed for
controlling the interaction between the host the microcomputer
and the correlator. The list of commands that provided the
necessary function in the DCP is: MEMORY, START, FETCH, TRANSMIT,
INITIATE, and BEGIN. Each function was coded in assembly
language as subroutines called by a control program. A cross
assembler produced the machine code as a string of hexadecimal
characters. These strings could be transmitted from the IBM 5100
through the MIKBUG port. Initialization data was transmitted as
part of the string. Once this transmission was completed, the
microcomputer would operate as a DCP.
     When the command))MEMORY is sent from either the terminal or
computer, the microcomputer then prepares for the memory
allocation for each channel. This allocation is done by an APL
function from the host or interactively from the terminal. The
command string))START invokes a subroutine in the microcomputer
that produces the necessary output signal levels to start the
correlator operation. When the correlator finishes taking a
data set, the information that that has happened is received by
the microcomputer as a flag.))FETCH   calls a subroutine to
read the correlator memory and store the hexadecimal
representation of the numbers in the DCP memory.))TRANSMIT
<argument> causes the microcomputer to transmit information to
either the host or the CRT. The command string))BEGIN is a
microcomputer call to the subroutine START and then TRANSMIT that
causes the correlator to run and when that step is completed,
causes the transfer of the data up into the host. The command
))INITIATE invokes a subroutine in the microcomputer that makes
the necessary links for a host to interact with the hierarchy.
The host must be able to handle block reception of the
data being transmitted from the microcomputer. The time
required for the 5100 to change from output to input mode is of
the order of 100 to 200 milliseconds and that was slow compared
to the microcomputer. However, the 5100 can be instructed to
take the last character of the output string as an input
prompt. The result was that the last character of the string
was not sent until the IBM 5100 had switched from output to
input. With this technique it was impossible for the 5100 to

miss any of the data strings being sent from the microcomputer.

Examples of APL/5100 functions to communicate with the M6800 microcomputer are available from the authors. Several levels of protocol are involved:bit level handshaking, shared variables conditioning of the serial I/O interface, and the APL defined functions. However, in the end only the APL defined functions need be used by the experimentalist in writing the functions for handling the various aspects of running an experiment.

Data, instructions and functions can be stored on magnetic tape. Usually, data storage on tape was organized with one file for each data set. A file name for each data set is stored in an array called LIBRARY specific for each workspace executing the control functions. The number of lines in LIBRARY tells the system how many files there are on that tape. The size of the files should be   known in advance so that the proper size can be marked on the   tape. If the size of the data sets to be stored are unknown, the   files are marked with the size of the largest data set expected. A number of functions were coded in APL to handle the   archiving of data automatically.

After each run or, alternately, after a series of runs, APL functions can be invoked to perform data workup calculations. one such calculation that must be done is the conversion of the hexadecimal code transmitted from the microcomputer into the IBM 5100 internal representation for numbers.   After that, the least squares curve fit of a run or a series of runs can be made automatically to the cumulant polynomial, eq. (2). A part of the   code is shown below.

```
K←C CUM N
T←ΔT×ιρR
B←(NR÷SIG)⊛R-C
A←(⍉((N+1),ρR)ρNR÷SIG)×(((ρR),N+1)ρ1,÷!ιN)×(-T)∘.*0,ιN
K←B⊞A
→0
⍝
⍝THE SET OF DELAY TIMES, T, IS COMPUTED GIVEN ΔT.
⍝THE FIRST ELEMENT OF R WAS DROPPED.
⍝THE WEIGHTED B VECTOR IS COMPUTED FROM THE LOG OF
⍝  THE CORRELATION FUNCTION SUBTRACTING OUT THE BASE LINE.
⍝ALL OF THE DERIVATIVES ARE COMPUTED AND ASSIGNED TO A.
⍝A IS AS LONG AS THE DATA SET AND AS WIDE AS THE NUMBER
⍝  OF CUMULANTS TO BE CALCULATED, N, PLUS ONE.
⍝B⊞A COMPUTES THE CUMULANTS
⍝CUM IS PART OF A SHORT FUNCTION THAT CONTROLS THE ITERATION.
```

To make memory available for large calculations, a system was designed whereby all the data acquisition programs were themselves stored on tape as canonical representations of the functions.   Only the first few lines of a calling function are

resident in the workspace. The rest are stored. The data
handling functions are invoked by the calling program and so are
cleared from the memory by the $\Box$EX function when it is
finished. Storing the functions and data on tape and having
two tape drives expands the available workspace memory to
approximately 400 K bytes. Obviously,the execution time is
slowed down when functions have to be read from tape.   Even
though the IBM 5100 execution time is slower on individual
functions than a larger time sharing system, it does not have
the transmission and sharing delays that a large system
requires. Operating at 1200 bits per second transmission, the
5100 can take and store a 400 point data set every 15 sec.   In
contrast, the Xerox Sigma 7 as a host exchanging data at 300
bits per second, required an average of 5 minutes to take and
store a data set. Even though the microcomputer is slower at
executing individual functions, its dedication to one user and
one experiment makes its overall throughput at least 5 to 10
times that of a conventional time sharing machine.

Results and Conclusions

The hierarchical system has been operating for six months
reliably and has been used by roughly a dozen different
experimenters. The effectiveness of the system is demonstrated
by a simple problem.
    In working up the autocorrelation function data to diffusion
coefficients (see the first section), the weight function for
the   cumulant analysis must be estimated. Edwards [7] has
constructed a model of the process that predicts a certain
variation of the   standard deviation of the correlation
function (σ_R) with delay   time.   A simple propagation-of-error
analysis will show that the   values of the cumulants are
sensitive to the variation of the   weight function when very
accurate estimates of the diffusion coefficient (<2%) and
higher cumulants are required.
    The form of the σ_R function was to be studied experimentally.
Replications of the correlation function had to be collected
under   closely controlled conditions. Histograms were
collected for each   of 400 points of the correlation function.
Fifty replications gave   reasonable distribution functions from
which   could be   calculated   for $\langle R \rangle$.
    The data collection proceeded rapidly since the signal to
noise   ratios were large enough that averaging required only
ca. 1 min.   for each run. A few seconds were required for
writing each data   set to a tape file. All of these steps were
handled by APL defined   functions sequenced appropriately by an
APL defined function. The   machine executed without operator
control during this tedious part   of the experiment.   The
operator then wrote   several lines of APL   code in a defined
function in order to fetch the data sets from   files, build up

the arrays from which the error data could be calculated and examined in plots of various kinds.

In one day, an experiment could be conceived and completed that with older techniques would require weeks of effort. Just the coding and debugging of the analysis program would have required about one man day of effort using FORTRAN and a batch system. In APL the coding and debugging was trivial.

We believe that the APL hierarchy has enhanced the productivity of the light scattering experiment by several orders of magnitude. Just automating the experiment accounts for an order of magnitude in the productivity of the experiment. Certainly, that improvement has been experienced by others with conventional computing systems and interfaces. However, the use of APL has cut the effort required to produce functions by an order of magnitude as well. This property of APL was especially appreciated when devising analysis algorithms.

The use of a hierarchy which had an IBM 5100 for most of the work and a large machine occasionally as hosts kept certain costs of operating the experiment in line. A large host can handle the role of the 5100 so long as telecommunication rates are above 300 baud. However, connect time is charged on most commercial systems at rates around $15 per hour and higher. The IBM 5100 requires only capitalization and maintenance. Further, commercial time sharing rates make the use of the large host in place of the IBM 5100 costly for data acquisition. However, the IBM 5100 executes large number crunching jobs slowly enough that they can be effectively done on a large host. Fortunately, it is easy to use the IBM 5100 for transferring data and functions to the host as well as fetching results from the host. The IBM 5100 can be a very bright terminal to the large host. It is able to make efficient use of the number crunching power of the large host since function development can be done in the small machine.

We believe that a hierarchical approach based on a APL as the driver language leads to the most effective compromise between the cost of hardware and the cost of writing software. This has proven to be true for our experimental work and there is evidence that the hypothesis is true generally for laboratory work. The very high cost of producing reliable software may make the hypothesis true for a much wider range of applications.

Acknowledgments

This work was supported by grants from NIH and NASA. We are happy to acknowledge the support of DATALOGICS, Cleveland, Ohio for time to develop several models for the operation of the DCP. We gratefully acknowledge the role that Drs. P. Friedl and J. Beaumont, IBM Palo Alto Scientific Center, have had in developing the IBM 5100 hierarchy as part of a joint study.

APPENDIX

Table 1 Summary Information of Some APL Systems

Computer	Response Time to Entry	Execution Speed	Workspace Size	Language Execution	Shared Variables	Suitability as a host for data acquisition	Human Engineering of system	Sign ON Protocol
IBM 5100	Good. A fine 1 person machine)SAVE is slow since mag. tape is used.	Slow	64kbytes maximum available This is minimum size for our applications.	Full APL. No known bugs.	Yes	Very good.	Very good First class visual fidelity is used.	Switch on power.
IBM 370/145	Good 1 sec.	Good	Virtual system default to 330k bytes or larger.	Full APL. No known bugs. Very effective.	Yes	Good. Block length limited to about 2kbytes on input from DCP.	Good	Simple

Computer	Response Time	Execution Speed	Workspace Size	Language Execution	Shared Variables	Suitability	Engineering	Sign ON Protocol
IBM 370/158 (Princeton Univ. Machine)	Good 1 sec.	Very good.	Virtual	Full APL. No known bugs. Very effective.	Yes	Good. Block length of input is fixed.	Good	Simple
SIGMA 7 (Datalogics, Cleveland, Ohio)	Good. Loads badly at times.	Good	128kbytes fixed work space size.	Full APL. □functions and variables implemented by $\bar{T}$ and I.	NO	Good.	OK	Awkward
HP3000 Ser II	Reasonable 1 - 5 sec.	Reasonable	Virtual	Full APL modeled after VSAPL. A few bugs are being fixed.	Yes but has not been fully implemented.	Good	OK	Simple
PDP 11- APL 11	Good	Reasonable (Benchmark would not run however).	Very Poor	Subset of Full APL Primitives missing.	NO	Poor. But may be acceptable with the extensive use of file I/O.	OK	Reasonable

Computer	Response Time	Execution Speed	Workspace Size	Language Execution	Shared Variables	Suitability	Engineering	Sign ON Protocol
DEC 10 APLSF	Has not been benchmarked.			Full APL.	NO. But there is an extensive file system.	NO comment.	No comment	No comment.
CDC (CYBERNET Services) a CYBER 73 machine was on line during benchmark.	Slow. Machine was loaded.	Good	Had to be adjusted through ⎕WA	Full APL.	NO	NO comment.	Poor during our one session.	reasonable.
Burroughs APL/700	It exists but we have not been able to use a system for benchmarking at this time.							
UNIVAC* 1100/11 UNIVAC APL	OK	OK	Must use ⎕WA and the maximum is about 256kbytes.	Subset of APL.	NO	NO	Very poor.	Very poor.

*The Univac APL processors were written at the University of Maryland or by Univac based on the University of Maryland processor. In our experience these processors are not up to modern standards.

Table 2 Comparison of Execution Times

The benchmark simulates the least squares fitting of 400 data points to a five parameter model. The timing was measured using the ⎕TS systems variable or the equivalent function. The following function was executed on the IBM machines, the HP3000 and the CDC machine.

```
TIMING
T←¯4↑⎕TS
A←?400 5 ρ100
B←?400ρ100
⎕←Z←B⊞A
1E¯03×-(1 60 60 1000 ⊥T)-1 60 60 1000 ⊥¯4↑⎕TS
Z←⎕
→1
```

Machine	Timing	Comments
IBM 370/158 (Princeton University)	0.6 – 2 sec.	(heavy loading)
CDC (Cybernet Services machine. A Cyber 73 machine was probably on line during the benchmark trial.)	1 – 17 sec.	(heavy loading)
SIGMA 7 (Datalogics, Cleveland, Ohio)	2 – 5 sec.	Moderate loading.
HP3000 Ser II Mod 5	23.5 sec.	One user at the time of the bench-mark. System was not fine-tuned for APL operation.
IBM 5100	90 sec.	
UNIVAC Systems	Would not execute. Either gave a workspace full or dropped out of APL.	Benchmark was attempted on several systems.

Literature Cited

1. Chu, B., "Laser Light Scattering," Academic Press, New York, 1975.
2. Berne, B. J. and Pecora, R., "Dynamic Light Scattering," John Wile and Sons, Inc., New York, 1976.
3. Mann, J. A. and McGregor, T. R., Colloid and Interface Science, V. III, 349, Academic Press, Inc., New York, 1976.
4. Roberson, D. A., Proceedings of the IEEE (1976), 64 (6), 994.
5. Lathwell, R. H., IBM J. Res. Develop. (1973) July, 353.
6. Gussen, N., IBM, Palo Alto Scientific Center, Private Communication.
7. Edwards, R. V., Private Communication.

A Distributed Minicomputer System for Process Calculations

A. I. JOHNSON, D. N. KIDD, and K. L. ROBERTS

University of Western Ontario, London, Canada

During the past decade one of the authors (Johnson) and his faculty colleagues and students have been developing, applying, and evaluating the modular approach to the steady state and dynamic behaviour of process systems. These studies have led to two executive systems, GEMCS (1) for steady state and DYNSYS (2) for dynamic systems studies which have academic and industrial use.

More recently a large timesharing computer, a DECsystem 10, has been used to create an integrated system for process analysis and design, INSYPS. This system offers optimization facilities and interfaces to the process designer or analyst through a graphics console (3). With the INSYPS system on the DECsystem 10 the process engineer can call, from one facility, upon the full range of executive programs for handling the various aspects of complex designs and greatly enhance his productivity and creativity.

INSYPS on a Large Computer

The original INSYPS deals with two concepts, the use of interactive graphics for input and output and automatic linkage between independent packages. The integration of packages is carried out in a modular fashion to enable one to add new systems or modify existing ones without affecting the entire structure. The areas considered for INSYPS are:

1. Computer Graphics
2. Steady State Simulation
3. Optimization
4. Dynamic Simulation

In theory one could make all four of these communicate with each other. Figure 1 shows the system, illustrating both the possible links and those actually implemented. Communication between packages is either a single step linkage or an iterative link. A single step linkage transfers information once per execution, as in the plotting of the results from a dynamic simulator. It can usually be accomplished by a data file. The iterative linkage, on the other hand, deals with a continuous flow of information between packages, such as the link between a simulator and the optimization packages. This type of linkage can only be ‑carried out by interfacing programs specially designed for the packages. Some of the characteristics of such a program would be:

1. Easy 'hook-up': that is, making a subsystem readily available for an application area with a flexible procedure and associated implementation technique.

2. Efficiency: this is required in running time, and is particularly desirable in iterative systems.

3. Automatic operation: once the link has been established the resulting system should be automatic in nature. The user should not be required to know the details of the linkage of the subsystem.

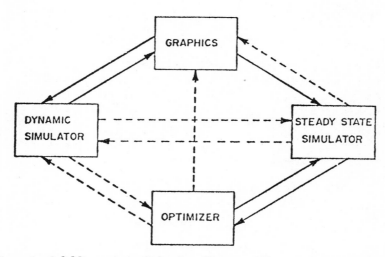

Figure 1.   Solid line: existing links; dotted line: possible extensions to the system

INSYPS was built with all of the above criteria in mind. It consists of four self-standing subsystems, four linking programs, and six data files. Figure 2 describes their layout. Since the subsystems are independent of each other they are not loaded together, except when the function to be optimized requires plant simulation.

Application of INSYPS

A chemical process is usually represented by a process flow sheet, which is made up of processing units joined by lines. The lines or streams represent flow of material or information. In general the flow sheet and the programs which simulate them deal with the equipment (or processing units) and the stream connections. One builds up the process by putting together the desired units, the shape and behaviour of which are pre-defined. A set of graphical symbols represents the unit computations and a diagram can be built to represent the information flow. Usually there is a one-to-one correspondence between the graphical symbol and the processing unit. Each graphical symbol corresponds to a unit computation subprogram in the library of the simulation system. In general the arrangement of the module symbols will be similar to those on the process flow diagram.

The designer constructs the flow sheet by selecting processing units from the menu. Each unit he selects is given a number and parameters. Stream connections are also defined by picking the appropriate stream functions. For every stream the designer gives its number, its source and destination units, its total flow, temperature, pressure, vapour fraction, and the component concentrations. By convention a material flow stream is shown by a solid line, an information flow stream by a dotted line. The other drawing or writing operations performed are mnemonic aids only and are not passed to the simulator.

On completion of the diagram the program understands the process topology – the interconnections of the components – and has a record of the input/output stream parameters for each processing unit in the diagram. The entire process information can be saved on the disk by executing the SAVE function on the menu.

The other aspect of the graphics subsystem is the graphical output. Since a person can evaluate a graph more quicky than he can a long list of numbers, this aspect of INSYPS greatly facilitates the study of transient systems. The designer can display a single

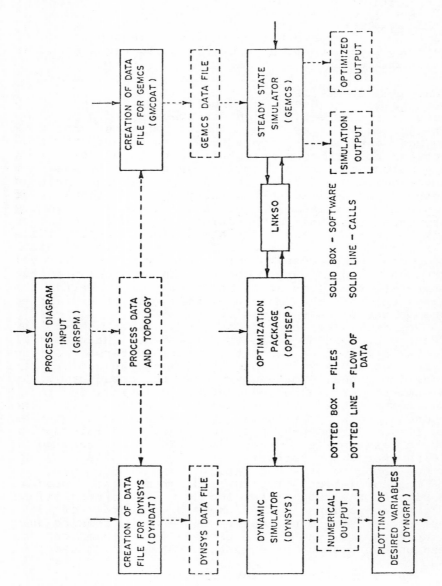

Figure 2

variable or a group of them together, and can point at any location on the graph and have its value typed out. He can also have the graph from the CRT plotted on a conventional plotter for better resolution or larger scale.

The designer of this system would start off by graphically creating the process flowsheet. (The same strategy is used for both steady state and dynamic systems.) He is expected to know the unit computations corresponding to his process. Any or all information on the process diagram (i.e. changes in equipment or streams or their parameters) can be updated graphically.

On completion of the input, the designer is provided with an information flow diagram and a data file to run the desired simulator. The results from the dynamic simulator are put on a disk file, and selected information from this can be graphed. Figure 3 illustrates the interaction of the user with the computer programs outlined above.

Control of a Simple Evaporator System

The problem presented was to control a one-component total vaporizer with two mode controllers. The study required determination of optimum settings and steady state operation.

A diagram of the process, presented in figure 4, shows the control configuration applied. The

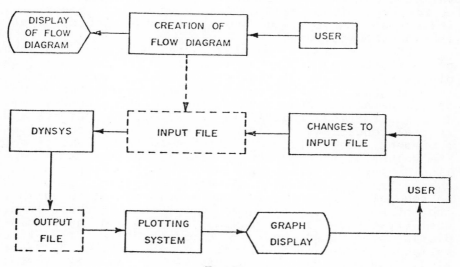

Figure 3

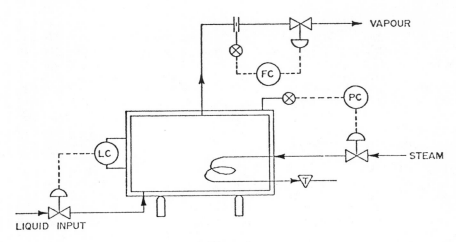

Figure 4

evaporator has a capacity for 800 lbs. of liquid
oprerating at normal level conditions. The equipment
is designed to handle 1700 lbs/hr of any component at
steady state operation. Three main variables have to
be controlled in order to control the entire process:
the level of liquid in the vaporizer, the output flow
of the vapour, and the pressure in the vessel. These
variables are controlled by manipulating
correspondingly: the liquid flow into the vaporizer,
the steam through the coil, and the flow of vapour
leaving the equipment.

Once the unit modules were designed and the
process configuration defined the information flow
diagram for the simulation was created. Figure 5 shows
the diagram as it appeared on the screen after it was
drawn, using the programs of the graphics subsystem.
The information provided in the streams represents the
initial conditions at time zero. All the given values
represent steady state operation conditions, except for
the values of the pressure in the vessel (stream 5) and
liquid level (stream 2) which will produce a step
change in the simulation of those variables. This can
be recognized by comparing the mentioned values against
the set point value assigned to the control they feed.
The first simulation run was started and the results
displayed on the screen as graphs. There were five
variables under observation: 1) Liquid flow, 2) Steam
flow, 3) Vapour flow, 4) Liquid level, and 5) Vessel
pressure. The basic criteria for control settings
were: recovery from perturbation to normal steady

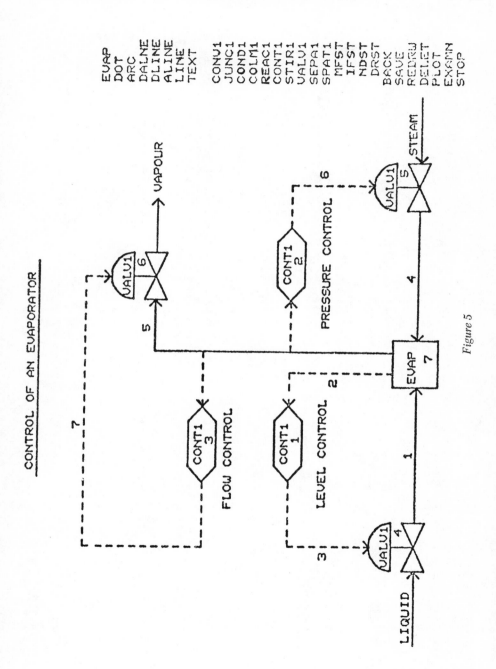

Figure 5

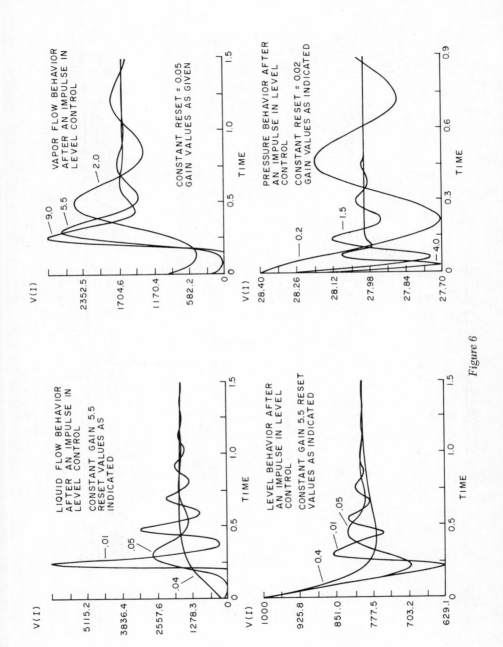

Figure 6

state as fast as possible, minimum amplitude of oscillation during recovery.

Sample comparative results for each of the variables mentioned are shown in Figure 6. The graphs describe the results of this example and at the same time illustrate the general procedure already mentioned. It is evident that in every set of curves representing specific values there is one that can be considered as the best in performance. A designer has to compromise at this point as to whether he wants faster response, sacrificing oscillation amplitudes and higher number of oscillations or slower response but in a smoother form.

An Integrated Process Analysis and Design Syntax on a Distributed Computer Assembly

Having demonstrated a potential opportunity to enhance the creativity and productivity of the process and design engineer with INSYPS, a distributed computer system is being developed.

The system is tentatively named GRAMPS. The analytical capabilities of this new system will be similar to those provided by INSYPS, but several performance benefits are expected:

1. Graphic operations response speedup. The new system incorporates a programmable graphics processor capable of performing all flow diagram editing operations, graph labelling, and the like.

2. Calculational response speedup. Process calculations will be performed on a dedicated minicomputer, providing better and more predictable response time than a large timeshared system.

3. Portability. The system is compact, and can be moved on-site for a period of intensive use by a chemical company's own engineering personnel.

4. Economy of Operation. The operating costs are relatively fixed, and known in advance; they are insensitive to the amount of analytical work done.

Configuration and Operation

The GRAMPS system (figure 7) consists of two minicomputers and various peripherals and communications links.

Graphics Computer: This is a 32K minicomputer which is programmed in GRAPPLE (4), a graphics

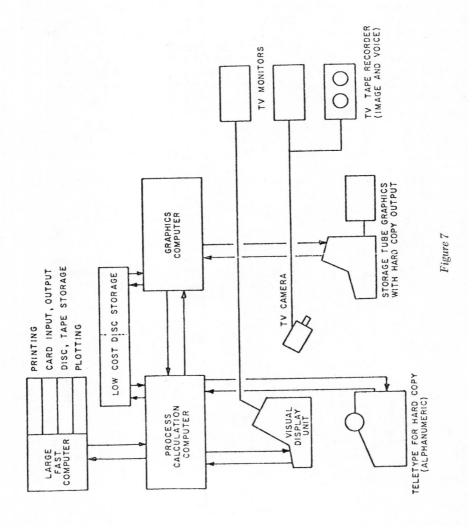

Figure 7

programming language similar in style to ALGOL. This system is manufactured by Systems Approach, Ltd. in Ottawa on license from Bell Northern Research, Ltd. It includes four floppy disk drives for local storage, and a Tektronix 4015 storage tube graphics terminal with plotter for hard-copy output or digitized input.

Process Calculations Computer: This is a 32K PDP-11/34 running under RT-11 and programmed in FORTRAN. It presently has two floppy disk drives for local storage and a teleprinter for hard-copy printout. Current plans call for this system to be expanded to 64K memory with addition of a floating point processor and cartridge disk storage. The GRAMPS system hardware cost is about $100,000.

The PDP-11 is the nucleus of the system; it has communication links with the GRAPPLE console, the DECsystem 10, and a teleprinter, and is responsible for overall system control and file routing.

When the INSYPS capabilities have been fully implemented in GRAMPS, the process flow sheet editing function will reside on the GRAPPLE console. When the flow sheet and parameters have been specified, the PDP-11 will be passed a file giving the process topology and the associated values. One or more analysis operations may be carried out on the PDP-11, with the results being written to files. Output files may then be transferred to the teleprinter for listing and/or to the GRAPPLE console for display as graphs.

At present the various analysis packages for steady state simulation, optimization, and dynamic simulation are operational on the PDP-11, and current emphasis is on the communications link between the GRAPPLE console and the PDP-11.

Research and Development Needs

The development of a modular process analysis and design system with a range of capabilities (e.g. steady state simulation, dynamic simulation, optimization, design and synthesis) on a distributed computing system has created some exciting opportunities for redesign of the system executive programs and for research into efficient data and program storage.

Low cost graphics terminals have been shown to greatly enhance the creativity and productivity of the design engineer. Yet much needs be learned about the quantity and quality of information to be presented on the screen, and the differing needs of a range of users. While all are familiar with graphical representation of data, new needs and opportunities for the presentation and manipulation of complex systems await development.

In the system under development the GRAPPLE console has a significant analysis capability. The best use of this requires further research.

It is apparent that easy communication between and among the computers of a distributed system is a key for their effective use. The units should be essentially parallel processors, taking full advantage of the independence and differing strengths of the computer systems. The communication needs are closely tied to the optimum use of the diskette and cartridge disk storage available. The diskettes provide convenient low cost, personal aids to program development and evaluation. Cartridge disks provide long-term, high-volume storage and faster access. The process calculation computer must serve as a communication link to remote computers when these can solve complex problems outside the capabilities of the local system. Distributed minicomputer-based systems open new dimensions for process analysis and design and encourage reconsideration of the existing design methodology.

Abstract

This paper describes a distributed minicomputer-based system for simulation and optimization studies of chemical process systems. The system provides an integrated analysis environment for the process engineer, including graphical input of flow sheets and display of performance curves. The system was initially developed on a large timesharing system and is now being re-developed on a distributed minicomputer system.

Literature Cited

1   ´GEMCS - General Engineering and Management Computation System´, (1971), A. I. Johnson and Associates, The University of Western Ontario, Faculty of Engineering Science, London, Canada.
2   ´DYNSYS User´s and Systems Manuals´, (1976), A. I. Johnson, J. Barney, R. S. Ahluwalia, available from SACDA, The University of Western Ontario, London, Canada.
3   Ahluwalia, R. S., Lopez, J., Johnson, A. I., Millares, R., ´Integrated Computer Aided Design System for Process Design´, Proceedings of the IFAC Symposium on Large Scale Systems Theory and Applications, Udine, Italy, June 1976.
4   Woolsey, L. G., ´Design for a High Level Graphics Language Machine´, Infor, vol. 13 1975), pp. 248-259.

A Computer Data Acquisition and Control System for an Atmospheric Cloud Chamber Facility

D. E. HAGEN, K. P. BERKBIGLER,* J.L. KASSNER, JR., and D. R. WHITE
Graduate Center for Cloud Physics Research, University of Missouri, Rolla, MO 65401

The Graduate Center for Cloud Physics Research is a multi-disciplinary research center devoted primarily to the study of the microphysical processes active in cloud and fog. The research tools from the disciplines of physics, chemistry, mechanical engineering, and electrical engineering are employed in this effort. Special emphasis is placed on laboratory experiment and theoretical work, complimented by some field measurement activity.

The purpose of this paper is to describe the hybrid mini/macro computer system that is used to support one of our experimental laboratory facilities, the cloud simulation chamber. The minicomputer is dedicated to serve the data acquisition and control needs of the chamber and is not used for general purpose batch job processing. It is just one of many peripheral subsystems used to support the cloud simulation chamber. The chamber and its peripherals are devoted to "classic" academic research and as a result are in a continuing state of evolution. This discussion will emphasize the present state of development of the computer/chamber system, with some discussion given to the near future plans for the system.

The cloud simulation facility which is supported by the computer system is shown in the block diagram in Fig. 1 and in the photograph in Fig. 2. At the heart of the system is the cloud simulation chamber. It is an expansion cloud chamber, one of the longest used and more important tools in the cloud physics laboratory. In this device a sample of moist aerosol-

---

* Present address: Sandia Laboratories, Livermore, Ca. 94550.

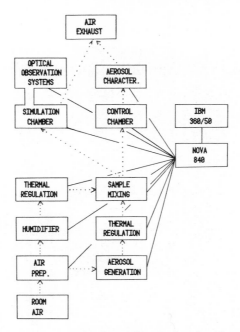

Figure 1. Cloud simulation chamber facility block diagram. · · · *air flow;* ——— *data flow and control.*

laden air is cooled by expansion. The air becomes
supersaturated with respect to water and the water
vapor condenses out on certain categories of the
particulates to form a cloud which can then be
studied. The expansion chamber is supported by a
variety of peripheral systems. An air preparation
system provides a supply of clean dry air. A bank
of humidifiers raises the vapor content of the air
to 100% relative humidity at a precisely known temperature. Aerosol generators provide a stable and
predictable aerosol to serve as condensation nuclei.
The control chamber allows for extensive analysis of
the sample gas and its aerosol at the initial simulation chamber conditions during the time the cloud
is being formed in the simulation chamber. The cloud
in the simulation chamber can be observed by several
optical systems: light attenuation, laser doppler
shift (1), Mie scattering, photography, and visual
observation by telescope. The aerosol characterization (critical activation supersaturation spectrum)
is accomplished with a variety of techniques: electric aerosol analyzer (2), continuous flow thermal

Figure 2.   Cloud simulation chamber facility photograph

diffusion chamber (3), Laktinov Chamber (4), and
a Gardner counter.

A major limitation of expansion cloud chambers
results from wall effects (5). The ordinary Wilson
expansion cloud chamber cools and supersaturates
the gas by means of a rapid expansion which is approximately adiabatic, but the chamber walls, whose heat
capacity is very high in comparison to the gas, remain at their initial temperature. Heat from the
walls flows into the gas and reduces the supersaturation, destroys the adiabaticity of the expansion,
and leads to errors in one's knowledge of the evolving thermodynamics. Furthermore, evaporation occurs
at all wet surfaces. Our simulation chamber has the
unique feature of cooling the chamber walls in unison
with the gas to remove this wall effect. The wall
cooling is accomplished by thermoelectric modules (6)
sandwiched between the chamber's interior wall and
an external heat sink. Control of the gas and wall
temperatures is one of the major real-time tasks of
the computer system. The control loop is complicated
by the fact that the gas temperature cannot be directly measured with sufficient accuracy (5), (7).
Instead it is calculated from thermodynamics (5) and
drop growth theory and measurements of pressure and
liquid water content.

The set of equations governing these processes
are given below:

$$\dot{T} = \frac{(nRT/P)\dot{P} - (L+\beta T)\, \dot{r}}{c_p + s\,(r_o - r)}, \qquad (1)$$

$$\dot{a}_j = \frac{D\rho\,\left[S - S_j{}^*\,(a_j)\right]}{a_j + \ell}, \qquad (\underline{8}) \quad (2)$$

$$r = r_o - \frac{4}{3}\,\pi\,\rho_L\,\sum_j\,N_j\,(a_j{}^3 - a_{oj}{}^3), \qquad (3)$$

where   T   denotes temperature,

         n   denotes the number of moles of gas,

         R   denotes the universal gas constant,

         P   denotes pressure,

         L   denotes the latent heat of vaporization
of water, it is temperature dependent,

         β denotes the coefficient in the linear de-
pendence of the specific heat of moist
air on its mixing ratio, ie. $\beta = dc_p/dr$.

r   denotes the mixing ratio for the moist
        air, ie. the number of grams of water
        vapor contained in one gram of dry air,

r_o denotes the initial mixing ratio,

c_p denotes the specific heat of moist air,
        it is temperature, pressure, and mixing
        ratio dependent,

s   denotes the specific heat of liquid water,
        it is temperature dependent,

a_j denotes the radius of a cloud drop in
        family j,

j   denotes the drop family, the cloud is
        broken down into a set of families based
        on the amount of condensation nuclei
        material contained within the drops,

D   denotes an effective diffusion constant,
        it is temperature and pressure dependent,

ρ denotes the equilibrium vapor density of
        water, it is temperature dependent,

S   denotes the ambient supersaturation ratio,
        it depends on temperature, pressure, and
        mixing ratio,

$S_j{}^*$ denotes the equilibrium supersaturation
        ratio for a drop in family j with radius
        a_j, it is temperature dependent,

ℓ denotes the kinetic coefficient in drop-
        let growth theory, it is temperature and
        pressure dependent,

ρ_L denotes the density of liquid water,

N_j denotes the number of droplets of family
        j in our sample (those contained in one
        gram of dry air),

a_{oj} denotes the initial radius of drops in
        family j.

The dot denotes differentiation with respect to time.
Eq. (1) describes the thermodynamic evolution of the
system, and Eq. (2) describes the diffusional growth
of the cloud drops. Eq. (2) represents a set of
equations, one for each cloud drop family. Normally
a system of 10 to 30 families is included in the
problem. Equations (1) and (2) are coupled through
Eq. (3). The gas temperature calculation involves
the numerical solution of this set of coupled differential equations.

The steps involved in a typical experiment are as follows. First a large sample of moist aerosol-laden air is prepared and used to thoroughly flush the chamber. The chamber is sealed and a stilling period is allowed for air motion to die down and equilibrium to be reached. During this time the initial temperature, pressure, relative humidity, and aerosol characteristics are determined. After the stilling period a slow expansion is performed, which simulates the expansion experienced by ascending air parcels in the real atmosphere, and the evolution of the resulting cloud is observed. The observations are then compared with theory during the post-mortem analysis.

In the near future our computer system will be used to support a second cloud simulation chamber facility as well as the present one. NASA is planning to put an Atmospheric Cloud Physics Laboratory (ACPL) on board Skylab in 1980. The ACPL will be patterned after our cloud simulation chamber facility. In support of the ACPL NASA has constructed a prototype facility, called the Science Simulator, which contains most of the hardware shown on Fig. 1. The NASA Ground Based Functional Science Simulator will be located at our research center and will be supported by the same computer system that services our simulation chamber. The Science Simulator will be used to: train the astronauts who will operate the ACPL, test new pieces of equipment before they are incorporated into the ACPL, and aid in the preparation of experiments for the ACPL.

Data acquisition is one of the computer's primary real-time duties. The simulation chamber and its peripheral subsystems generate a variety of analog and digital data. Approximately 100 temperature points are measured throughout the system, with analog temperature signals derived from transistor thermometers, (9), thermocouples, and thermistors. Other analog signals are generated by air flow meters, a pressure transducer, a valve position indicator, a photomultiplier tube, a silicon photodiode, and several voltages from the wall temperature controllers. Digital data sources are a Hewlett Packard quartz crystal thermometer, a laser scattering counter, optical particle counters, and an external digital clock. In total the computer system services 152 analog data inputs, 128 from the UMR simulation chamber, and 32 from the NASA Science Simulator; and 80 bits of digital input data, 48 from the UMR system. and 32 from the NASA system.

Control is the computer's other real-time responsibility. Numerous air flow control valves are involved in the system shown in Fig. 1, and these are all digitally controlled. The NASA chamber's analog data input hardware has an external multiplexer built into it, and it is digitally controlled through our digital output unit. Both chambers have camera/flash optical systems under digital control. The continuous flow diffusion chamber requires analog temperature control and digital control for its optical particle counters.

During the expansion we want the gas and wall temperatures to track each other accurately in order to minimize wall effects. Causing this to happen is our most difficult control problem. Because of its high heat capacity and slow response time the wall temperature is made to track a pre-determined time profile. The desired time dependent wall temperature signal is generated by the NOVA and output through its D/A. The entire wall is broken down into 28 individually controlled sections. The sectionalization of the chamber aids in reducing thermal differences from place to place on the surface of the chamber. These are isolated from one another with 28 linear analog isolators. During the experiment we then measure the wall temperature and the thermodynamic parameters that determine the gas temperature, calculate the gas temperature, and then control the gas pressure so as to keep the gas at the wall temperature at all times.

We have two distinct systems available for the gas temperature control during the expansion. The first is a hybrid digital/analog controller (10). Here the gas temperature is approximated by the sum of a dry adiabatic temperature term plus a latent heat term due to condensed cloud droplets. The dry adiabatic temperature is calculated via a small analog computer. The latent heat term is calculated digitally and the result is output through a D/A channel. The two temperature components are then summed with an analog summation amplifier, compensated analog, and then the result is used to drive a three-way (chamber, high pressure reservoir, low pressure reservoir) rotary valve driven by a servo motor. This hybrid system was the earliest to be put into operation; however, it suffers from the usual difficulties with analog systems, drift and inaccuracy. Also its range of accurate operation limited it to relatively small expansions, those with a temperature change of 2°C or less. Much larger expansions are desired.

The second gas temperature controller, now
being completed is a purely digital system, with the
computer doing all of the pressure-temperature calculations and control compensation. Fig. 3 contains
a block diagram of the control scheme. P denotes
pressure, T_{wall} denotes the measured wall temperature, and the X's denote other measured parameters
which vary from experiment to experiment. A discrete
time optimal tracking technique is used. The control
signal is sent through the digital output system to
a stepper motor driving a three-way rotary valve.
The number from the digital output is sent to a
specially designed interface which then emits that
number of pulses at 900 Hz to the stepper motor.
   Several reasons were behind the decision to use
digital data acquisition and control rather than the
combination manual-analog systems used on previous
fast expansion chambers (11). First of all, the
accuracies required in the control related computations are beyond those available with analog transfer function generators. In order to take full

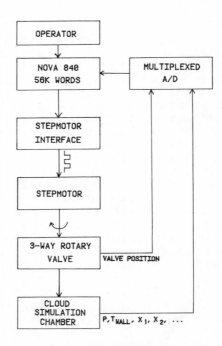

*Figure 3.   Expansion control loop block
diagram*

advantage of the accuracies of the wall temperature and the chamber pressure measurements, the gas temperature should be calculated to an accuracy of 0.001 °C. Analog devices could not meet this requirement. Furthermore, the cost of the less accurate analog system is comparable to that of the digital system if not more expensive. The cost of the digitizing equipment must be included in either approach since the data has to be in digital form in order to be stored and analyzed. Moreover the multiplexing capability of the digital system reduces the overall cost considerably.

Another major advantage of the digital system is its versatility. The simulation chamber can be used for a wide variety of experiments. With a computer based control and data acquisition system the nature of the experiment can be changed substantially by making only simple software changes to the computer program, with little or no hardware changes. Such changes are faster and less expensive than analog hardware changes and readjustments. This feature greatly increases the versatility of the chamber and increases the number of experiments which the chamber can perform per unit time. It also makes it easier for more than one experimenter to use the chamber.

Computer System

Figure 4 shows a block diagram of the computer system used for cloud chamber support. Fig. 5 shows a photograph of the computer system. The NOVA 840 system is dedicated to our two cloud chamber facilities and is not used for the batch processing of general jobs. The cable link is a hard wire 19.2 K-baud link to the UMR IBM 360/50 through the UMR mini-network (12). The IBM 360/50 features 524, 288 bytes of core storage, 5 IBM 2314 Disk Drives, 2 IBM 2415 magnetic tape units, 2 IBM 1403N1 printers, an IBM 2540 card reader/punch, an IBM 2501 card reader, and an IBM 2701 transmission control unit for data transmission lines to the University of Missouri IBM 370/168 and 370/158 computers. The IBM 370 is not used for the direct real time support of our cloud simulation chamber effort. It is used for general modelling, software development, and the experiment's post-mortem analysis.

Our NOVA minicomputer system was acquired over a period of several years at a total cost of $73,500.

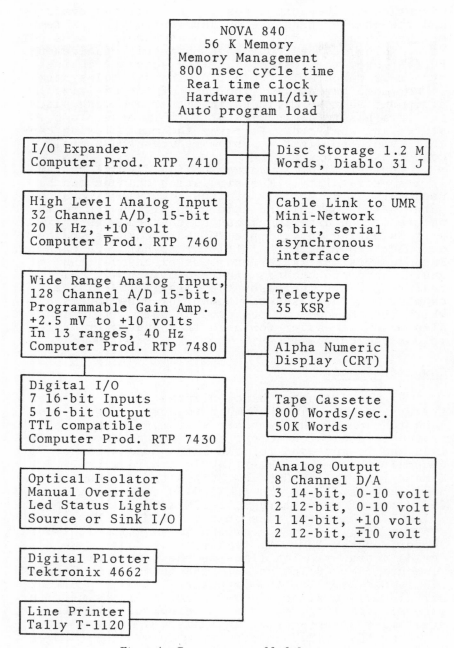

Figure 4.   Computer system block diagram

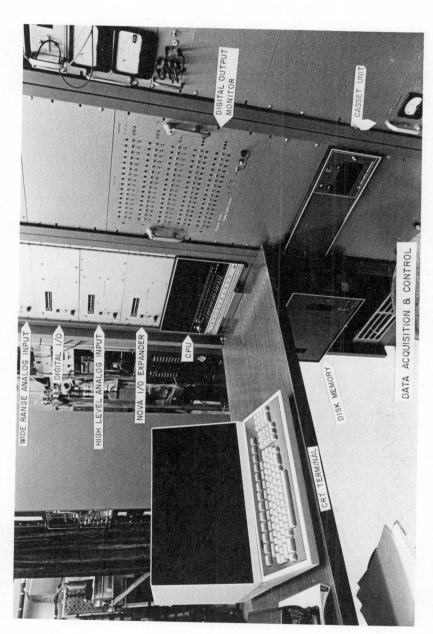

Figure 5.   Computer system photograph

Maintenance is handled by our Center's electrical engineering staff at a cost of approximately $100/month. The computer system has proven quite reliable. In its 2½ years of operation it has rarely caused the shutdown of the cloud chamber facility. Our campus operates ten of the NOVA 800 series mini-computers. A staff member in the electrical engineering department handles the more sophisticated repair and interfacing problems for all the NOVAs on campus. The optical isolators attached to the digital I/O are homemade units that cost about $3500.

The NOVA's operating system is RDOS (Real time disc operating system). The memory management and protection option divides the computer into three partitions that are hardware protected from each other. The operating system resides in one, and two independent programs can be run in a time sharing mode in the other two partitions. Hence, we can run the two cloud chambers simultaneously, or run one chamber and edit programs for the other, etc. The partitioning feature has proven quite useful. Our cloud chamber support programming is done in Fortran, Basic, and Assembler. Most of the chamber operation programs are in Fortran, all of the subroutines which handle our peripherals (A/D, D/A, etc.) are in Assembler and are Fortran callable.

The IBM 360/50 services the entire UMR campus and handles both batch jobs and real time service of the mini-network. It is a $1,000,000 machine with a $2,000/month maintenance cost. It uses the OS 360 MVT Rel. 21 operating system and the mini-network is accessed with the BTAM method. All of our usage of the IBM 360 is done under Fortran.

Computer System Role in Expansion Control

There is a distinct division of labor between the NOVA and the IBM 360 during an experiment. The 360 is involved in Chamber operation because we need to calculate the gas temperature (the gas temperature cannot be directly measured with sufficient accuracy due to condensation on the sensors (5,7)) in order to properly control the experiment (make the gas temperature track the wall temperature). The gas temperature is calculated via a numerical cloud model that solves a set of simultaneous differential equations (Eqs. (1-3)), describing the thermodynamics and cloud droplet growth. This cloud model is too large and runs too slow for the NOVA to handle.

Inputs to the cloud model are the initial temperature (T_o), pressure (P_o), supersaturation ratio (S_o), the aerosol's critical supersaturation spectrum, and the pressure vs. time ($P(t)$) profile during the experiment. The output from the cloud model is the time dependent temperature, $T(t)$, plus drop sizes and other thermodynamic information. Ideally the cloud model should be run in real time using the initial conditions and aerosol characterization measured just before the expansion plus the measured real time pressure profile as inputs. However this is not practical for a machine of the NOVA's size and speed. Instead we use a "perturbation" type of approach. The NOVA collects the initial thermodynamic and aerosol starting conditions. We know in advance the approximate pressure profile that will occur during the experiment since our goal is to make the gas track the wall temperature, and this defines a pressure profile. The wall temperature profile is predetermined to the extent that we can make the walls track a desired temperature profile. The cloud model is (Eqs. (1-3)) is run on the 360 for the measured initial conditions and the expected pressure profile. The resulting temperature profile is approximately what will occur during the actual experiment. All we need to calculate in real time is the deviation from this anticipated behavior due to deviations in the other measured parameters during the experiment. To accomplish this the IBM 360 performs a functional fit; the gas temperature is expressed as a simple function of measured parameters. Various options are available for which parameters are used (liquid water content, mixing ratio, light attenuation, pressure, etc.) depending on the type of experiment. These functional fits are found to be quite accurate (on the order of 0.001 °C) but are valid only for the exact experiment for which they were calculated. They must be recalculated for each experiment. The 360 transmits the results of the functional fit back to the NOVA. This information is then used in the NOVA for its time control calculations. Since simple functions were used in the functional fit they can be evaluated in real time on the NOVA.

The following list summarizes the steps taken by the two linked computer systems in order to accomplish an experiment.

1) The NOVA oversees the preparation of the exper-
    iment and the measurement of the initial condi-
    tions of the system (T_o, P_o, S_o, and aerosol).

2) The information taken in step 1 plus the expect-
    ed pressure profile, P(t), is transmitted from
    the NOVA to the IBM 360.

3) The cloud model is then run on the IBM 360,
    yielding the temperature profile T(t).

4) A functional fit is performed on the IBM 360,
    yielding T (P, x_1, x_2, ...), ie. temperature as
    a function of the measurable parameters P,
    x_1, x_2, ... P denotes pressure, and x_1,
    x_2, ... the other measurable parameters selected
    for this experiment.

5) The function T(P, x_1, x_2, ...) is transmitted
    from the IBM 360 to the NOVA.

6) The NOVA uses the function T(P, x_1, x_2, ...) for
    its real time control calculations during the
    experiment, as shown in Fig. 3.

Steps 3 and 4 are run on the IBM 360 during the
stilling period following the flushing of the chamber
with the aerosol-laden moist air.

Cloud Simulation Chamber Program

     In this section we describe the computer program
that runs on the NOVA and oversees the cloud chamber
operation during an experiment. The program is
written in Fortran and makes extensive use of Data
General Fortran's multitasking feature. During an
experiment various activities (take temperature data,
take laser data, output wall temperature control
signal, etc.) must be done periodically. The multi-
tasking feature allows each activity to be designated
as a task, each with its own priority and frequency
of execution. Various tasks can be active simultaneously. They compete for system resources based on
need and priority.

     The overall simulation chamber software is too
large to fit into the available core, so it is broken
down into four programs corresponding to four con-
secutive phases of experimental activity: preparation of the chamber, closing of the chamber, the
expansion, and the post-expansion clean-up. Chaining
is used to automatically transfer from one program
to the next; upon completion of its duties the

phase one program deletes itself, causes the phase
two program to be loaded into core from disc, and
begins its execution, and so on down the line.

PART 1 - Preparation. This program collects
input information from the operator via the CRT
keyboard that defines the experiment to be done.
Questions are displayed on the CRT and the operator
responds. Then the program reads disc files containing the desired wall temperature profile and the
cloud model functional fit result, $T (P, X_1, X_2, ..)$.

Up to this point in time a manual chamber flush with
dry air has been in progress. All of our valves
that control air flow have a manual override. The
computer now switches valve control digital output
bits to the dry flush position and asks to have all
the valves changed from manual to computer control.
Then at the operator's signal, the computer initial-
izes a chamber flush with moist aerosol-laden air,
and it takes periodic data readings (temperature,
light scattering, etc.) and stores the results on the
disc and displays them on the CRT. When the operator
decides that the flush is sufficient, he signals the
computer and it then chains to the phase 2 program.

PART 2 - Closing of the chamber. Here the
computer takes one set of thermometer readings,
stores them on the disc, and displays them on the
CRT. Then the temporal length of the wet flush is
recorded, the chamber valves are closed, and the
stilling period begins. During this time the initial
readings (T_o, P_o, S_o, aerosol, etc.) are taken and
transmitted to the IBM 360. When the 360's cloud
model results are received and the operator signals
that he is ready for the expansion to begin, the
program chains to the phase 3 program.

PART 3 - Expansion. This phase of the experiment is handled with multitasking. PART 3 activates
five tasks and then simply waits for the duration of
the expansion to pass. TASK 1 takes periodic wall
temperature and gas pressure readings, TASK 2 takes
periodic laser (Mie and Doppler) light scattering
data, TASK 3 displays current information on the
CRT, TASK 4 outputs an updated wall temperature control signal, and TASK 5 outputs an updated gas temperature control signal. When the time allotted for
the expansion elapses, the computer aborts all five
tasks and chains to the phase 4 program.

PART 4 - Post-expansion. Under this phase the
computer re-opens the chamber and begins a chamber

flush with clean dry air for a given amount of time.
Disc data files resulting from this experiment are
secured for the post-experiment analysis.

Independent programs are then run on the NOVA
after the experiment to perform some analysis on the
raw data stored on disc files. They produce written
listings and graphical output that records the experimental data in permanent form. Then some of the
raw data files are transmitted to the IBM 360 via
the mininetwork link and are stored on cards. The
subsequent post-mortem analysis using the cloud
model and other physics or chemistry models for the
process under study are performed on the IBM 360 or
the IBM 370 as batch jobs.

Acknowledgement

This work was supported by the Office of Naval
Research, ONR-N00014-75-C-0182, and by the National
Aeronautics and Space Administration, NAS8-31849.

Abstract

The Graduate Center for Cloud Physics Research
operates an experimental cloud simulation chamber
facility designed for the study of atmospheric micro-
physics and chemistry. The Marshall Space Flight
Center is constructing a miniaturized version of
this facility as a ground based science simulator in
support of an Atmospheric Cloud Physics Laboratory
which is planned for the Space Shuttle. These two
facilities are supported by a hybrid NOVA 840 -
IBM 360/50 computer system for data acquisition and
control purposes.

Literature Cited

1. Hagen, D. E., Hale, M. H., and Carter, J., Proc.
    Electro-Optical Systems Design Conf., Anaheim,
    CA, 1975, p. 373.
2. Whitby, K. T., Liu, B. Y. H., Husar, R. B., and
    Barsic, N. J., J. Colloid Interface Sci., (1972),
    39, 136.
3. Sinnarawalla, A. M. and Alofs, D. J., J. Appl.
    Meteor., (1973), 12, 831.
4. Laktinov, A. G., English Translation Atmos. and
    Oceanic Phys., (1972), 8, 382.
5. Kassner, J. L. Jr., Carstens, J. C., and Allen,
    L. B., J. Atmos. Sci., (1968), 25, 919.
6. "Thermoelectric Handbook," Cambridge Thermionic
    Corp., Cambridge, Mass., 1972

7. Kassner, J. L. Jr., Carstens, J. C., and Allen, L. B., J. Recherches Atmospheriques, (1968), 3, 25.
8. Carstens, J. C., Podzimek, J., and Saad, A., J. Atmos. Sci., (1974), 31, 592.
9. Pease, R. A., Instruments and Control Systems, (1972), 45, (6), 80.
10. Hagen, D. E., Tebelak, A. C., and Kassner, J. L. Jr., Rev. Sci. Instrum., (1974), 45, 195.
11. Allen, L. B., "An Experimental Determination of the Homogeneous Nucleation Rate of Water Vapor in Argon and Helium," Ph. D. Dissertation, University of Missouri-Rolla, 1968.
12. Beistel, D. W., Mollenkamp, R. A., Pottinger, H. J., de Good, J. S., and Tracey, J. H., in "Computer Networking and Chemistry," ACS Symposium Series 19, (1975), ed. by P. Lykos, p. 118.

7

The Minicomputer and X-Ray Crystallography

ROBERT A. SPARKS

Syntex Analytical Instruments, Inc., Cupertino, CA 95014

One of the first analytical instruments automated was the
single crystal x-ray diffractometer. Because of the rather
complex angular settings required (for each diffraction measurement 3 or 4 angles must be set with an accuracy of about 0.01-
0.02°) and because of the length of the experiment (typically
24 hours per day for 2-7 days)early diffractometers were punched
card-controlled or paper tape-controlled. The controlling
equipment consisted primarily of electrical relays. With the
advent of the minicomputer the diffractometer became computer-
controlled. Early computer-controlled diffractometers were built
at IBM Research (1) and at the Oakridge National Laboratory (2).
Today all commercially available diffractometers are controlled
by small minicomputers. With the availabilty of higher-level
languages (primarily FORTRAN) and the development of some new
algorithms the computer-controlled single crystal x-ray
diffractometer has become a very flexible tool. A review of the
algorithms for the diffractometer was presented by Sparks (3).
The computer requirements for the control of the diffractometer
are: 4-8K of 16-bit core memory and an IBM compatible magnetic
tape drive for programs which have been written in assembly
language. For a FORTRAN version, 24K of 16-bit core memory, a
1.25M word disk, and an IBM compatible magnetic tape drive are
required. Because the diffractometer is a slow device the Central
Processing Unit does not have to be very fast and floating point
hardware is not necessary.

Minicomputer for Structure Determination Calculations.

Traditionally the crystallographer has taken the data
produced by the diffractometer to a large computer and has then
used the large computer for all the necessary structure
determination calculations. A few crystallographers have used
the small computer for some crystallographic calculations (4).
However, until recently that calculation (least squares refinement
of atomic parameters) which requires 80% of all computer time

94

for crystal structure determination(5) could not be done on the small computer.

Recent developments in the minicomputer industry have changed this situation markedly. Fast floating point hardware and FORTRAN compilers which generate efficient code are now readily available for minicomputers. In 1972 (6) Syntex announced that they were developing a Structure Determination System based on the Data General Nova 1200 computer which is the same computer used to control the Syntex P2₁ Diffractometer. The first Syntex XTL Structure Determination System was delivered in early 1974. Since then Syntex has developed an E-XTL Structure Determination System based on the Data General Eclipse computer. Three other commercial manufacturers offer similar systems. The four companies and the minimum computer configurations are as follows.

TABLE I

Syntex Analytical Instruments	a) 24K Nova 1200 or 24K Nova 800 - 1.25M word disk - 12.5 ips magnetic tape drive
	b) 32K Eclipse 2 - 1.25M word disks -12.5 ips magnetic tape drive
Enraf-Nonius (Holland)	28K PDP 11/40 or 11/45 or 11/35 1.25M word disk - 12.5 ips magnetic tape drive
Philips (Holland)	Philips PM 855
Computer-Systemtechnik (Germany)	32K Eclipse 5M work disk

All of the computers have a 16-bit word length. A very useful option is a line printer-plotter. Syntex provides a Versatec 11" printer-plotter. For the Syntex system prices include all of the structure determination software and range from about $62,000 to $100,000. Syntex has delivered more than thirty systems and I would estimate that including a few individually built systems there are now over fifty crystallographic structure determination systems on mimicomputers throughout the world.

To compare the performance of the minicomputer and the large computers Sparks (7) used the FORTRAN benchmark shown in Table II.

The code from statement 30 to statement 5001 forms the normal equation matrix, A, from the derivative vectors, DV, one reflection at a time. This or similar codes are used in all the crystallographic full matrix least squares routines on large computers. For reasons which will be discussed this algorithm is not used on any of the minicomputers mentioned above. The benchmark is meant to compare the efficiency of hardware and

TABLE II

```
              COMMON A(2500), DV(100)
101           FORMAT(1H ,7E10,4)

              DO 10 I=1,2500
10            A(I)=0.0
              ACCEPT "N,NREF,IPR=",N,NREF,IPR
              M=N+1
              MM=M+1
              DO 6001 IP=1,NREF
              DO 20 I=1,M
20            DV(I)=I*IP*0.9
              K=1
30            DO 5001 J=1,N
              B=DV(J)
              IF(B.NE.O) GO TO 5002
              K=K+MM-J
              GO TO 5001
5002          DO 5003 L=J,M
              A(K)=A(K)+DV(L)*B
5003          K=K+1
5001          CONTINUE
6001          CONTINUE
              K=K-1
              IF(IPR.EQ.O)GO TO 6002
              WRITE(10,101)(A(I),I=1,K)
              STOP
6002          WRITE(10,101)A(K)
              STOP
              END
```

FORTRAN test program (N=64, NREF=100)

code generated by the various FORTRAN compilers. The execution times for this benchmark for various computers is shown in Table III.

The computer programs for the dedicated minicomputer system are similar to those for the large computer. Most of the major programs for the Syntex XTL are modifications of the programs written for the large computers. All programs are written in FORTRAN. Because of the limited amount of core, the programs are more disk oriented than are those on the large computer. All program files, data files and scratch files reside on disk. Because more than one data set can reside on disk at any one time, the data files contain as part of their names a four letter code identifying the structure to which they belong. A list of the data files and their contents are shown in Table IV.

Special care was exercised to make user input as simple and error-free as possible. XTL and E-XTL programs are conversational

TABLE III

Comparison of time for least squares inner loop

Computer	Compiler	Time
CDC 7600	FTN-OP2	0.175 secs
	FTN-OP1	0.402
CDC 6600	OP2	0.93
	OP1	1.164
IBM 370/155		7.5
Eclipse	FORTRAN V	7.7
PDP 11/50 MOS MEMORY FORTRAN IV PLUS		11.0
PDP 11/45 CORE MEMORY FORTRAN IV PLUS		16.6
Syntex XTL (NOVA 800)	FORTRAN IV	28.4
HP 2100A	FORTRAN IV	29.0
Enraf Nonius SDP(PDP 11/45)	FORTRAN IV-DOS 9	35.0
Syntex XTL (NOVA 1200)	FORTRAN IV	41.0
PDP 11/40	FORTRAN IV	59.8
PDP 8E-floating hardware	FORTRAN IV	64.0

and utilize unformatted (or free-form) input. The user is
prompted on each input by a print-out of possible responses. An
automatic updating of the primary data file minimizes user
instruction and eliminates redundant user inputs and calculation
by individual programs. Frequently used input parameters (e.g.
cell dimensions, space group information, etc.) need only be
entered once. Since files are rewritten automatically as new
information is available, calculations made by one program can be
utilized by the others. The user rarely needs to intervene in
going from one program to the next. In most cases, the specification of the program name, the data file identifier, and a small
number of input parameters are all that is required to run any
program in the system. Extensive discussions among all the
programmers (who were also crystallographers) were held on all
input and output procedures and formats. An example of the input
and output is shown in Table V.

The XTL program file interaction is shown in Table VI. The
names of the major programs are shown in rectangles, the files
in ovals.

Large programs like MULTAN and the Full Matrix Least Squares
(FMLS) must be divided into many overlays so that each part will
fit in 24K of core memory. MULTAN requires 15 segments and FMLS
requires 5 on the Nova 1200 and 7 on the Eclipse. To minimize
the number of disk transfers (which are time consuming) a very
thorough understanding of the program is necessary in order to
make an efficient division into segments.

FMLS requires a large storage area for the normal equation
matrix. As mentioned above, programs which run on large computers
form the normal equations as shown in the benchmark. All of

TABLE IV

List of the data files and their contents

File	Name	File Contents
Primary Data File	DØUSER.DA	Title, cell dimensions, space group equivalences, scattering factor types, overall scale and temperature factors, weighting scheme, atomic coordinates, etc.
Reflection Data File	D1USER.DA	h,k,l,E,F,σ,A_c,B_c, scattering factors, etc.
E phase Data File	D2USER.DA	E phases for each MULTAN solution
Peak File	D3USER.DA	Peak information generated by Fourier, E-map, or Patterson
H,K,L File	D6USER.DA	File of h,k,l values for $P2_1$ FORTRAN programs
$P2_1$ Parameter File	D7USER.DA	Orientation matrix, wave lengths, centering, indexing, collection, etc. parameters for $P2_1$ FORTRAN programs
Check Reflection File	D8USER.DA	h,k,l, intensity, time for check reflections
Raw Intensity Data File	D9USER.DA	h,k,l, intensity, σ
Scattering Factor File	SAIASF.TB	Cromer-Weber scattering factor tables
Normal Equation File	NORMAL.TM	Full-matrix normal equations

TABLE V

PRIME

S.A.I. XTL PROGRAM   PRIMARY DATA FILE SETUP (2)

ENTER DATA FILE ID (4 CHAR.): <u>TEST</u>
ENTER COMPOUND NAME (3Ø CHAR. MAX): <u>NEW TEST CRYSTAL</u>
WHAT KIND OF X-RADIATION? (CU,MO,AG,FE,CR): <u>MO</u>

ENTER CELL CONSTANTS TO AS MUCH PRECISION AS POSSIBLE
WITH LENGTHS IN ANGSTROMS AND ANGLES IN DEGREES
ORDER - A,B,C,ALPHA,BETA,GAMMA - SEPARATE WITH COMMA'S
:<u>13.712,15.241,1Ø.334,9Ø,92.17,9Ø</u>
ENTER STD. DEV. FOR CELL DIMENSIONS
:<u>.ØØ1,.ØØ2,.ØØ1,Ø,.Ø2,Ø</u>
IS THIS SECTION CORRECT? (YES OR NO): <u>YES</u>

ENTER SPACE GROUP SYMBOL: <u>P 21/C</u>
    CRYSTAL CLASS: MONOCLINIC   LAUE GROUP: P 2/M   CENTROSYMMETRIC
    NUMBER OF GENERAL POSITIONS: 4   POLAR AXIS: NONE
    UNIQUE 2-FOLD AXIS: Y

    EQUIVALENT POSITIONS:
          X,   Y,   Z,   -X, 1/2+Y, 1/2-Z,

ENTER ATOMIC NAMES IN STANDARD FORMAT. GIVE THE NUMBER OF EACH
IN THE ASYMMETRIC UNIT WHEN REQUESTED.   FINISH WITH "END".

ATOM TYPE: <u>FE+2</u>
HOW MANY? <u>2</u>
ATOM TYPE: <u>C</u>
HOW MANY? <u>18</u>
ATOM TYPE: <u>O</u>
HOW MANY? <u>3</u>
ATOM TYPE: <u>H</u>
HOW MANY? <u>8</u>
ATOM TYPE: <u>END</u>
IS THIS SECTION CORRECT? (YES OR NO): <u>YES</u>

ATOM LIST

COMPOUND: NEW TEST CRYSTAL   IDENT: TEST

	A	B	C	ALPHA	BETA	GAMMA	VOLUME
CELL DIMENSIONS:	13.712	15.241	1Ø.334	9Ø.ØØ	92.17	9Ø.ØØ	2158.1

ATOM	NUMBER/ CELL	ATOMIC NUMBER	ATOMIC WEIGHT	WEIGHT (%)	ABSORPTION COEFF.
FE+2	8.	26.	55.85	29.1	13.2
C	72.	6.	12.Ø1	56.3	Ø.4
O	12.	8.	16.ØØ	12.5	Ø.2
H	32.	1.	1.Ø1	2.1	Ø.Ø

TABLE V (cont)

```
NUMBER OF ATOMS IN THE UNIT CELL = 124.
UNIT CELL SCATTERING F (ØØØ) =      768. ELECTRONS
UNIT CELL VOLUME =                 2185.1 A3
UNIT CELL MASS =                   1535.8 AMU
CALCULATED DENSITY =                 1.18 G/CM3
ABSORPTION COEFFICIENT =            13.9 CM(-1)
```

PRIMARY DATA FILE SETUP COMPLETE   FILENAME: DØTEST.DA

R

Underlined items are the user input.

the normal equation matrix (really only the upper or lower
triangular part) resides in the core memory of such computers.
Traditionally, crystallographers have measured the size of their
central computer by the size of the normal equation matrix that
can be handled. Thus, Ibers(8) states that no more than 240
variables can be refined on his CDC 6400. The maximum size for
the CDC 7600 at the Lawrence Radiation Laboratory in Berkeley
is 832 parameters, although a more practical limit is 722
parameters(9). In the Syntex XTL, the normal equation matrix
is stored in a large contiguous block on disk. Since typically
40-50% of the execution time of a full matrix least squares
program (or 32-40% of all crystallographic computing time) is
spent in formation of the normal equation matrix, whatever effort
is spend on optimizing this part of the code will pay large
dividends. For the Nova 1200 and Nova 800 XTL systems special
floating point hardware was designed to execute Data General's
FORTRAN IV efficiently and to make it possible to write a very
fast machine language subroutine for this part of the program.
Instead of the algorithm indicated in the benchmark the following
algorithm was developed. Derivative vectors for three reflections
are generated and stored in core. Then one half-track (768
elements) of the normal equation matrix are read into core from
disk. As soon as the first element arrives in core the three
corresponding products from the three derivative vectors are
added to it. The next element is then processed in the same way.
The arithmetic operations (three floating point multiplies and
adds) are slower than the disk transfer rate. As soon as the
disk has transfered the first half-track it reads in the second
half-track into a second array in core. At the end of reading
the second half-track the processing for the first half-track
will be finished and can be written back onto the disk. Finally
at the end of processing the second half-track it also is written
back onto the disk. The floating point processor operates
independently of the central processing unit and the program is

TABLE VI
XTL PROGRAM-FILE INTERACTION

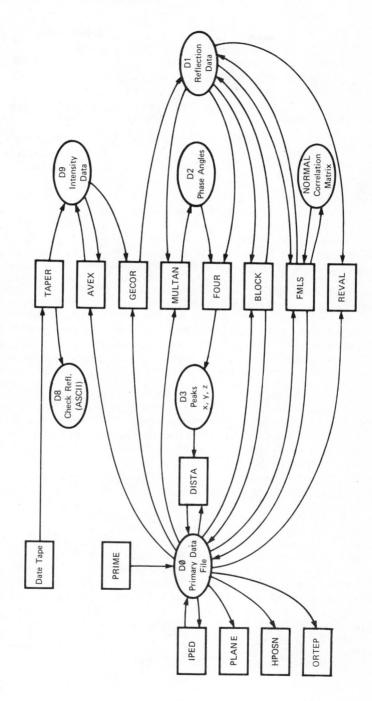

written so that time for the address arithmetic calculations
(done by the CPU) are almost completely overlapped by the
floating point processor time. Thus, the floating point processor
is busy about 80% of the time.

The Eclipse floating point processor is considerably faster
than the special processor designed for the Nova 1200 and Nova
800; however, the disk transfer rate is the same for all of these
computers. Therefore, for the E-XTL it is necessary to process
more than three derivative vectors at a time. The algorithm
used in the E-XTL is the following. Derivative vectors for many
reflections (several hundred) are written onto a disk file.
When this file is filled a block of the normal equation matrix
(3072 elements) is transferred to core. This block is then
updated with contributions from all of the vectors in the
derivative file. Then that block of the normal equation matrix
is written back on disk. The derivative vector must be read for
each 3072 element block of the normal equation matrix. Depending
on the total number of reflections the derivative vector file
may have to be written more than once and each time the normal
equation matrix must be updated. To minimize disk seek times,
it is necessary to have the derivative vector file and the normal
equation file on different disks.

On the Nova 1200 version of the Syntex XTL two cycles of a
217 parameter, acentric problem with four equivalent positions and
1152 reflections took 117 minutes. It took 96 minutes on the
Nova 800 XTL and 44 minutes on the Eclipse E-XTL.

Up to 500 parameters can be handled by the current XTL and
E-XTL Full Matrix Least Squares programs.

Almost all of the programs normally run by crystallographers
in connection with structure determination of molecules (other
than protein and other macromolecules) are included in the XTL and
E-XTL and in the systems provided by other manufacturers listed
above. These few programs not now included can easily be added
to the various packages.

Protein and Other Macromolecular Crystallographic Calculations.

The commercially available systems described above do not now
have very many programs which can be used for large molecules.
However, one cyrstallographic group which has a Syntex Nova 800
XTL has written many programs including structure factor
calculations, phase angle refinement, and structure refinement
by difference Fourier methods. Except for the calculation and
plotting of the Fourier maps they do all of their protein
calculations on the Nova 800. Much development work (mostly on
large computers) on algorithms for protein structure refinement
is now taking place. I am confident that all or almost all
protein calculations will be performed on minicomputers not very
different from those described above.

Time-sharing of the Diffractometer with Structure Determination
Calculations.

Although a number of Syntex customers have systems that will
run either the $P2_1$ diffractometer or the XTL Structure Determination System, they cannot run both simultaneously. Enraf-Nonius
does offer a time-sharing system. This system has a PDP 8 computer
operating the CAD-4 diffractometer and a PDP 11 operating the
Structure Determination Package. The PDP 8 and PDP 11 are tied
together and the PDP 11 sends diffractometer commands to the
PDP 8 and collects data from the PDP 8.

There is a slight degradation of the structure determination
calculations when the diffractometer is operating in this system.
The cost differential between this system and a stand-alone
diffractometer plus a stand-alone Structure Determination Package
is small (approximately $16,000 for an extra magnetic tape drive
and disk drive, compared to an approximate cost depending on
accessories of $130,000 for the time-shared system). The
stand-alone approach offers the advantage that the diffractometer
can still be operational even if the PDP 11 is not.

Comparison of the Large Computer with the Minicomputer.

Because of differences in FORTRAN compilers transportability
of large programs from one large computer to another has at times
been a problem. However, it is much more difficult to take a
large program written for a large computer and make it run
efficiently on a small computer. A very thorough understanding
of the algorithm is necessary in order to determine how the
program must be segmented into overlays and to decide which arrays
can be put on disk without vastly increasing execution time. Some
minicomputers have a virtual memory scheme which makes the
user think that he has a very large core memory when actually
the computer is using a paging technique to swap parts of the
program between core and disk memories. Still the user must be
cautious that the way the program accesses elements in large
arrays is not causing excessive and very inefficient paging.
Clearly, these problems are much more serious for the minicomputer
programmer than for his counterpart on the large computer.

Debugging new programs written originally for a minicomputer
is a less difficult problem. Debugging aids are still not as
good as those found on the best large computers. From my own
experience the most efficient debugging I have ever done has
been on a time-sharing system on a large computer.

With a dedicated minicomputer it is possible to choose
computer hardware and design algorithms so that the computation
will be done in the most cost effective way. It is also possible
to design special hardware to make certain critical parts of
the programs execute as fast as possible. It is much more
difficult to do these things on a large general purpose computer.

One must always be aware of the fact that pressures from other users of the large system can cause the system to change either in hardware, operating system, or charging algorithms in such a way that his programs are no longer cost effective and in extreme cases no longer run at all.

Very large problems can be run on the minicomputer. As indicated above, the largest number of parameters that can be handled in the Full Matrix Least Squares program on the CDC 7600 is 833. With an addition of 16K of core and a change of some of the dimension statements the E-XTL can handle more than 1000 parameters. One cycle of Full Matrix Least Squares on such a problem would take about 50 hours. Of course, it would be possible to program the CDC 7600 to use peripheral memory for the normal equations in the same fashion as was done for the E-XTL.

The major consideration between the choice of a dedicated minicomputer or the use of a large computer must be cost. The cost of crystallographic computing varies greatly throughout the world. A survey (10) of all institutions showed that the average computer cost was $5,400 per structure (real money - not phoney money as used in some central facilities). The cost of the minimum dedicated minicomputer system is about equivalent to the cost of computer time for 12 structures. The cost of the maximum system is equivalent to about 19 structures. Two computer controlled x-ray diffractometers can collect 100 data sets per year (one laboratory in the USSR is currently collecting this much data). The Syntex E-XTL can easily keep up with this volume. Service and operating costs are not very different from those of the computer controlled diffractometer.

Most of the dedicated minicomputer systems for crystallography are located outside the United States. The reasons are that in many parts of the world the minicomputers are as powerful or more powerful than the central large computer facilities available and secondly, that in the United States restrictive policies by the national funding agencies and central computing facilities have prevented the wide spread use of dedicated minicomputers.

In any case, the dedicated minicomputer promises to play an increasingly important role in all crystallographic calculations.

Literature Cited

1. Cole, H., Okaya, Y. & Chambers, F.W., Rev. Sci. Instr., (1963) 34, 872.
2. Busing, W.R., Ellison, R.D. & Levy, H.A., Abstracts of the American Crystallographic Association, (1965) 59.
3. Sparks, R.A., "Trends in Minicomputer Hardware and Software Part I", pp 452-467, Munksgaard, Copenhagen, 1976.
4. Shino, R.,"Crystallographic Computing", pp 312-315, ed. F. R. Ahmed, Munksgaard, Copenhagen, 1970.

5. Hamilton, W., "Computational Needs and Resources in
    Crystallography", pp 9-17, Washington, D.C.: National
    Academy of Sciences, 1973.
6. Sparks, R.A., "Computational Needs and Resources in
    Crystallography", pp 66-75, Washington, D.C.: National
    Academy of Sciences, 1973.
7. Ibid., pp 66-75.
8. Ibers, J.A., "Computational Needs and Resources in
    Crystallography", pp 18-27, Washington, D.C.: National
    Academy of Sciences, 1973.
9. Zalkin, A., private communication, 1977.
10. Hamilton, W., loc. cit.

8

Description of a High Speed Vector Processor

J. N. BÉRUBÉ and H. L. BUIJS

Bomen, Inc., 2371 Nicolas Pinel, Ste.-Foy, Québec, Canada

A high speed vector processor has been developed which, coupled with a low level minicomputer or microprocessor, provides an efficient data reduction facility for Fourier Transform Spectrometry. The vector processor performs the dot product of two arrays at high speed and very high precision. Since in many data reduction applications the computation of dot products present the greatest load to the data processing system, the vector processor will be found useful for a wide range of tasks.

In Fourier Transform Spectroscopy the vector processor is used to perform high speed numerical filtering and fourier transformation.

Numerical Filter

Modern spectrometric applications sometimes demand very high spectral resolution over a relatively large optical bandwidth. A model DA3.003 Fourier Transform Spectrometer manufactured by Bomem Inc. is capable of providing spectral resolution of $0.003 cm^{-1}$ over the visible to millimeter wavelength region. A large amount of data (millions of elements) is produced when such resolution is recorded over a large optical bandwidths. Fortunately, it is seldom required that such large bandwidths must be analysed completely at one time; in the vast majority of cases it is preferred to limit the analysis to a succession of rather narrow portions of the spectrum which have been judiciously chosen because of the particular information contents of the spectrum. In such cases the interferogram vector, the raw data from the instrument, may be numerically filtered such that only the information contents of the selected portion of the spectrum are retained. This results in reduced number of data points to be Fourier Transformed in order to produce the spectrum.

In applications where limited time is available for measurement, such as in analysing substances in chemical reaction, the rate of information generated may become greater than the storage rate normally available using data storage devices such as

magnetic tape or flexible disc systems. Real time numerical filtering can be applied to reduce the data storage rate to that
compatible with the storage system. Numerical filtering also reduces the volume of data storage required for a given set of
experiments.

The high speed vector processor, developed for the above mentioned application, permits real time numerical filtering to be
performed with input data rates up to 200,000 data points per
second. The numerical filtering process used consists of numerically convolving the input data with the impulse response of a
filter function having near unity gain over the desired spectral
region ($\sigma_0 \pm \sigma_r/2$) and high signal rejection outside this region.
Such a filter is generally classified as "non-recursive" or
"finite impulse response". The general input-output relationship
is of the form:

$$Y_n = \sum_{k=0}^{N-1} a_k \cdot x_{n-k} \qquad\qquad (1)$$

where $\{X_n\}$ is the input data sequence, $\{Y_n\}$ the output data sequence, and $\{a_k\}$ the coefficients of the filter, (i.e. the impulse
response function).

It may be noted here that non-recursive numerical filtering
presents several unique characteristics which are of use to Fourier
Transform Spectroscopy and other applications. Primarily, the
filter function is applied to data in the digital sampled domain,
the transfer function operates therefore on the signal as determined by the sample source. In the modern Fourier Transform
Spectrometer, sampling is controlled very precisely from a reference interferogram generated by a stable monochromatic light
source. Since the numerical filter operates on the sampled data,
errors due to phase shifts and time frequency variations are not
injected during the filter process. This attribute would be applicable to other applications where signal variation and therefore sampling interval are functions of parameters other than time.
A second characteristic of use to Fourier Transform Spectroscopy
is the ability to shift the output sampling function with respect
to the signal. This allows centering of the output sample function with respect to singular signals.

Fourier Transform

The raw data from the interferometer portion of a Fourier
Transform Spectrometer is the autocorrelation function of the incident radiation. Once the filtering process, bandlimiting and
sample function centering has been performed, the spectrum may be
computed. Fast Fourier Transform (FFT) algorithms are often used
for this since they provide means for transforming spectra with a
minimum of numerical operations. General computing facilities

with fast hardware multiply/divide and random access data storage
capacity comparable to the vector length can perform the FFT quite
rapidly.

Consider however the general equation for the Discrete Fourier
Transform (DFT) :

$$A_r = \sum_{k=0}^{N-1} X_k \cdot \exp\ (-2\pi jrk/N) \tag{2}$$

where A_r is the rth coefficient of the transformed vector (spectrum) and X_k is the Kth sample of the input vector (filtered interferogram). One can see that the structure of the DFT is identical to that of the numerical filter. If a high speed vector
processor is needed for numerical filtering, the same processor
can be used to perform Fourier transformation by using the DFT
algorithm.

Discrete Fourier Transformation has several advantages with
respect to Fast Fourier Transformation. Some examples particularly related to spectroscopy follow:

1. Fourier Transformation by DFT involves only sequential access
to the data to be transformed whereas the FFT algorithm requires
repeated access to different portions of the original vector and
to intermediate results. The DFT can therefore be efficiently
performed from sequential access devices such as digital magnetic
tape or flexible disc whereas for efficient application of the
FFT, either large random access memory or very high speed discs
must be used.

2. Using the DFT any portion of the total spectral range may be
computed and the spectral interval and sample positions may be
chosen at will. It is sometimes possible, therefore, to compute
a portion of the spectrum and begin plotting that portion while
the computation of other portions of the spectrum continues.

3. Computation of one spectral point or several isolated points
is also possible, this is sometimes useful for monitoring chemical
reactions or mixtures. The processing format of the FFT, on the
other hand, is relatively fixed; in order to compute one point in
the spectrum, all of the points must be computed and the spectral
interval and sampling positions are also fixed.

4. Calculation of the sine or cosine transformation using the
DFT is performed in one-fourth the operations required for complex
transformation. This is not true when the FFT is used.

Performance for DFT

As mentioned previously, the Fast Fourier Transform is often
chosen for spectrum computation since it provides a minimal number
of required operations (n log₄n complex multiplications and addi-
tions in radix 4 system) in order to arrive at a complete transformed spectrum. The DFT requires n^2 operations to fully trans-

form a real vector using the sine or cosine transform and $4n^2$ operations for transformation of a complex asymetric vector of n points. Clearly, when long vectors are to be totally transformed the number of operations becomes very large and the time required increases. The relatively high speed of the vector processor is used to keep the processing time to a reasonnable value for vectors of commonly used length (plotting restrictions often limit length of output vector) and, where very wide spectral intervals are to be transformed, the numerical filter is used to first separate the interval into sections such that computing time is held within acceptable limits. Table I illustrates the computation times for direct transformation using the high speed vector processor. 32 bit, floating point, spectral data is assumed and I/O is assumed to be via standard IBM compatible Floppy Disc.

Hardware

The high speed vector processor is configured for ease of interface to most minicomputers or higher-level microprocessors. Its function is to perform high speed, high precision, multiplication and accumulation in one or more registers. The control of the system is performed by the host computer with a minimum number of control transfers. Serial data input in 16 bit floating point format may be accommodated directly from an external source or may be transferred via the host computer. Output data is normally in 32 bit floating point format for DFT and 16 bit floating point format when numerical filtering is performed.

A functional block diagram of the system is shown in Figure 1. The hardware is composed of the following:
- a high speed, high precision multiplier, 0.5µs for 40 bit products, 0.8µs for 64 bit product.
- one programmable length accumulator of up to 64 bits
- floating to fixed point input converter
- fixed point to floating point output converter
- 4K x 16 bit memory organized as FIFO (first-in-first-out)
- 4K x 16 bit memory for storage of filter coefficients
- sine/cosine generator for up to 64K different values
- control logic for automatic operation as determined by host computer
- host computer including at least 8K bytes of read/write memory, DMA capability, and, peripheral storage unit such as floppy disc or digital magnetic tape recorder.

The control information for the vector processor can be readily generated using any programming language. Computation of the filter coefficients is also a straight forward task for scientific programmers. For use with Fourier Transform Spectrometers the Digital Equipment Corporation LSI-11 has been found quite useful. The LSI-11 has sufficient computing power to be useful for general tasks such as control of other instruments, scientific computation, process control, etc. It supports the time-tested DEC RT-11

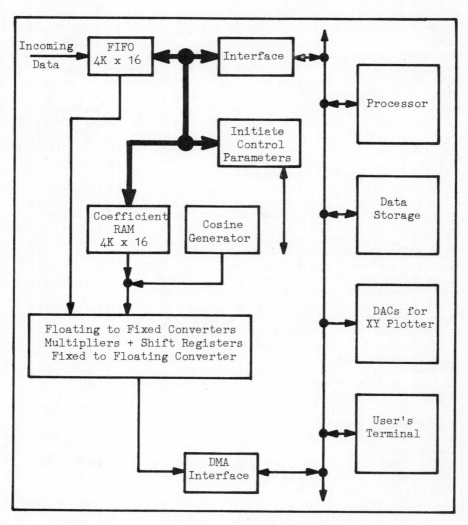

Figure 1. Vector processor block diagram

Table I.   Computation times for direct transformation using the
high speed vector processor.

Points in vector to be transformed	1)time to compute at least one and up to 200 spectral elements.*	2)time to compute 2048 spectral elements.	3)time to compute same number of spectral elements as interferogram points.
4K	1 s	4.2 s	8.5 s
8K	2 s	8.5 s	34 s .
16K	4 s	17 s	2 min 30 s
32K	8 s	34 s	9 min 40 s
64K	16 s	1 min 10 s	36 min 30 s
128K	32 s	2 min 20 s	2 h 30 min
256K	64 s	4 min 40 s	10 h 5 min

* This computation time is limited by floppy disc input/output time
The first group of computation times is useful for quick turn
around monitoring of a very restricted spectral region. The second group of computation times indicates the rate at which reasonable sized plotter page sets of data may be generated, and the
third group gives times of maximum computing effort for a given
size interferogram.

operating system and Fortran compiler. These have been used to
supply control to the high speed vector processor.
    While the system was primarily designed to provide superlative
processing accuracy and relatively high speed it also provides an
economical means for accomplishing these tasks.

Conclusions

    The high speed vector processor has been shown to be a high
performance device for implementation of numerical filtering and
for performing Fourier Transformation by DFT. Since both of
these functions are repetitive applications of dot product computation the system may find application whenever calculation of
a dot product is required. Examples are correlation analysis,
signal convolution, autocorrelation, spectral signature analysis,
and of course general vector operations.

9

The Potential of 16 Bit Minicomputers for Molecular Orbital Calculations

MARIE C. FLANIGAN and JAMES W. McIVER, JR.

Department of Chemistry, State University of New York at Buffalo, Buffalo, NY 14214

The number cruncher is being squeezed out of University computing centers. The dramatically increasing pressure of small student jobs and the concommitant shift of policy to relieve this pressure have made it so. The number cruncher sits endlessly in queues at the bottom of the priority pile. He can raise his priority by paying more "real" money but the resources he needs for his mammoth jobs (compared to undergraduate student jobs) are just not available. His turn around time is appalling. He can run fewer jobs each year, so his research output is affected. The good old days of number crunching in Universities are gone.

The formation of the National Computing Laboratory in Chemistry is an implicit admission of this, as well as a recognition of the importance of computing in chemistry. However, one other alternative is also being explored; namely the use of a minicomputer for number crunching. This symposium is a testimony to the importance of this possibility.

By minicomputer we mean a relatively inexpensive system (less than $100,000) with a 16 bit or smaller word length. Minicomputers can support a small number of users interactively. More often they are found interfaced to one or more instruments where they are used for data acquisition and control of experiments. They are not designed for the multiple precision, compute-bound jobs that characterize number crunching.

Much of the number crunching in Chemistry is concerned with quantum mechanical calculations of molecular properties. Indeed, one often finds in the experimental literature, reports of molecular orbital calculations together with other chemical and structural data. Although the usefulness of these calculations is sometimes questioned, there is no denying their ubiquity. Can minicomputers be used for this type of calculation? If so, will they be cost effective?

To address this question, we prepared a benchmark consisting of a semi-empirical SCF molecular orbital program and two supplementary programs designed to separately mimic the numerical and mass storage features of the molecular orbital program. The benchmark was then run for several molecules, for which comput-

ing times and accuracy were reported. The runs were made on the
State University of New York at Buffalo's Control Data Cyber 173
system. The same runs were also carried out on a Data General
S/200 ECLIPSE minicomputer kindly made available to us by Dr.
Stanley Bruckenstein for this purpose. This paper describes the
benchmark, some of our experiences in developing it, and the
rather surprising results of our study.

Cyber and Eclipse Hardware and Software Differences

    The CDC CYBER 173 hardware consists of the Central Process-
ing Unit (CPU), 131,072 decimal words of .4 microsecond Central
Memory (CM), fourteen Peripheral Processing Units (PPU), and
associated peripheral equipment such as card readers, printers,
etc. The CPU has no I/O capability but communicates with the
external world through the CM. The peripheral processors read and
write to CM and provide communication paths between the CPU and
individual peripheral equipment. This is in contrast to the
ECLIPSE where the I/O bus with I/O devices attached to it are
directly connected to the CPU. Both machines have disk drives
for random access mass storage, with the CYBER's PPU's handling
the transfer of data between the CM and the disks. Thus, a
significant hardware distinction between the two machines is that
the ECLIPSE's single processor must perform the functions of
both CPU and PPU of the CYBER.
    Perhaps the most critical difference between the CYBER and
the ECLIPSE is the difference in word length. The CYBER has a 60
bit word. Floating point single precision numbers have a sign
bit, an 11 bit biased exponent field and a 48 bit mantissa
field. This gives a range of about 10^{-293} to 10^{+322} with approximately 14 significant decimal digits. A 60 bit word can hold
any positive decimal integer up to $2^{60} = 10^{18}$. This is the
number of words of memory one can directly address. The ECLIPSE,
however, has a 16 bit word of which only 15 bits can be used for
direct addressing. Thus only 32,768 (=32K) decimal words of
memory can be directly addressed. In addition to the 32K direct
access memory, the particular ECLIPSE we used has 16,384 (=16K)
of "extended memory" and a hardware device allowing access to
this memory. The total amount of extended memory can reach up to
131,072 (=128K) words.
    In contrast to the 60 bit word on the CYBER, the ECLIPSE
"single precision" floating point number is made up of two 16 bit
words with a sign bit, a 7 bit biased exponent field (hexadecimal)
and a 24 bit mantissa field. A "double precision" floating point
number on the ECLIPSE is made up of four 16 bit words (64 bits
total) with a sign bit, a 7 bit biased exponent field and a 56
bit mantissa. The range of both single and double precision
words is approximately 5×10^{-79} to 7×10^{75}. There are 6-7
significant decimal digits in single precision whereas double
precision gives 13-15 significant digits. The maximum number of

directly addressable single and double precision numbers is
16,384 and 8,192 respectively. Actual space available to the
user is even less since normally, the core resident portion of
the Real Time Operating System (RDOS) demands on the order of 11-
15K words out of the 32K available. However, if the Mapped RDOS
system (MRDOS) is used which requires one 16K unit of extended
memory (bringing the total to 48K), then the core resident portion of the operating system resides in the upper 16K leaving 32K
directly addressable words available to the user.

Since the total memory requirements of a program very often
exceed the amount of user address space, various means are
available under RDOS and MRDOS to segment user programs and
extend the amount of user address space. Unmapped systems
(RDOS), make use of program swaps and chains, and user overlays.
Mapped systems (MRDOS), in addition to these three methods of
program segmentation, also employ virtual overlaying and window
mapping. These require the use of extended address space. For
both methods, it is the address at which data is found that is
changed, no true data transfer occurs, resulting in a substantial
increase in speed over normal disk I/O while performing essentially the same functions. Virtual overlaying differs from normal
overlaying in that the overlays are loaded into extended memory
and there is no reading and writing of programs to and from disk
as in normal overlaying. Window mapping makes use of extended
memory in much the same way only for data instead of programs.
One or more 1K blocks in the lower 32K portion of memory are
reserved for the window which is then used to slide up and down
the extended memory in such a way that the contents within the
window change. This situation is illustrated in Figure 1, using
a 2 block window. Here the window originally contains blocks 0
and 1 of "extended" memory. A REMAP operation changes the position of this window to have it contain blocks 3 and 4. Thus,
while the window mapping feature does not allow the direct addressing of more than 32K words, it does allow the user to select
(via the FORTRAN call to the REMAP operation) which 32K of the
total memory is to be accessed. In FORTRAN, access to the window
is through a COMMON statement.

An alternative means of handling large amounts of data is,
of course, reading and writing to and from disk, although this
introduces more overhead. This overhead can be minimized,
however, if contiguous disk files are used rather than random or
sequential to reduce seek time on the disk. The range for this
seek time is 15-135 milliseconds. The user disk to which we are
referring is a Model 33, 2200 BPI, 12 sector/ track disk. A
complete revolution of the disk cartridge requires 40 milliseconds and a disk block read requires 3.33 milliseconds.

The remaining hardware items of the ECLIPSE used in the
benchmark are a CRT terminal, hardware multiple precision floating point arithmetic units, a TALLY 300 line per minute printer
and a Diablo dual disk drive. The compiler used on the ECLIPSE

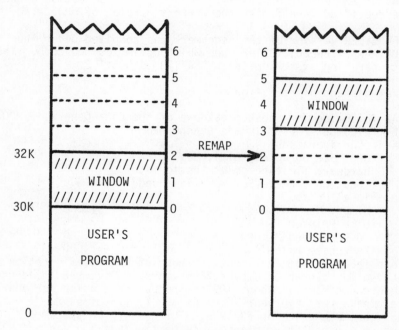

Figure 1. Window mapping on the ECLIPSE

was the optimizing FORTRAN 5 compiler (Revision 4.01 - Pre-
release). The FORTRAN 5 language has quite a few attractive
features such as conversational I/O, selective compilation (or
exclusion) of certain code, PAUSE statements, etc. However, in
the interest of machine transferability and in order to keep both
versions of the benchmark as similar as possible, standard FORTRAN
IV was used. With regard to the reliability of the operating
system, we experienced problems with system bugs in earlier
versions of the operating system. However, this situation appears
to have rectified itself with the current version of MRDOS (Rev.
5).

The CYBER version of the benchmark was compiled under the
FTN (FORTRAN EXTENDED), OPT=2 mode which optimizes the code. The
current operating system on the CYBER 173 is NOS 1.2.

Cost Analysis and Depreciation

The following is a cost breakdown of the Data General S/200
ECLIPSE minicomputer used in the benchmark:

Basic Configuration	Cost
CPU, 32K words (16 bit), dual disk hardware floating point (basic math functions),CRT, (Software included)	$42,000
Additional Units:	
Memory Map Unit	$1,000
Line Printer	$3,500
16K Extended Memory	$5,000
Total Purchase Price	$51,500

To establish a general cost per hour of this configuration,
the machine was depreciated over five years. Since the standard
maintenance contract is about 10% of the purchase price per year,
this becomes, over five years, approximately 1.5 times the
original purchase price or $77,250. To account for system
maintenance, preventative maintenance on the hardware and actual
down time for repairs, the system was assumed to be available to
the user 80% of the time over the five years. Therefore, the
five year price divided by 80% of the number of hours in five
years gives a cost per hour of $2.20 or $.00061 per second. This
we refer to as plan A.

Because the system actually used was maintained by inhouse
personnel and therefore required no maintenance contract, a somewhat revised cost analysis would be more realistic for our installation. The actual cost of replacement parts over the two
years the machine has been in service was $250 which, when pro-
jected over five years becomes $625. This figure plus the pur-
chase price gives $52,125 as the labor-free cost of the machine.
In two years the down time for repairs totaled approximately 60
hours. Preventative hardware maintenance (running test programs)
averages two hours per month and software maintenance requires
about one eight-hour day per month. Therefore, the total time in

one year that the machine is not available to the user is 150
hours or 750 hours over five years. Dividing $52,125 by 43,050
(total hours in 5 years minus 750) gives a cost per hour of $1.21
($3.36 x 10^{-4}/sec). This is cost plan B.

Cost plans intermediate between A and B can easily be constructed by noting that machine repairs were carried out by a
trained electronics technician and that software maintenance and
preventative hardware maintenance were carried out by graduate
students. Also, in both cost plans A and B, it has been assumed
that the machine will not be idle, but will always be busy running user's jobs. One can account for any deviation from this
assumption by simple dividing the cost by the fraction of available time the machine will be used.

The cost of running the benchmark on the CYBER was obtained
directly from the University Computing Center's charging algorithm which was designed to "reflect, as accurately as possible,
the actual cost of running the job". Since this cost includes
that of personnel salaries, and since about one half of the
center's budget is personnel, an alternative price can be obtained by dividing by two the calculated cost obtained from the
charging algorithm.

The CYBER rate schedule divides the computer cost/hour into
contributions from various sources. The major contribution of
interest with respect to the benchmark is the $200/hour charge
for CPU time. Field length usage during the time a job is
active in central memory costs $0.75 per central memory kiloword-
hour, and mass storage charges add an additional $0.015 per
kilopru of disk I/O. There are of course, additional charges for
cards, tape mounts, plotter use, etc., which are irrelevent to
the benchmark in question and so will not be discussed here. An
analysis of individual job costs for execution of the benchmark
as well as cost ratios for the two machines will be discussed in
a later section.

Description of the Benchmark

A proper evaluation of the efficiency of a computer should
involve running the actual programs used. For this reason, the
semi-empirical SCF molecular orbital program MINDO/2([1]) (with
options for executing INDO([2])) was programmed on both the ECLIPSE
and the CYBER.

The starting point for the general SCF molecular orbital
problem is the molecular electronic Schroedinger equation

$$H\Psi = E\Psi \qquad (1)$$

an eigenvalue problem with the set of Ψ_n's and E_n's to be determined. The majority of ways of generating solutions to (1) involve
basis set expansions of the Ψ_n's with variationally determined
coefficients. The net effect is the transformation of (1) into

a (usually non-linear) matrix pseudoeigenvalue problem.

$$F(C) \; C = S \; C \; E \qquad\qquad (2)$$

$$C^\dagger \; S \; C = 1$$

A typical calculation can generally be analyzed in two steps. The first involves the initial evaluation of integrals used in the construction of F and S and the second involves the solution of (2), usually by iterative methods. In terms of computational effort, various methods divide themselves into two classes: <u>ab-initio</u> methods in which steps (1) and (2) take very roughly equal amounts of computer time, and semi-empirical methods in which step (1) consumes neglibible computer time relative to step (2). The solution of Eq. (2) (step 2) for semi-empirical methods (for which S = 1) involves principally the repeated diagonalization of F(C) until self-consistency is obtained. This iterative portion of the program requires the most time and memory. As a result, this part of the semi-empirical SCF program MINDO was the most critical from the programming standpoint.

Because of the limited amount of extended memory (16K) on the minicomputer available, the window mapping and virtual over-laying options for data and program storage could not be tested in the actual SCF benchmark. Therefore, normal user overlays and contiguous reads and writes to and from disk were used. However, a short window mapping test program was executed to verify the performance of this feature.

The SCF program consists of a very small main program which contains a few short COMMON blocks and calls to the nine over-lays. Only the main program and any one overlay are core resi-dent at any given time. A brief descripton of each overlay follows:

1.   Input Overlay. Introduces cartesian coordinates and atomic numbers for each atom in the molecule, sets print options and specifies type of calculation (MINDO or INDO).

2.   Initialization Overlay. Sets up various tables of constants used in other overlays and stores them on disk.

3.   Coulomb Overlay. Calculates two-electron integrals and writes them to disk.

4.   Overlap Overlay. Evaluates overlap integrals and stores them on disk.

5.   Guess Overlay. Generates an initial guess of the density matrix which is written to disk.

6.   Core Hamiltonian Overlay. Generates the one electron part of the F matrix and writes it to disk.

7.   SCF Overlay. This iteratively solves Eq. 2.

8.   Overlap Derivative Overlay. Calculates the derivatives of the overlap integral with respect to the x, y, and z coordin-ates of each atom and writes them to disk. Although it is more efficient to evaluate these with the overlap integrals themselves,

space limitations precluded this.

    9.   Gradient Overlay. Calculates the total energy and its derivatives with respect to the x, y and z coordinates of each atom.

The entire program consists of 62 subroutines each of which must be compiled separately on the ECLIPSE. The slow, optimizing compiler of the ECLIPSE required several hours for the task. We found that a hobby such as embroidery is useful while waiting for the routines to compile.

    The SCF program was dimensioned to 50 orbitals and run for several molecules of various sizes. Execution times were tabulated for both the CYBER and the ECLIPSE. At first sight, the measurement of execution times on either machine would seem to be straightforward. This is not the case. On the ECLIPSE, the only time available is that of a real time clock, i.e., the elapsed time one would ideally obtain with a stop-watch. The elapsed time obtained in this benchmark is the sum of the time the system spends performing two functions: the numerical calculations, and the mass storage transfers of data and programs (overlay overhead). No effort was made to overlap these two functions. The time spent in mass storage transfers was measured by running for each molecule, that part of the benchmark that duplicates the mass storage transfers without performing the calculations. This was run only on the ECLIPSE and will be referred to as the mass storage benchmark.

    On the CYBER, the only time easily available is the central processor execution time, i.e., the time the CPU spends executing a program. The mass storage transfers are handled by peripheral processors during which time the central processor is performing housekeeping operations or working on another program. The actual "time on the machine" or turn-around time on the CYBER is difficult to obtain and varies so widely, depending on the load on the machine, as to be worthless as a performance measure.

    Finally, in order to obtain a reliable estimate of actual execution time with a minimum of overhead from the operating system as well as from sources described above, a simple benchmark designed to mimic the most time consuming portion of the typical SCF calculation was run on the ECLIPSE, the CYBER 173, and the CDC 6400.   As mentioned earlier, for semi-empirical methods the solution of Eq. (2) involves principally the repeated diagonalization of F(C) until self-consistency is obtained. Thus, a benchmark involving the repeated diagonalization of F plus some matrix multiplications should closely resemble step 2. This execution benchmark, then, consisted of the diagonalization of F which was an array filled with real numbers ranging from -10^5 to $+10^5$ with magnitudes varying from 10^{-5} to 10^{+5}, followed by the back-transformation of F to recover the original matrix. We refer to this as the diagonalization benchmark. The numerical precision for various word lengths (i.e., single vs. double precision) was determined by subtracting the value of each

element in the back-transformed maxtrix F from the original
matrix F. The largest value of this difference matrix then, gave
an estimate of the machine accuracy.

Execution times for the diagonalization benchmark were
conducted for varying array sizes. The purpose of varying the
dimension of the matrices was to eliminate the effects of operating system overhead expenses and to provide a basis for extra-
polating execution times to larger matrices. The entire diagonalization benchmark was placed in a FORTRAN DO loop and executed
100 times for each array size. The time at the start of execution and the time at the end of execution were printed. Printing
of the arrays was suppressed in this series of runs so that I/O
time was not a factor.

Results and Discussion

In this section we seek answers to the following:

1.   Can a more or less "standard" molecular orbital program
with the ability to handle 50 basis functions be made to run at
all on a minicomputer? If so, how much trouble is it to "bring
up" such a program?

2.   Will execution times or, more appropriately, turnaround times be reasonable?

3.   Will the costs be competitive with alternative computing sources?

The first of these three questions has been answered in the
previous section. By using program overlaying and disk mass
storage for temporarily holding arrays, a 50 orbital basis semi-
empirical molecular orbital program can be made to fit in 32K of
16 bit words. Of course, one can effectively increase the size
of the program by making even more extensive use of the disk.
But this would entail a drastic change in the program and, as we
shall see shortly, would increase the mass storage overhead to
intolerable limits.

As was discussed earlier, the iterative part of the SCF
problem is the most time consuming and has the largest core
requirements for both data and code. The size of the largest
overlay is of particular importance on the ECLIPSE since the area
in core reserved as an overlay area is preset at load time to the
size needed to contain the largest overlay in the corresponding
segment of the user overlay file. This area is reserved in core
throughout execution regardless of whether succeeding overlays
are smaller or not, unlike the CYBER. The size of the SCF overlay, which determined the size of the overlay area, was 26.6K
which left a little over 5K for the main overlay and run-time
stack (expandable area for temporary storage of variables and
intermediate results, e.g., non-common variables). The final
program required 31,778 words out of the 32,768 available under
MRDOS to load.

A word might be said here regarding the internal clocks

provided by the ECLIPSE operating system. The clock interrupt frequency can be selected at 10, 100, or 1000 hertz. Although only a 6% variation of elapsed time was found between the 10 hertz and the 1000 hertz clocks, this perturbation of the system argues in favor of using an external clock for time measurements. This "clock frequency effect" was not observed for the mass storage benchmark since very little processor time is used.

In preparing the benchmark, we encountered an interesting and important difference in the way array indexing is handled by the two computers. The ECLIPSE FORTRAN manual emphatically cautions the user to ensure that the first index of arrays within a nest of DO loops corresponds to the index of the innermost loop of the nest. Complying with this, however, would have entailed a major revision of the molecular orbital program. We investigated this problem by executing each of the four programs shown in Table I, 10,000 times and recording the execution times on each machine. (The statements in the square brackets were not included in the 10,000 executions of each program). Comparing the ECLIPSE execution times for programs I and III, it is seen that the warning in the ECLIPSE manual is justified. The ECLIPSE results for programs II and IV show that this problem can be easily circumvented by referencing the array with a single subscript and handling the double subscript indexing in FORTRAN with the aid of the "look up table" INJ. When implemented in the diagonalization benchmark, a 30% reduction of execution time occurred. It was thus included in the SCF overlay of the molecular orbital benchmark.

The ECLIPSE results in Table I can be understood when it is recognized that the compiler computes a single index address by the equivalent of the formula

$$IJ = I + 50 * (J-1)$$

and that it "optimizes" the code by removing constant expressions from loops. Thus the optimized revision of program III would be

```
DO 1 I = 1,50
  K = 50 * (I-1)
  DO 1 J = 1,50
1 A(K + J) = 1.0
```

which requires only 50 multiplications (the slowest operation in the program) rather than the 2500 of program I. Programs II and IV require no multiplications, with program IV requiring 2450 fewer table look-ups than II.

The CYBER results are puzzling in this context since the CYBER compiler also optimizes the source code and uses the same formula for the single subscript IJ as does the ECLIPSE. The results of II and IV are nearly twice as long as I and III(which are now comparable) on the CYBER as on the ECLIPSE. The explana-

TABLE I

COMPARISON OF INDEXING METHODS

	EXECUTION TIME (SEC)	
FORTRAN CODE	ECLIPSE	CYBER

```
I.   [DIMENSION A(50,50)]                785          66
        DO 1 I = 1,50
        DO 1 J = 1,50
      1 A(I,J) = 1.0



II.  [DIMENSION A(2500),INJ(50)          625          120
        DO 5 K = 1,50
      5 INJ(K) = 50*(K-1)]

        DO 1 I = 1,50
        DO 1 J = 1,50
        IJ = I + INJ(J)
      1 A(IJ) = 1.0



III. [DIMENSION A(50,50)]                549          70
        DO 1 I = 1,50
        DO 1 J = 1,50
      1 A(J,I) = 1.0



IV.  [DIMENSION A(2500),INJ(50)          550          103
        DO 5 K = 1,50
      5 INJ(K) = 50*(K-1)]

        DO 1 I = 1,50
        DO 1 J = 1,50
        JI = J + INJ(I)
      1 A(JI) = 1.0
```

tion for this lies in the fact that the multiplications $50*(I-1)$ are effectively eliminated by the compiler. This is accomplished by using the princple that any positive integer can be expressed as a linear combination of powers of 2 with coefficients of plus or minus one. Thus, in our example, the integer 50 (which is known to the compiler from the DIMENSION statement) can be written as $2^6 - 2^4 + 2^1$. Multiplication of any integer $(I-1)$ by 2^n can be very rapidly carried out on the CYBER by simply shifting the bits of the integer n spaces to the left. Thus the multiplication by 50 is replaced by three bit shifts, an integer additon and an integer subtraction. The impact of using singly dimensioned arrays on the CYBER version of the molecular orbital benchmark can be estimated from the fact that the diagonalization benchmark took 10% more time to execute when the arrays were made linear.

The double precision 64 bit word on the ECLIPSE gave a noticeable improvement in precision compared to the 32 bit single precision floating point word. The largest error in the diagonalization benchmark (with tolerence set to 10^{-8}) was 0.2×10^{-8} for the double precision word and 0.0004 for the single precison version. The CYBER (60 bit word) gave an error of 6.0×10^{-8}.

Various execution times for the molecular orbital benchmark are shown in Table II. As discussed earlier for the ECLIPSE, the total execution time is the "real time", i.e., the sum of processing time and mass storage transfer time. The contribution of overlay overhead to the latter averages about 6 seconds and is a constant independent of both the molecule and the number of iterations. Therefore, disk I/O in the form of data transfers accounts for the balance of the mass storage time.

The ratio of total ECLIPSE execution time to CYBER CPU time shown in Table II varies from 25 for C_2H_4 to 7.3 for C_6H_8 where it appears to be leveling off. This is a result of the diminishing importance of the mass storage transfer time for the larger molecules.

The mass storage overhead could easily be eliminated if sufficient extended memory were available to us. Results of a short test program using window mapping for data transfers indicated that 20,000 REMAP operations using a 2K window can be performed in three seconds. The number of data transfers to disk for the molecules executed in the SCF program varied between 43 and 51 depending on the number of iterations. Therefore, using REMAPS instead of disk reads and writes would entail almost zero overhead. The mass storage overhead then would be due soley to overlaying and this is a known constant (6 seconds).

One can easily estimate the SCF ECLIPSE execution time which would be the equivalent of the CYBER CPU time by subtracting the total mass storage times obtained from the mass storage benchmark from the total ECLIPSE execution times. These times are listed in Table II as Δ. The ratio of Δ to CYBER CPU time varies from 3.8 for C_2H_4 to 4.7 for C_6H_8. These can be compared

TABLE II

COMPARISON OF EXECUTION TIMES

MOLECULE	C_2H_4	C_3H_6	C_4H_6	C_5H_{10}	C_6H_8
# ORBITALS	12	18	22	30	32
# ITERATIONS IN SCF	9	13	11	10	13
ECLIPSE					
TOTAL TIME (SEC)	72	98	106	151	188
MASS STORAGE TIME	61	68	65	62	68
Δ (TOTAL - MASS STORAGE)	11	30	41	89	120
CYBER					
CPU TIME (SEC)	2.88	6.73	9.06	18.81	25.70
ECLIPSE/CYBER RATIOS					
TOTAL TIME/CPU TIME	25.0	14.5	11.7	8.0	7.3
Δ/CPU TIME	3.8	4.5	4.5	4.7	4.7

to the ECLIPSE/CYBER execution ratios obtained in the diagonalization benchmark (which has no mass storage calls), thus providing an independent check of our assumption that Δ corresponds to the CYBER CPU time. The diagonalization benchmark was executed for both singly and doubly subscripted arrays because, although single subscripting was shown to be faster than double, the SCF program used a combination of both. For single subscripting, the ratios obtained in the diagonalization benchmark varied from 3.7 (15 x 15 matrix) to 3.8 (35 x 35 matrix) while those for double varied from 4.6 (15 x 15 matrix) to 5.0 (35 x 35 matrix). The ratios of Δ to CYBER CPU time given above falls well within the range 3.7 to 5.0.

The evaluation of the cost effectiveness of anything is beset with many difficulties and the effectiveness of carrying out molecular orbital calculations on a mincomputer is no exception. Some of these difficulties have been discussed in the section on cost analysis. We venture no further discussion here other than to remark that the results presented in this section must be regarded as crude.

Table III shows the CYBER cost (as given by the University's charging algorithm) for each molecule and the ratios of the CYBER costs to the ECLIPSE costs (as computed under the cost plans A and B described earlier). Table III also includes the estimated ratios of CYBER costs to the costs obtained on an ECLIPSE with 65K of extended memory. This is sufficient memory to eliminate the disk I/O from the molecular orbital benchmark. This estimate was obtained by first modifying cost plans A and B to include the cost of the additional memory (and its maintenance) in the total five year price of the machine. The execution times on this hypothetical ECLIPSE were estimated by adding six seconds (the fixed cost of the disk overlaying overhead) to the Δ's of Table II.

According to the results shown in Table III it is far cheaper to use an ECLIPSE for these calculations than the CYBER. Even in the worst case shown, the CYBER is nearly ten times more expensive to use than the ECLIPSE. Moreover, the results also show that the additional extended memory on the ECLIPSE is well worth the extra investment, although the differences for the two ECLIPSE configurations are not great for the larger molecules.

Conclusions

The surprising aspect of this work is not that a molecular orbital program could be run on a 16 bit minicomputer. Given a suitable length floating point word, such programs can be highly overlayed and at the worst, the array dimensions can be lowered. We believe that even <u>ab-initio</u> programs can be made to run on the ECLIPSE, although the basis set size might be limited and mass storage overhead somewhat high. What was surprising to us was the sheer power of the ECLIPSE. The results of the diagonaliza-

TABLE III

COMPARISON OF COSTS

MOLECULE	C_2H_4	C_3H_6	C_4H_6	C_5H_{10}	C_6H_8
CYBER CHARGE	$0.41	$0.74	$0.91	$1.76	$3.28
CYBER/ECLIPSE					
PLAN A	9.3	12.3	14.0	19.0	28.5
PLAN B	16.9	22.4	25.5	31.6	51.9
CYBER/EXTENDED ECLIPSE					
PLAN A	32.4	26.0	24.5	23.4	33.0
PLAN B	59.1	47.5	44.7	42.8	60.1

tion benchmark showed that the ECLIPSE is only 4 to 5 times slower than the CYBER 173, even though the ECLIPSE uses a 64 bit floating point word. For a further comparison, we found via the diagonalization benchmark, that the CYBER 173 is 30 to 50% faster than the CDC6400.

Because a minicomputer used in this fashion is a dedicated "hands on" machine, with the only delay due to printing, the turn-around time will often be much better than that of the CYBER.

Provided that the usage demand is sufficiently high, we believe that the use of a minicomputer is both a highly convenient and cost effective alternative to using University computer centers for the type of calculation described in this paper.

Acknowledgement

We are very grateful to Dr. Stanley Bruckenstein for the use of his ECLIPSE. We also thank Mr. Greg Martinchek as well as other members of Dr. Bruckenstein's group for their valuable assistance in using this machine.

Literature Cited

(1) Dewar, M. S. and Haselbach, E., J. Amer. Chem. Soc.,(1970) 92, 1285.
(2) Pople, J. A., Beveridge, D. L. and Dobosh, P. A., J. Chem. Phys., (1967) 47, 2026.

A Minicomputer Numbercruncher

A. LINDGÅRD, P. GRAAE SORENSEN, and J. OXENBOLL

Chemistry Laboratory III, H. C. Orsted Institutet, University of Copenhagen, Universitetsparken 5, DK-2100 København O

Due to the low price of small minicomputer configurations they have become very popular in computerized instrumentation for chemistry and physics. Large scale scientific computing has not been much influenced by this, but has mostly been done on large computers. An example of use of a monoprogrammed minicomputer for quantum chemistry is found at Berkeley (Miller and Schaefer, 1973), but the configuration with plenty of main memory, backing store etc. is not typical for minicomputer systems. On the other hand the small stand alone systems are not suited for program development due to the lack of powerful peripherals. Only interpreters like BASIC can be used with a reasonable turn around time for program development, and BASIC is certainly not suited for anything but small programs.

A problem with the large machines is that they are very expensive for jobs having large cpu-time requirements. Monte-Carlo calculations in statistical mechanics can often require weeks of cpu-time, but do not require much backingstore or use of peripherals.

Considering these cpu-bound problems it became clear that a dedicated minicomputer with a reasonable amount of fast store would be sufficient to do these type of calculations at a very low cost, the only problem being how to develop programs and get data in and out of the memory.

At the H. C. Ørsted Institute there was a need for handling problems in statistical mechanics and chemical kinetics requiring weeks to months of cpu-time. Core requirements for these jobs are low. These jobs could of course run on our medium size multiprogrammed RC4000 computer (Brinch Hansen, 1967), but not in a reasonable

way. Either other users would have problems getting a
decent turnaround time for their computational jobs,
and the RC4000 would be less attractive for doing small
jobs like editing, compiling and running small programs
from a terminal, or the turnaround time for the time
comsuming job would have been so long that it could not
have been realized.

System design.

The purpose of the system is to make long cpu-
bound computations feasible. Typically a program will
run for a few hours before it needs attention from the
RC4000 for storing away data. The program will then go
on making a new computation. This cycle may continue
for weeks.
From the point of view of the minicomputer the
RC4000 is a backing store. The computed data may be
stored by an RC4000 control program on the backing
store ie. the disc. The final security of the data is
assured by the security dump of the whole backing store
on a magnetic tape, which is done once every day.

Selecting the minicomputer.

The primary criteria used in selecting the minicomputer for this project were processing rate, instruction repertoire and cost.
It was decided that hardware multiply/divide was
essential for most applications, but that floating
point arithmetic would be used in a few cases only. It
was expected that a large amount of processing time
would be used for bit manipulation and memory addressing, and an advanced addressing scheme with easy use
of index registers was important.
The Texas Instrument 980A was selected as a
reasonable compromise between the abovementioned requirements. For instance, the shift instruction can handle
a variable number of positions and the hardware multi-
ply/divide is not too difficult to use for multilength
integer arithmetic. Further, the protection system of
the TI980A was considered as an advantage. Software
support from the manufacturer was not considered,
because we already have a general assembler for any
minicomputer and microcomputer, and program development
should not be done on the minicomputer.

Connecting the minicomputer to the RC4000.

The minicomputer may be connected either as an independent machine having a terminal for the user and only using the RC4000 as backingstore, or as a slave computer completely controlled by the RC4000, with no other peripherals. We favor the last solution as it makes hardware and software simpler. A slave computer is like any other completely controlled peripheral. The difference is that a general purpose minicomputer can do very complex data transformations while other peripherals generally can not.

The minicomputer should not have any character oriented peripherals connected. Character input/output requires a lot of software. If a terminal had been connected, users would furthermore have felt inclined to use the minicomputer for developing, editing and assembling of programs. This requires a command interpreter and some program to determine whether this could be done locally or involve the RC4000. We would certainly use the same command language on the minicomputer as on the RC4000, which implies that we had to develop a lot of software. It is much simpler to force the user to use the RC4000 for editing, assembling and loading programs and have no conventional peripherals on the minicomputer.

A slave computer is simple to handle. It can always be put into a well defined state, it cannot harm the RC4000 as it cannot do anything on its own but has to ask the RC4000 to do it, by sending a signal.

The TI980A controller.

Communication between the RC4000 and the TI980A takes place via the low-speed and the high-speed (DMA) data channels of the RC4000, but only via the DMA port of the TI980A. Besides the DMA capability, this port has an instruction controlled output feature and an interrupt input. These features made it easy to build the TI980A interface, because it was only necessary to implement one peripheral device to the minicomputer, namely RC4000 through the DMA port.

The interface can logically be divided into two parts, a control system and a DMA data transfer system. In the control system the TI980A is connected to the instruction controlled low-speed data channel of the RC4000 and functions as a slave computer. The RC4000 uses five instructions to control the minicomputer: 1) reset, 2) stop, 3) start, 4) single instruction execution and 5) interrupt. Implementation of the first

four instructions is performed by connecting the output
of the RC4000 controller to the front panel board of
the minicomputer and then simply simulating the front
panel switches. The interrupt instruction is connected
to the DMA port.

The DMA system controls the data transfers between
the two computers. A word is loaded from the memory of
one computer through its DMA port, stored temporarily
in a one word buffer, and then the second computer is
requested to store this word in its memory through its
DMA port. In one RC4000 24 bit word only one 16 bit
TI980A word is stored. No attempt has been made to make
a more efficient packing, because it would complicate
both software and hardware.

The DMA transfer can only be initialized by the
RC4000, which has four instructions for this purpose:
1) load the RC4000 adress counter for input, 2) load
the RC4000 adress counter for output, 3) load the
TI980A adress counter and 4) load the word number
counter. Execution of the last instruction also starts
the data transfer, which is now controlled by the
interface.

The automatic transfer instruction (ATI) of the
minicomputer is used for activating the instruction
controlled output at the DMA port. This instuction is
normally used to initialize a DMA transfer to a
peripheral device (e.g. a disc) when the minicomputer
is used in a stand alone system. Here the output is
used for a low speed communication from the TI980A to
the RC4000. The DMA port does not have an input
feature, so low-speed communication the opposite way is
not implemented. The ATI instruction can load two 16
bit TI980A words to peripheral registers, and sends at
the same time an interrupt to the RC4000. This can read
the two registers by sense instructions. The remaining
bits which can be read by a sense instruction are used
for status.

Software.

The communication and control software developed
for this project consists of the following programs:
1.   A handler as a part of the RC4000 monitor
      (Brinch Hansen, 1973) which together with a
      process description is the peripheral process
      "ti980a".
2.   Initialisation code in the RC4000. This is only
      executed at system restart in the RC4000.
3.   A monitor in the TI980A. This includes a
      handler for the RC4000 known as "rc4000".

The TI980A monitor provides a control and communication structure similar to that of the RC4000 monitor. The TI980A user area and register file dump is conceptually a process similar to the internal process of the RC4000 monitor (Brinch Hansen, 1973). The process it may communicate with is the peripheral process "rc4000" (see figure 1) and it does so using a message buffer technique equivalent to that in the RC4000 system. Thus multibuffering of input/output is a built-in feature. The structure allows us to implement multiprogramming on the TI980A without changing external conventions and with a relatively small effort in software development.

Communication in the TI980A.

When the TI980A user program wants the attention of the RC4000 user program it sends a message. This is done by calling a procedure "send message". A buffer within the TI980A monitor is selected and the message is copied from the user program to the message buffer. The buffer address is returned to the TI980A user program. The latter may send a new message or may wait for an answer to the message send (see figure 2b for an example). Calling the TI980A monitor procedure "wait answer" delays the TI980A user program until the RC4000 has sent an answer back to the TI980A. The answer from the RC4000 arrives in the same message buffer as used by "send message" and is copied by "wait answer" into

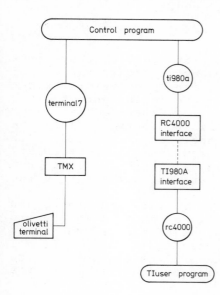

Figure 1. Structure of a simple job using the TI980A showing the communication and control paths. Rectangular boxes are interface hardware; circles are peripheral processes.

an answer area in the TI980A user program. The TI980A
user program can call the TI980A monitor to examine
whether an answer has arrived.

Communication in the RC4000.

When the RC4000 user program has loaded and
started the TI980A, the TI980A user program may send a
message to the handler telling the handler to queue up
the message buffer until a message arrives from the
TI980A user program. When it arrives the message is
copied from the TI980A to the selected message buffer
in the RC4000. The RC4000 user program will get the
TI980A message copied into its answer area by executing
wait answer. An answer to the message from the TI980A
can be send by the RC4000 user by executing a new "send
message", "wait answer" sequence, (see figure 2a).

Control.

The RC4000 user program is an operating system for
the TI980A user program. It can do block input/output
to the user area at any time. It can start and stop the
TI980A user program and when finished remove the TI980A
user program. This is done by sending messages to the
handler. The TI980A user program and even the TI980A
monitor can do nothing to harm the RC4000 and the
activities therein. The control both in hardware and in
software is exclusive to the RC4000.

Survival.

For long term computations, it would be convenient
if the minicomputer could survive most kinds of
troubles in the host system, irrespective of whether
they are caused by hardware malfunctioning or by new
development of hardware and basic software.
In hardware the TI980A is protected against the
RC4000. The communication channel is separated both
from the RC4000 data channels and from the TI980A data
channel through two controllers. The TI980A can run
even when there is no power on the controller in the
RC4000.
In the design of the TI980A monitor and the RC4000
handler it was possible to design a safe strategy to
keep the TI980A going independant of system deadstarts
in the RC4000. This is done by having a copy of all
state variables in both the TI980A monitor and the
RC4000 peripheral process. At system deadstart in the

```
rcusercomm
  1  27 4 76
  1  begin
  2  comment rc4000 user program for control and
  3    communication with ti980a;
  4  integer i;
  5  integer array M,A(1:8),image(1:256),register(1:9);
  6
  6  comment fetch translated tiuser program from dis ;
  7  careaproc(<:tiusercomm:>);
  8   M(1):=3 shift 12; comment input operation;
  9   M(2):=firstaddr(image);
 10   M(3):=M(2)+2*256-2;
 11   M(4):=1; comment relative segment for code;
 12  waitanswer(sendmessage(<:tiusercomm:>,M),A);
 13  comment the tiuser program is now in image;
 14
 14  comment reserve ti980a and move code to ti980a;
 15  reserveproc(<:ti980a:>,0);
 16   M(1):=5 shift 12; comment output;
 17   comment M(2) and M(3) are unchanged;
 18   M(4):=0; comment first address in ti980;
 19  waitanswer(sendmessage(<:ti980a:>,M),A);
 20
 20  comment set  registers and start ti980a;
 21  register(8):=register(9):=0;
 22  comment TIprogramcounter:=TIstatusregister:=0;
 23   M(1):=5 shift 12+2; comment set registers and start;
 24   M(2):=firstaddr(register);
 25  waitanswer(sendmessage(<:ti980a:>,M),A);
 26
 26  comment wait for 5 messages and generate answers;
 27  for i:=1 step 1 until 5 do begin
 28     M(1):=14 shift 12; comment wait message(<:ti980a:>);
 29     waitanswer(sendmessage(<:ti980a:>,M),A);
 30     comment a message has arrived. generate an answer;
 31     M(1):=10 shift 12; comment send answer(<:ti980a:>);
 32     M(2):=A(2); comment copy TI buffer address ;
 33     waitanswer(sendmessage(<:ti980a:>,M),A);
 34     end loop;
 35
 35  comment removeprogram and release ti980a;
 36   M(1):=16 shift 12;
 37  waitanswer(sendmessage(<:ti980a:>,M),A);
 38  end

algol end 15
```

Figure 2a. Model operating system written in the ALGOL6 dialect (Lauesen, 1969). The program reads the translated TI980A user program from the RC4000 backing store and moves it to the user area of the TI980A (lines 6–19). The TI980A register file is loaded and the minicomputer started (lines 20–25). A number of messages and answers are exchanged (lines 26–34). The minicomputer is released (lines 35–37).

RC4000 the initialization code reads the state
variables from the TI980A monitor into the RC4000
peripheral process. Loading the TI980A monitor is a
privileged operation which a normal user cannot execute.

The major problem that arises when handling a
survival problem lies in the multiprogrammed RC4000
computer. After deadstart only the person who has last
reserved the TI980A should be allowed to control it
again, if a TI980A user program is running. The
reservation scheme is extended as follows. When the
TI980A is free, any RC4000 process may reserve the
TI980A. The name of the reserving process is moved to
the TI980A monitor. At system deadstart it is copied
from the TI980A monitor into the peripheral process.
Only an RC4000 process with the same name as the
original reserver can now reserve the TI980A. The
disadvantage of this scheme is that the RC4000 user
process explicitly has to release the "ti980a" process.

A user can take advantage of the automatic process
start up facility in one of the operating systems
(Graae Sørensen and Lindgård, 1973). The RC4000 user
program can easily examine the state of the TI980A and
the program therein, making the coding of an start up
mechanism relatively easy.

How to use the TI980A.

In figure 2a is given a simple example of an
operating RC4000 algol program and in figure 2b a
TI980A assembly language program. The operating program
fetches the assembled code as generated by the general
assembler (Bang, 1974). The TI980A is loaded with the
program after reservation has taken place and the
TI980A user program is started. The TI980A user program
and the RC4000 user program exchange a number of
messages. Finally the RC4000 user program releases the
TI980A.

The control model program in figure 2a is a short
program and it is easy to extend it to a realistic
control program by including some input/output and test
of the communications. Such a program will only be a
few pages long and rather trivial to write. The TI980A
model program in figure 2b is very short. It has indeed
been the scope of the design to make life easy for the
programmer when handling communications. Assembly language coding should be kept at a minimum. Although the
communication primitives looks different in the TI980A
they work basicly the same way as in the RC4000. In an

```
tiuser
 0
 0   rep:  ldx=message         ;
 1         trap 3              ; send message(<:rc4000:>,message);
 2         ste bufferaddress;  bufferaddress:=
 3
 3
 3   ;     comment computations and/or other communications
 3   ;        may take place here;
 3
 3         ldx=answer          ;
 4         lde bufferaddress;
 5         trap 4              ; wait answer(bufferaddress,answer);
 6         bru    rep          ; goto rep;
 7
 7   bufferaddress: 0          ;
 8   message:            0,r.6 ; message area
14   answer:             0,r.6 ; answer area
20
```

Figure 2b. Model program for the TI980A showing how to communicate with the RC4000

RC4000 assembly language program, the comments would have been the same.

Discussion.

    Starting out with the model operating system (figure 2a) it is a rather trivial task to write an operating system for a specific application.

    The system has already been succesfully used to solve scientific problems in statistical mechanics (Rotne and Heilmann, 1976) for polymers on a grid.

    The cost per run is very low compared with the cost on a large, fast machine considering the difference in speed. The stability of the system is extremely good. The TI980A has not failed at least in the past year.

    The total hardware development cost is around half the price of the minicomputer. The basic software development cost was around two person months.

Acknowledgement.

    The grant from Statens Naturvidenskabelige Forskningsråd to purchase the TI980A is gratefully acknowledged. Jørgen Bang designed and implemented the general assembler. Heinrich Bjerregaard implemented the basic software.

Abstract.

   The low price of minicomputers makes them attractive
for timeconsuming jobs which are only cpu-bound, like
Monte Carlo simulations. At the H. C. Ørsted Institute
a minicomputer with 12 k main memory has been connected
to the multiprogrammed RC4000 computer. All program
development is done on the RC4000 and so is the control
of the minicomputer.

Literature cited.

Bang, J., (1974), Report 74/15, Datalogisk Institut,
København.

Brinch Hansen, P. (1967), Bit 7 191-199

Brinch Hansen, P. (1973), Operating Systems Principles,
Prentice-Hall, Englewood Cliffs, N. J.

Graae Sørensen, P. and Lindgård, A. (1973),
Computers in Chemical Research and
Ed. Hadzi, Elsevier, Amsterdam.

Lauesen, S. (1969), ALGOL5 User's Manual, RCSL 55-D42
Regnecentralen, København.

Miller, W.H. and Schaefer, H.F. (1973),
Quarterly Reports,
Department of Chemistry, University of California,
Berkeley, California.

Rotne, J. and Heilmann, O.J. (1976),
Proc. VIIth International Congress on Rheology,
Gothenburg.

Molecular Dynamics Calculations on a Minicomputer

PAUL A. FLINN

Physics and Metallurgy Departments, Carnegie-Mellon University, Pittsburgh, PA 15213

Since its introduction by Rahman in 1964 (1), the technique of computer simulation of motion in liquids, generally known as "molecular dynamics", has played a vital role in increasing our understanding of the real nature of the liquid state. Applications of the technique to various liquids have been reviewed by McDonald and Singer (2), Rahman (3), and Fisher and Watts (4). The results of the calculations have been in excellent agreement with a variety of experimental measurements of the properties of liquids: the equation of state, the radial distribution function, inelastic scattering of neutrons, and diffusion. The molecular dynamics results also provide valuable tests of the adequacy of various approximate analytic theories of liquids. A major limitation of the technique has been economic: the calculations have required large amounts of time on large, expensive, computers. Fortunately, it is possible to carry out useful molecular dynamics calculations at greatly reduced cost on a minicomputer (or microcomputer); much more widespread use, including instructional use, of the technique, should now be possible.

The calculation is, in principle, quite simple; it consists of numerical integration of the simultaneous nonlinear differential equations of motions for a number of particles constituting a small sample of the liquid. In the original work the Newtonian form of the equations of motion was used:

$$m \frac{d^2 \vec{r}_i}{dt^2} = \sum_{j \neq i} f(r_{ij})$$

where m is the particle mass, r_i is the position of the i th particle, $\vec{r}_{ij}$ is the distance between the centers of particles i and j, and f is the force acting between particle i and j. For the work described here, it was more convenient to use the Hamiltonian equations:

$$\frac{d\vec{p}_i}{dt} = \sum_{i \neq j} f(r_{ij}) \qquad \frac{d\vec{r}_i}{dt} = \frac{\vec{p}_i}{m}$$

where $\vec{p}_i$ is the momentum of the i th particle. The potential used for a given liquid is generally of a form suggested by theoretical arguments, but with parameters obtained from experimental data on the material. To illustrate the method we use the case of argon, with a Lennard-Jones potential:

$$V(r) = 4\epsilon \left[(\sigma/r)^{12} - (\sigma/r)^6 \right]$$

and parameter values $\epsilon = 1.65 \times 10^{-21}$ J, $\sigma = 3.4$ Å taken from the work of Rahman.

Basic Principles of Minicomputer Use.

The characteristic features of most minicomputers are small word size (16 bits), limited memory, and reasonable speed for integer arithemetic. Floating point operations usually require subroutines and are quite slow. The usefulness of minicomputers for molecular dynamics calculations results from the fact that the range of values of the variables needed is sufficiently limited that integer arithmetic can be used, and 16 bit precision is adequate. The only potential difficulties arise in connection with the interatomic force function, which may be of complicated form, and has an unbounded magnitude. These problems can be fairly easily circumvented: the interatomic force function is evaluated and tabulated at the beginning of the calculation; in the body of the calculation determination of the force is simply a look-up operation. The wide range of the magnitude of the force does not represent any real problem, since the force becomes inconveniently large only at distances considerably shorter than those which actually exist when the liquid is at or near equilibrium. We can, therefore, truncate the magnitude of the force to a constant value for distances less than some r_s. We also, as is customary, limit the range of interaction by setting the force equal to zero for distances beyond the cutoff distance. Our force law then has the form:

$$r < r_s \qquad f(r) = f(r_s)$$
$$r_s \leq r \leq r_c \qquad f(r) = c_1 r^{-13} - c_2 r^{-7}$$
$$r > r_c \qquad f(r) = 0$$

and the lookup table need cover only the range $r_r \leq r \leq r_c$. For this calculation, r_s was taken as 2.82 Å, and r_c as 5.07 Å.

System Hardware.

The minicomputer used for this work was a Texas Instruments 960A, borrowed from its normal use as a Mössbauer spectrometer and data processor (5). The system includes 8192 words (16 bit) of semiconductor memory, an interface to a teletype with paper tape punch and reader, and a CRT display. The optional extended instruction set of the 960A includes the following hardware operations: multiply two 16 bit words, 32 bit (double word) product; divide double word by single word, single word quotient and single word remainder; double word add; double word subtract; double word left and right shift operations. The display is provided by a Tektronix 603 storage display unit, driven by two Datel DAC 4910B 10 bit analog to digital converters, interfaced through the communications register unit (CRU) of the computer. Alphameric display is provided by software; no character generating hardware is used. The original cost of the computer was about $7000 (1972). The 960A is no longer made, but equipment with similar performance can now be obtained at a much lower cost.

For integer arithmetic, the 960A is only moderately slower than typical large computers, such as the Univac 1108. The times in microseconds for some typical instructions are:

	960A	1108
Add	3.583	1.50
Subtract	3.583	1.50
Multiply	8.583	3.125
Divide	10.417	3.875
Load	3.333	1.50
Store	3.583	1.50

System Software.

The operating system used for this work was one originally written for the Mössbauer spectrometer application, and described in more detail elsewhere (5). It consists of a monitor, I/O routines, and a floating point arithmetic package. The monitor provides for the loading of programs from paper tape, initiation of execution, recovery from error traps, dump, patch, and debug facilities. The I/O routines provide for teletype input and output of decimal, hexadecimal, and alphanumeric data, and CRT display of alphanumeric data by software character generation. The floating point package includes addition, subtraction, multiplication, division, integer to floating point, and floating point to integer conversion. A fixed point square root routine was written and included for this calculation. The system

software occupies 2128 words, with an additional 82 words for the
square root routine. All programming was done in assembly
language, and converted to object code by a macro instruction
processor and a cross assembler run on an IBM 360/67.

Molecular Dynamics Program.

The working program consists of several parts: initialization, cooling, integration, calculation of statistics, CRT
display, and teletype output. The program storage requirements,
in 16 bit words, are: initialization, 210; cooling, 38;
integration, 192; statistics, 100; display and output, 48; total,
588. The data storage requirements are: force table, 1024;
position, momentum, initial position and initial momentum, 384
each; correlation functions, 1024; total data 3584. The overall
space required is 4172 words.

Units and Scaling.

It is customary in molecular dynamics calculations to use a
system of units based on the properties of the system under study:
following the choice of Tsung and Maclin (6), we take the particle
mass as the unit of mass, the parameter σ as the unit of length,
and a conveniently short time (10^{-13} sec.) as the unit of time.
With this convention, the momentum is numerically equal to the
velocity.

In order to avoid unnecessary loss of precision in the
integer arithmetic, it is necessary to scale the variables of the
problem into proper integer units. We consider first the length
scale: we have a system of N particles, with a volume V per
particle, for a total volume NV, in a cube of side $(NV)^{1/3}$. To
use the full precision of the computer we represent this length
by 2^{16}. We choose our unit of time for one integration step as
62.5 femtoseconds; this is scaled as 1/16 of an integer unit,
since multiplication by Δt is accomplished by a shift of 4 binary
places to the right. One integer unit of time is therefore 0.1
picosecond. This choice of distance and time scales fixes the
velocity (and momentum) scales. We define the "temperature" of
the system in terms of the kinetic energy:

$$T = 3k/m\langle v^2 \rangle.$$

Startup of Calculation.

The first step in the calculation is the generation of the
force lookup table for the range of R needed (10234 to 18426).
Since the memory space available was quite limited, steps of 8
were used, so that only 1024 locations were required.
Interpolation from the table was planned for intermediate values
of R, but proved to be unnecessary.

Next, the initial configuration of the system is constructed by assigning random values to the position and momentum coordinates of the particles. Random numbers are generated by the multiplicative congruence method: repeated multiplication by 3125 and retention of the least significant half of the double word product. This initial configuration has, of course, an extremely high energy. It is necessary to "cool" the system by gradually removing kinetic energy. This is done by periodically reducing the magnitude of each component of momentum of each particle by some fraction of its value. The cooling must be done gradually to avoid freezing in a nonequilibrium state; the cooling rate should not exceed the rate at which the initially extremely high potential energy of the system can be converted into kinetic energy, so that approximate equipartition is maintained.

Main Calculation Loop.

The calculation proper is carried out in a nest of three loops. The outermost (T loop) is a time loop; each execution corresponds to one time integration step. The intermediate loop (J loop) is over all particles; one execution corresponds to a calculation of the net force on one particle, and an updating of the position and momentum of that particle. The innermost loop (I loop) is also over all particles; one execution corresponds to a calculation of the force on one particle due to one other particle.

We use the following notation to describe the calculation: $X1(I)$, $X2(I)$, $X3(I)$: position coordinates of the I'th particle. $P1(I)$, $P2(I)$, $P3(I)$: momentum coordinates of the I'th particle. DX1, DX2, DX3: components of the vector from particle J to particle I; e.g., $DX1 = X1(I) - X1(J)$. R: the distance from particle J to particle I. F: the force exerted by particle I on particle J. F1, F2, F3: the components of the net force on particle J; this is calculated as a running sum over the I particles in the inner loop.

The calculation proceeds as follows:
Zero the time register and enter the T loop.
    Initialize the J register and enter the J loop.
    Clear F1, F2, F3 to zero.
        Initialize the I register and enter the I loop.
        Test and skip if $I = J$.
        Calculate $RR = DX1**2 + DX2**2 + DX3**2$ as a double word sum.
        Test and skip if $RR > RRC$. (Separation beyond cutoff range).
        Calculate $R = SQRT(RR)$ and store.
        Form R-RS and set equal to zero if negative.
        Shift right 3 places (divide by 8) and use as index to look up F.
        Form the components of F: $(F*DX1/R)$, $(F*DX2/R)$, $(F*DX3/R)$, and add to F1, F2, F3.

Increment I and continue.

On exit from I loop calculate momentum changes as F1, F2, F3 shifted right 4 places (divided by 16, corresponding to $\Delta t = 1/16$) and update P1(J), P2(J), and P3(J).

Calculate position changes as P1(J), P2(J), and P3(J), shifted right 4 places, and update X1(J), X2(J), and X3(J).

Display new position.

Increment J and continue.

On exit from J loop, store panel switches and test for exit to monitor, cooling, or temperature calculation.

Increment T register and continue.

Display and Output of Results.

The calculations produce two sorts of results: particle positions as a function of time, and statistical functions of the system. The particle positions as a function of time are displayed on the storage CRT. For reasons of clarity, only those particles in the first octant (all components of position positive) are displayed. After the new position of the J'th particle is calculated, the three components of position are tested, and, if all are positive, the x and y components of position are transmitted through the CRU to the 10 bit analog to digital converters which drive the CRT display unit. We thus display the projection on the x-y plane of the content of the first octant. Placing the display unit in storage mode results in the development of traces of the paths of the centers of the particles. Some typical traces after varying lengths of time (0.36 ps, 0.9 ps, 1.8 ps) are shown in Figures 1, 2 and 3. Such displays are quite valuable for visualising the nature of a liquid (it rapidly becomes obvious that a liquid is neither gas-like nor solid-like), but, obviously some quantitative characteristics are needed.

Two widely used statistics of a liquid are the mean square displacement function, and the velocity autocorrelation function. We take the mean square displacement function, $x^2(t)$, as the ensemble average:

$$x^2(t) = \langle x_i(o)x_i(t)\rangle_i$$

It is, of course, equal to the time average for any particle:

$$x^2(t) = \langle x(\tau)x(t + \tau)\rangle_\tau$$

but the first form is more convenient here. To evaluate it, we choose a starting time after the system has reached equilibrium, as determined by the constancy of the "temperature". We take this time as t = 0, and store the values of X1, X2, and X3 for all the

Figure 1. Projection on the x-y plane of the tracer of the motion of the center of simulated argon atoms in the first octant of the system. Temperature is 90 K; elapsed time 0.36 picoseconds; computation time, 2 minutes.

Figure 2. Projection of tracer of motion of argon atoms as in Figure 1, but after total elapsed time of 0.9 picoseconds; computation time, 5 minutes

Figure 3. Projection of tracer of motion of argon atoms as in Figures 1 and 2, but after total elapsed time of 1.8 picoseconds; computation time, 10 minutes

particles as XS1, XS2, and XS3. At each time step, after
completion of the J loop, the current value of $x^2(t)$ is evaluated
by summing (X1(I) - XS1(I))**2 + (X2(I) - XS2(I))**2 + (X3(I)
- XS3(I))**2 over all particles and dividing by N. The resulting
function can be displayed at any time on the CRT or punched out on
paper tape at the conclusion of a run for plotting on a pen and
ink plotter. A typical plot is shown in Figure 4.

The normalized velocity autocorrelation function is calculated in a similar way. It is defined as:

$$\psi(t) = \langle \vec{v}(0) \cdot \vec{v}(t) \rangle / \langle v^2(0) \rangle .$$

At the t = 0 chosen as described above, we store the values of
P1, P2, P3 for all the particles as PS1, PS2, PS3. After each
time step we form P1*PS1 + P2*PS2 + P3*PS3 for each particle,
sum over all particles, and normalize by division by the sum of
PS1**2 + PS2**2 + PS3**2 for all particles. This function also
can be displayed on the CRT or punched out for external plotting.
A typical plot of this function is shown in Figure 5.

Comparison with Standard Calculations.

The results obtained in this investigation are consistent
with those obtained in conventional large machine calculations,
but the cost per computation is very much lower. The qualitative
features seen in Figures 1-5 are the same as those reported for
the standard calculations; a quantitative test is provided by the
diffusion coefficient, which is a sensitive test of the technique.
Levesque and Verlet (6) have summarized the results of their
calculations for argon with the empirical formula in reduced
units:

$$D = 0.006423 \ T/\rho^2 + 0.0222 - 0.0280 \ \rho .$$

Converted to SI units, this becomes:

$$D = 5.639 \times 10^{-5} \ T/\rho^2 + 8.270 \times 10^{-9} - 6.207 \times 10^{-12} \ \rho .$$

For the conditions corresponding to the data shown in Figure 4,
T = 113 K, and $\rho = 1.446 \times 10^{-9}$ m²/s, their equation predicts
D = 2.34 × 10^{-9} m²/s. The data of Figure 2 correspond to a
D = 2.77 × 10^{-9} m²/s. This difference is of the same order as the
scatter of standard calculations, and the discrepancy between
calculation and experiment.

The speed of the calculation was quite reasonable: 282 time
steps in 10 minutes, or 1692 steps per hour. Each second of
machine time corresponds to 3 × 10^{-15} seconds in argon. For
comparison, the reported rate achieved on a large machine, a
CDC 6600, was 1500 steps per hour for a somewhat larger system
(864 particles) (2). With proper programming, the calculation

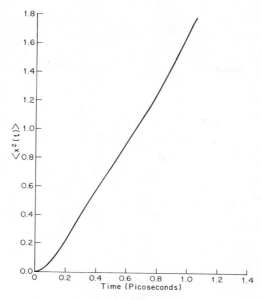

Figure 4. Mean square displacement of simulated argon atoms at 113 K as a function of time

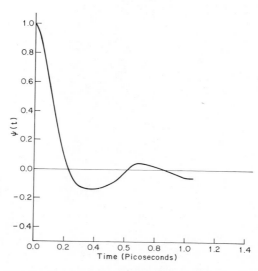

Figure 5. Normalized velocity autocorrelation function of simulated argon atoms at 113 K

time varies approximately as N. With this allowance, it appears
that calculation on a minicomputer is slower by roughly a factor
of 6 than on a large machine.

To estimate the relative cost of computation, we take the
initial cost of the system and distribute it over three years (a
conservative procedure, since our machine has been in continuous
use for five years with no maintenance contract and neglible
servicing). This corresponds to a cost of $6.40 a day or $0.27
per hour. If we assume a large machine cost of about $100 per
hour, the cost of equivalent calculations is lower on the small
machine by a factor of about 50.

Future Prospects.

The use of currently available hardware, instead of the
obsolete 960A, would make possible both greater savings and much
more ambitious calculations. In particular, a three dimensional
array of microprocessors (such as the TI 9900), each assigned a
portion of the volume under study, could be used to increase the
speed of calculation by more than an order of magnitude for a cost
increase of about a factor of two.

Literature Cited.

(1) Rahman, A., Phys. Rev. (1964), 136, A405.
(2) McDonald, I. R. and Singer, K., Quart. Rev. (1970), 24, 238.
(3) Rahman, A. in "Interatomic Potentials and Simulation of
     Lattice Defects", ed. by Gehlen, P. C., Beeler, J. R. Jr.,
     and Jaffee, R. I., p. 233, Plenum, N.Y., 1972.
(4) Fisher, R. A. and Watts, R. O., Aust. J. Phys. (1972), 25,
     529.
(5) Flinn, P. A., in "Mössbauer Effect Methodology", vol. 9,
     ed. by Gruverman, I. J., Seidel, C. W., and Dieterly,
     p. 245, Plenum, N.Y. 1974.
(6) Levesque, D. and Verlet, L., Phys. Rev. (1971), A2, 2514.

Many-Atom Molecular Dynamics with an Array Processor

KENT R. WILSON

Department of Chemistry, University of California—San Diego, La Jolla, CA 92093

"The change of motion is proportional to the motive force impressed; and is made in the direction of the right line in which the force is impressed." Sir Isaac Newton, Philosophiae Naturalis Principia Mathematica, 1687.

I. Introduction and History

A. Theoretical Instruments. We chemists traditionally have built specialized instrumentation for experimental studies. We are now beginning also to build specialized instrumentation for theory (1). While we are accustomed to designing and building, for example, special spectrometers or molecular beam machines to efficiently probe the experimental side of a particular class of chemical questions, it is now becoming clear that with comparable effort we can also design and build specialized computational systems which will efficiently probe particular classes of theoretical problems. The reasons for building specialized instrumentation in either case are similar; that we want to explore chemical questions beyond the range of what we can learn using general purpose commercial instrumentation which must sacrifice specific efficiency to generalized applicability.

B. Plastic Hardware. We are accustomed to thinking of computer software as plastic, malleable; employed to adapt a general purpose computer to our specific needs. The advance of computer science and technology has now softened hardware as well, making it also plastic, moldable to effectively fit the task at hand. But while hardware is plastic, it still has restraints. It flows more easily in some directions than in others. Thus, the initial task is to find those chemical problems which are best suited to this natural direction of hardware flow.

For example, it is now cheaper to replicate many identical hardware units than to produce even a few different units. Therefore, one direction of hardware flow is toward structures composed of many identical units, working in parallel (2-4). The

147

congruent chemistry involves those theoretical problems which
can be cast into forms involving many simultaneous parallel
streams of computation.

C. Mechanical Molecules. One such chemical area is the
classical mechanical treatment of how nuclei, or roughly speaking
atoms, interact on a Born-Oppenheimer potential surface. The
idea that the forces among a collection of particles determine
both their static configuration (molecular struct re) and their
motions (molecular dynamics) is an old one. Newt n, in the 17th
century, already understood the fundamental concepts of classically interacting particles and considered that macroscopic
properties might result from microscopic interactions. By the
19th century, with the acceptance of the atomic theory, the view
that chemistry should ultimately be an exercise in mechanics became a popular one.
     The nature of the underlying mechanics became apparent fifty
years ago with the development of quantum mechanics; it is now
clear that what the electrons are doing is inherently a quantum
problem, but given a potential surface derived either from a
theoretical quantum computation of electronic energy or from a
fit to experimental measurements, that what the nuclei are doing
both in terms of molecular structure and molecular dynamics can
be handled in most cases reasonably well by that approximate
form of quantum mechanics called classical mechanics. (In a
sense this is unfortunate, for chemistry would be an even more
subtle and interesting puzzle if Planck's constant were larger.)
     We will thus concentrate here on the advantages which com-
puter hardware plasticity can bring to classical molecular dynamics. (Molecular statics or molecular structure will be viewed
in this context as that subset of molecular dynamics for which
the energy has been reduced to a global minimum.) The structure
of the computation is exceedingly simple, a desirable situation
for a first essay into a different mode of solution. Given N
atoms, we have, from Newton's Second Law,

$$\underset{\sim}{F}_i = m_i \frac{d^2 \underset{\sim}{r}_i}{dt^2} \; ; \quad i = 1, \ldots, N \tag{1}$$

$$\underset{\sim}{F}_i = \underset{\sim}{F}_i(\underset{\sim}{r}_1, \ldots, \underset{\sim}{r}_N) = -\underset{\sim}{\nabla}_i V(\underset{\sim}{r}_1, \ldots, \underset{\sim}{r}_N) \tag{2}$$

in which $\underset{\sim}{F}_i$, the force on the ith atom, located at $\underset{\sim}{r}_i$, is a function of the positions, $\underset{\sim}{r}_1, \ldots, \underset{\sim}{r}_N$, of the set of atoms whose
masses are $m_1, \ldots, m_N$, and V is the Born-Oppenheimer potential
surface seen by the nuclei.

D. Two Molecular Dynamics. Strangely, the application of
this viewpoint, that chemistry may be understood as the detailed
mechanics of atomic motions, has led to two quite distinct fields,
each called by the same name, molecular dynamics, which have remained quite separate for twenty years. Both fields, which are
compared in Table I, grew up in the late 1950's, one (5) out of
statistical mechanics (SM), largely (but not exclusively) concerned with equilibrium and steady state properties, usually of
fluids composed of many simple particles: hard spheres, atoms
or simplified molecules. The breakthrough which triggered the
development of the field was computational, the ability provided
by the electronic computer to actually calculate the trajectories
of many interacting particles.

TABLE I. Comparison of two fields called molecular dynamics

Category	Molecular Dynamics (SM)	Molecular Dynamics (CK)
historical antecedents	statistical mechanics	chemical kinetics
initiating breakthrough	computational	experimental
major application	equilibrium and steady state	chemical reactions
number of atoms	many	few
major state	liquid	vacuum (isolated molecules)

The other molecular dynamics (6, 7) grew out of chemical
kinetics (CK) and has been concerned with understanding the
detailed mechanics of the mechanisms of chemical reactions, usually involving relatively few atoms, smaller molecules colliding
and reacting in isolation, the "vacuum" phase. The development
of the field was initiated by experimental advances, the ability
provided by molecular beam and infrared chemiluminescence techniques to measure the results of individual chemical reaction
events.

What we are now attempting is a synthesis drawing from both
fields of molecular dynamics, a computational advance which will
allow through mechanics the study of the detailed mechanisms of
chemical reactions involving many atoms, often occurring in
solution.

E. Difficulties and Directions. Given that the structure of Eqs. (1) and (2) is so simple, why isn't the detailed mechanism of many-atom chemical reactions routinely studied by computing the trajectories of the atoms? Three major difficulties are as follows.

1. Potential surface. In reality, we know quantitatively relatively little about the basic determinant of molecular structure and dynamics, the forces among atoms. If we would have to compute from first principles the potential surface to chemical accuracy separately for each large molecule of interest along with all the interactions with surrounding solvent molecules, the problem would seem insurmountable. Our chemical experience, conceptualization, nomenclature and system of cataloging of molecules, however, is based on the faith that molecules can be analyzed into functional groups which retain their approximate identity and nature from molecule to molecule. Thus the force functions, $F_i(r_1, \ldots, r_N)$, to a first approximation should be decomposable into i) local force functions which describe chemical functional groups and which are approximately transferable from molecule to molecule and ii) terms which describe the interaction among functional groups. This transferable force function approach has been extensively developed in vibrational spectroscopy (8), organic chemistry (9-12) and biochemistry (13, 14) and the wide extent of its applicability is stressed in a recent review by Warshel (15), who describes both the usual type of fully empirical potential surface treatment and a version in which π electrons are treated in a formulation derived from semiempirical quantum mechanics.

Thus a reasonable approach to potential surfaces is the patient collection and refinement with respect to theoretical calculations and comparison of computed to measured parameters of a library of force functions which should be at least approximately transferable from molecule to molecule.

2. Computational speed. If one wishes to study the detailed molecular dynamics of reactions of even simple molecules in solution, one must consider at least a single solvation shell around each molecule, and thus at least the order of 100 atoms. Given x, y and z components for Eqs. (1) and (2), one must solve the order of 300 coupled differential equations, integrating forward for thousands or perhaps millions of time steps. The number of arithmetic operations involved is therefore inevitably large. If one wishes to interact with the on-going calculations, viewing the trajectories of the atoms and seeing the results of modifications of parameters within a reasonable waiting time, the processing system must be a rapid one even by today's large computer standards. This difficulty, however, is overshadowed by an even more demanding and subtle one.

3. Initial conditions. Unfortunately, we usually do not
know in advance where to start, which set of initial positions
and velocities for the atoms will lead, as time proceeds, to
the chemical process of interest. For most chemical reactions
we can't just assemble our molecules and allow them to rattle
around toward equilibrium, for on the time scale of internal
molecular motion most chemical reactions of interest will almost never occur in an equilibrium system. Thus a random approach doesn't solve the problem.

A quick calculation shows that a brute force systematic
approach won't solve it either. Consider a systematic search
through just 10 different initial position vectors and 10 different initial velocity vectors for each of 100 atoms. This
would give $100^{100} = 10^{200}$ (a number greater than the estimated
number of atoms in the universe), different initial phase space
points, each of which would have to be integrated forward in
time to decide if it did indeed lead to the reaction of interest.
Such a brute force approach is now and will always remain in-
feasible.

If neither random nor brute force systematic approaches
are generally feasible, what can be done? One possible approach is the development of techniques to automatically identify critical configurations or saddle points (or more precisely
surfaces or regions in phase space (16) through which reaction
trajectories must pass). If one can identify such a phase
space region, one can then integrate both forward and backward
in time to trace out the entire trajectory, and one can explore
neighboring trajectories as well. This approach can be straightforward for systems with sufficient symmetry, such as defect
jumps in crystals (17), and its extension to more complex molecular systems can also be expected to be pursued.

Another alternative, perhaps complementary to the above,
is to try to use the human chemist's accumulated understanding
of the mechanisms of chemical reactions to guide the machine's
calculations. We chemists at least think we have some knowledge of the way to relatively orient two molecules and how to
shove them at one another to get them to react. We think we
have some feeling for the reaction pathway from reactants to
products, for the bonds which must change and for the critical
configurations (transition states, activated complexes) which
must be traversed. Unfortunately, this chemists's understanding
is largely pictorial and intuitive, but our computers need numerical guidance as to positions and velocities in order to proceed. This need to bring together the chemist's non-numerical
mechanistic understanding of the reaction pathway with the
machine's ability to calculate forward and backward along the
reaction trajectory once given the potential surface and the
atomic positions and velocities at any given point on the trajectory has led us to work on techniques of closer man-machine
interaction.

The first need is vision. In order to comprehend the molecular dynamics of reactions involving a hundred or more atoms, it is imperative to be able to watch the motions, the three-dimensional (3D) trajectories of the atoms involved. Fortunately this is a well-solved problem, with several specialized display systems now being commercially available which make feasible the visualization of the 3D motions of hundreds or even thousands of atoms in real time (human, not molecular) and even in color and/or stereo, if desired. In addition, films can easily be made using even relatively simple display terminals which can allow the off-line visualization of molecular dynamics.

We quickly discovered, however, that vision alone is insufficient. We want to manipulate atoms, fragments within molecules or entire molecules which are closely surrounded by other atoms, fragments and molecules, in order to arrive at some point on a reaction-path phase-space trajectory. To do this we must remain within the energy range which is thermally allowed. However in a dense system, as is well known in Monte Carlo calculations (18), almost all randomly chosen new configurations are energetically inaccessible, because the atoms are almost all already up against hard repulsive walls (19) and a random displacement will almost always send the energy too high. Thus, just as potential surface referenced importance sampling (18) is used to guide the choice of new configurations in Monte Carlo calculations, some feedback from the potential energy surface is needed to guide the human chemist in manipulating atoms, fragments and molecules to reach a point on the reaction path. We have found that vision is a poor feedback tool for maneuvering on a multidimensional potential surface and we believe that this is at least in part because touch rather than vision is the natural human sense when forces and torques are to be perceived. This has led us to the development of man-machine touch interfaces (1, 20) to more closely link man and machine beyond what is possible with vision alone.

F. Goal. Our goal thus is to develop and use an "instrument for theory" which we call NEWTON, a closer man-machine symbiosis focused on the understanding of the molecular dynamics of many-atom chemical reactions, a machine which opens a window to the microscopic world of the 3D trajectories of moving atoms, visualized as we wish, elements labeled, bonds shown. We wish to be able to build up the system of interest from atoms, fragments and molecules, adjusting the positions and velocities to correspond to our understanding of mechanism, reaction path and critical configuration in order to initiate the desired chemical reaction. We want to control energy, temperature and pressure by the turn of knobs and to display the calculated values as the process proceeds. Our viewpoint (angle and zoom) should be variable, as well as which atoms are to be displayed. One should be able to control the speed of passage of computed time; increasing (up to the computational limit), decreasing, freeze framing, or backing up and then readjusting parameters and restudying. One would like to calculate and display derived parameters such as bond lengths and angles, progress along a defined reaction coordinate or computed spectra to compare with measured spectra. In addition, a record of the run, including all input parameters and atomic trajectories, should be stored for future additional analysis.

As we will see in the following section, most of these instrumental goals have been achieved, at least, in a preliminary fashion.

II.   Instrumentation

Two versions of NEWTON have now been built and tested, the earlier version able to handle a few atoms and the present one a hundred or more atoms.

A.   Initial Version. The first implementation of the NEWTON concept is shown schematically in Figure 1. As it is described elsewhere (1), it will only briefly be mentioned here. The equations of motion are integrated in a minicomputer, the moving atoms are displayed on an Evans and Sutherland (E & S) Picture System and the user can control the position and velocity of any selected atom by using the "Touchy-Feely" touch interface, feeling the forces imparted by neighboring atoms. This system served to show that such an instrument could be built, but was only adequate to handle a few interacting atoms and manipulate them atom by atom.

B.   Present Version. The current system, which can handle a hundred interacting atoms fast enough for interactive use (at approximately 10 integration time steps per second) is shown as a block diagram in Figure 2 and as a photograph in Figure 3. Several hundred atoms can be handled at reduced speed. The equations of motion are integrated in a Floating Point Systems (FPS) AP120B Array Processor which runs for our application at a through-put of several floating point operations per microsecond and which forms, with the help of its host, essentially a general-purpose processor capable of several simultaneous operations, with parallel and pipelined floating point adder and multiplier. At present, it lacks direct higher level language capability. Its approximate relative power may be judged by comparisons indicating a speed 3 to 4 times slower (21) than a Control Data Corporation (CDC) 7600 and 10 to 50 times faster (22) than a Data General (DG) Eclipse under Fortran V. It should be realized that all such comparisons are a function of program mix and efficiency of coding.

Visual interaction with the user is through a dynamic 3D

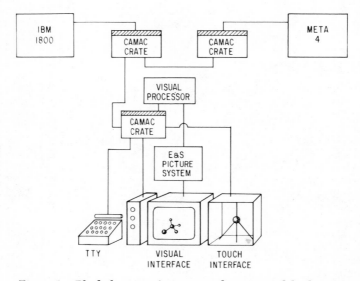

Figure 1.   Block diagram of system used to test crudely the concept of NEWTON. The touchstone of the touch interface drives
the central carbon atom of a methane molecule, allowing it to
be moved and the forces on it from the other atoms to be felt
by the user. The molecule is displayed on the Evans & Sutherland (E&S) Picture System, and the differential equations are
integrated in real (human) time by the Digital Scientific Meta-4
computer to give the trajectories displayed on the Picture System.
The Meta-4 is linked through three CAMAC crates and an IBM
1800 to the California Data Processors (CDP) 135 emulating a
Digital Equipment Corporation (DEC) PDP 11/40 which in turn
runs symbiotically with the Picture System processor.

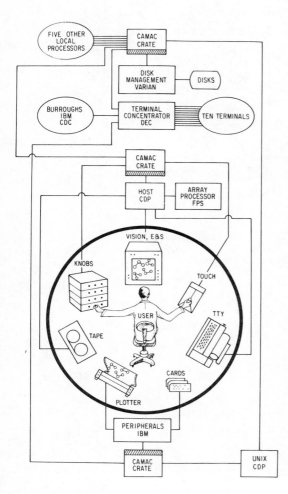

Figure 2. Block diagram of present NEWTON instrument designed for interactive study of the molecular dynamics of chemical reactions involving a hundred or more atoms. The user interacts with NEWTON by setting parameters such as temperature, pressure, and time step through knobs and teletype, by watching the motion of the atoms and the values of calculated parameters on the screen of the E&S Picture System and by adjusting the positions and velocities of atoms with the touch interface. The coupled differential equations (Newton's Second Law) are integrated in the Floating Point Systems (FPS) Array Processor to calculate the atomic trajectories. Other parts of the Chemistry Department Computer Facility (into which NEWTON is integrated) which are used as part of NEWTON include a CDP 135 emulating a DEC PDP 11/40 which serves as host for the Array Processor and the Picture System and a Varian 72 which handles disk management.

Figure 3. Photograph of NEWTON showing E&S Picture System screen on the left, control knobs and FPS Array Processor in the background

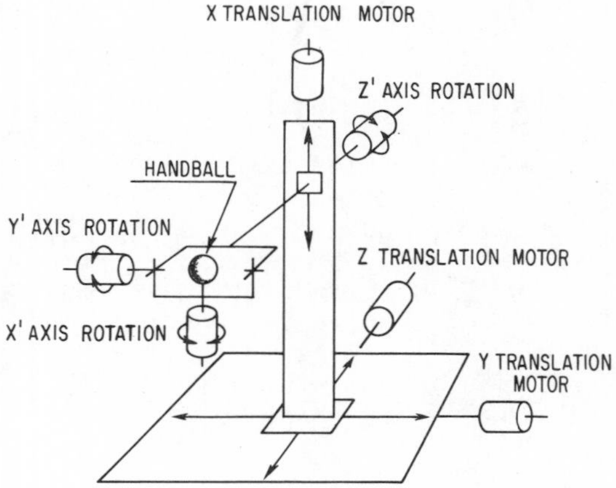

X TRANSLATION MOTOR

Z' AXIS ROTATION

HANDBALL

Y' AXIS ROTATION

Z TRANSLATION MOTOR

X' AXIS ROTATION

Y TRANSLATION MOTOR

Figure 4. Schematic of "Touchy-Twisty" designed for force–torque–position–orientation man–machine communication, a touch interface to assemble and manipulate three-dimensional objects. A handball containing force-torque vector sensors is driven to position and orientation by three nester computer-driven rotational stages carried by three nested computer-driven translational stages.

display using an Evans and Sutherland Picture System which allows
the motions of the appropriately labeled atoms to be seen as
they are calculated. A California Data Processors (CDP) 135
emulating a Digital Equipment Corporation (DEC) PDP 11/40 serves
as host for both the Array Processor and the Picture System.
Binocular stereo and color presentations are available by visual
fusion of spinning-disk controlled sequential images, but in
practice are only rarely used. Rotation of the system of molecules is a better depth cue and labeling of atoms is a sufficient
identifier. Orientation of view, angular velocity of rotation
and zoom are all controllable by knobs and buttons. Temperature
is varied by knob-controlled, mass-weighted viscosity which
removes energy as viscosity is increased or adds energy if viscosity is formally made negative. External pressure is controlled
by changing the size of an elastic-walled boundary cube. Other
boundary conditions, for example, periodic repetition or a free-
floating drop are also possible. Temperature and pressure are
calculated from atomic velocities, forces and positions and are
displayed on the Picture System screen.

NEWTON is integrated into the Chemistry Department Computer
Facility, which includes a dozen processors interconnected
through a system based on the CAMAC convention. Others of these
processors which are used in conjunction with NEWTON include a
Varian 72 which handles disk management, an IBM 1800 which controls peripherals and a second CDP 135 emulating a DEC PDP 11/40
which runs a UNIX time-shared operating system used for program
editing and file manipulation.

C. Touch Interface. We wish to build up our chemical
systems of interest not just atom by atom, but from fragments
and whole molecules and we wish also to be able to reach into
the simulated volume and guide fragments and molecules into the
desired coordinates and velocities to arrive at a point along
the reactive trajectory for the chemical process of interest.
The atom by atom touch interface described above, involving force
and position (1,20), is no longer sufficient if we wish to
assemble and manipulate three dimensional objects such as fragments and molecules involving force, torque, position and orientation. Therefore we are building (20) what we call a "Touchy-
Twisty" which is shown in Figures 4-6. A ball for the user's
hand (the handball) is driven by three nested computer-controlled
translational stages carrying three nested computer-controlled
rotational stages to follow the x,y,z position of the center
of mass as well as the orientation of three defined axes within
a designated fragment or molecule.

The force and torque vectors exerted by the user on the
handball will be sensed by internal flexing members with strain
gauge pickups (see Figure 6) and will be added appropriately to
the forces already exerted by surrounding atoms on each atom of
the designated molecule, and will therefore affect the on-going

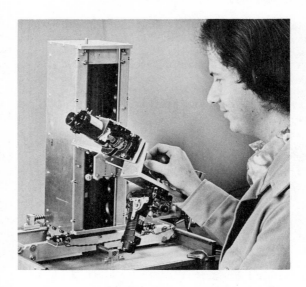

Figure 5.   Photograph of "Touchy-Twisty," partially
constructed

Figure 6.   Photograph of force–torque resolver in-
side handball, under construction. Strain gauges
will be mounted on the flexing members to pick up
components of force and torque.

calculation of that molecule's trajectory. Thus, as the user tries to translate or rotate the handball-molecule in a way which matches chemical possibility as described by the potential surface, it will move relatively freely, being unhindered by opposing forces from surrounding atoms. Conversely, if one tries to translate or rotate the handball-molecule so that repulsive walls of surrounding atoms are impinged upon, it will move only with difficulty, as these atoms must be shoved out of the way to proceed. This type of touch interface is designed specifically to interact with a dynamic system, as its communication with the user is intimately linked to the computer's ability to simultaneously integrate the equations of motion of the objects involved in the dynamic simulation.

III. Chemical Applications

While the mechanical molecule approach to the molecular dynamics of many-atom chemical reactions is in principle applicable to almost any chemical reaction, our lack of sufficient general quantitative knowledge of interatomic forces makes it wise to concentrate, at least initially, on cases in which the many-atom complexity arises largely from the repetition of simple units, for example polymers in which the monomer is the repeated unit and reactions of smaller molecules in solution in which the solvent molecule is repeated, so that the number of force parameters to be determined remains manageable. Two of our current interests are therefore dynamic approaches to vibrational spectra in solution and to the microscopic understanding of solvation.

A. Dynamic Approach to Vibrational Spectra. If we observe a small molecule, the vibrational spectrum (infrared or Raman) is a series of well-defined lines, and we know how to invert such spectra to gain information on the potential surface near the equilibrium geometry (8, 23). If we go to many-atom systems, i.e. large molecules or collections of closely interacting molecules as in a liquid, instead of well-defined lines we find broad continuous bands and we can no longer invert to the potential surface in the same direct way. However, we can still proceed in the opposite direction, calculating the vibrational spectrum from the potential energy surface. (Such an approach was perhaps better known before the day of modern computers when actual mechanical models of molecules were constructed from springs and masses and driven by an eccentric disk on a motor whose speed was varied to find the resonances corresponding to the normal frequencies (24, 25).)

For example, we can use linear response theory (26-31) to relate the spectrum of the natural fluctuations of a parameter in a system at equilibrium to the response spectrum we would find if we drove that parameter with a weak external

perturbation. Thus we can start with a potential surface
$V(r_1, \ldots, r_N)$, calculate the trajectories $r_1(t), \ldots, r_N(t)$
of atoms upon it at equilibrium at a chosen temperature, calculate (for example, in the first approximation by assigning
partial atomic charges) the time varying dipole moment $\mu(t)$
from the trajectories, and then calculate the infrared spectrum
from the power spectrum or from the Fourier transform of the
time correlation of the dipole moment ($\underline{29}$, $\underline{30}$).

$$V(r_1, \ldots, r_N) \longrightarrow r_1(t), \ldots, r_N(t) \longrightarrow \mu(t) \longrightarrow A(\omega) \qquad (3)$$

Similarly, by assigning an approximate relationship between polarizability and atomic coordinates, one should be
able to compute Raman spectra.
    For example, we have used the Lemberg-Stillinger potential
($\underline{32}$) for water to calculate infrared spectra at approximately
room temperature for equilibrated isolated water molecules
and then for larger and larger clusters. The spectrum shifts
smoothly from the gas-phase line spectrum toward the broad bands
characteristic of the liquid phase, the bending (scissors)
vibration moving up in energy and broadening as expected and
the asymmetric and symmetric stretches moving down in energy
and melding together to form what in the liquid is a single
broad peak. The Lemberg-Stillinger potential was designed
for somewhat different ends, and by its nature as a central
force approximation, a sum of two body terms, V_{HH}, V_{OH} and V_{OO},
it cannot accurately reproduce the isolated molecule spectrum.
Nonetheless, it is instructive to see that the expected gas
to liquid shifts are taking place as the cluster size grows.
Similar calculations with more realistic potentials are in
preparation for several liquids.
    There are two purposes to such calculations. The first
is to improve our knowledge of interatomic forces, in particular non-bonded and intermolecular forces, which we need for
further molecular dynamics studies. For example, we can set
up a parameterized potential function which is constrained in
regards to that which we know such as equilibrium bond lengths
and angles and dissociation energies, but which contains adjustable parameters such as those describing non-bonded interactions.
Then we can iteratively change the adjustable parameters to try
to gain better agreement between calculated and measured spectra,
hopefully converging on an improved potential surface.
    The second purpose is to try to change our present under-
standing of liquid state vibrational spectra, which is mainly
qualitative, into quantitative understanding based on potential
surfaces and molecular dynamics. For example, if we believe we
have a reasonable potential surface, we should be able to assign

spectral features by driving the simulated system of molecules
with a simulated electric field oscillating at the frequency of
the spectral feature and then watching and analyzing the actual
computed trajectories which the atoms follow in response to this
perturbation.   Such an approach is not really a new one, as it
resembles the technique (33) used forty years ago to analyze
stroboscopically the normal motions of molecules modelled
mechanically by masses and springs and driven by an external
mechanical oscillatory perturbation.   The advent of systematic
procedures for the analysis of vibrational line spectra (8, 23)
has made such mechanical molecule approaches unnecessary for few
atom systems, but has not solved the problem for many-atom
systems.   With the present availability of very fast computing
systems such as our array processor and our ability to visually
recognize complex motions with the aid of dynamic computer
graphics, we can now apply this mechanical molecule approach in a
new form to many-atom spectra, in particular spectra in solution.

   B.   Dynamics of Solvation.   A second area of application is
the understanding of solvation in terms of the trajectories of
the atoms.   Most reactions of interest to chemists and most of
the chemistry in living systems occur in solution, yet we understand very little of solvation, and even less of chemical
reactions in solution, in terms of a quantitative microscopic
picture involving atomic motions.   The modelling of the molecular
dynamics of solvation in isolated droplets of up to hundreds of
solvent molecules is relatively straightforward; the large
difficulty comes in trying to match the properties of bulk
solutions with calculations involving finite numbers of molecules.
The key to the latter appears to be in the boundary conditions:
whether to choose, for example, periodic boundary conditions, a
dielectric-surrounded cavity or a surface layer which is fixed in
the configuration of bulk solvent (34).
   In the illustrations shown in Figures 7-9 we have chosen the
easy way out, by modelling isolated droplets.   These stereo pairs,
which may be seen by most people in depth by a slight crossing of
the eyes, represent individual frames from the calculated time
history of a water cluster, the solvation of a chloride ion in
water and the process of dissolution and solvation of an ultra-
crystallite of NaCl in water.   The water potential is again
Lemberg-Stillinger (32) with electrostatic interactions and
approximate repulsive cores for the interactions with and among
the ions.

IV.   Some Thoughts on the Future

   A.   Future Applications.   The author suspects that in the
long run, the most interesting many-atom molecular dynamics is
likely to be found in biomolecular reactions.   While up to the
present, biochemistry and molecular biology have concentrated on

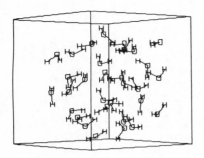
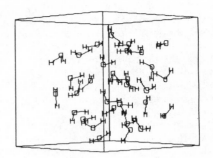

Figure 7.   A time-step in the evolution of a cluster of 31 water molecules

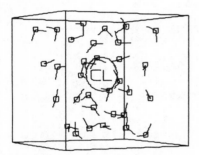
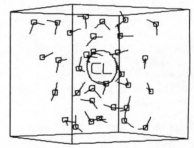

Figure 8.   A time-step in the history of a chloride ion solvated in an isolated water droplet

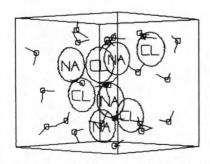
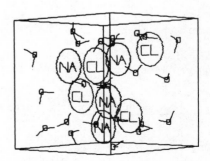

Figure 9.   A time-step in the dissolution and ion solvation of a crystallite of NaCl

statics, i.e. the relationship of structure and function, it seems clear that the functioning of at least many of the most interesting biomolecules must be understood in terms of dynamics, their time evolution. A very long period of selection has undoubtedly moulded many biomolecules into very efficient machines whose dynamics as yet is largely speculative. Examples of such biomachinery are to be found in enzymic action (35) and allosteric effects, muscle contraction, membrane transport (particularly active transport), aspects of drug-receptor inter-action, and biomolecular self-assembly. Perhaps as the past twenty years have seen such great progress in the understanding of biomolecular structure-function relationships, the next twenty years may see similar progress in understanding the more complete picture of biomolecular structure-dynamics-function.

While some molecular dynamic calculations on biomolecules are already in progress in batch mode, for example retinal photo-isomerization (36), water around a dipeptide to study the difference in dynamics near hydrophilic and hydrophobic sites (37) and motions of a simplified small protein, pancreatic tryp-sin inhibitor (38), such calculations are severely hindered by limits to available computational speed. How can such limits be transcended?

B. Faster Computation. With a few more orders of magnitude in computer speed, the mechanism of most reactions of interest to chemists would be accessible to study by many-atom molecular dynamics. How can such speed increases be achieved?* Two directions are apparent: more powerful elements (integrated circuits) and the interconnection of these elements in archi-tectures which more efficiently match the problem to be solved.

It is thought that there is another factor of 30 still to be realized in linear shrinkage in metal oxide semiconductor (MOS) technology before fundamental physical limits are reached (39). This translates into a 30^2 increase in packing density on a chip and another factor of 30 in speed, for a total gain of perhaps four orders of magnitude. Thus we can look forward to continuing substantial gains in computational power per element by this and probably by other routes as well.

A complementary approach is the architecture of interconnect-ing the elements. The classical mechanics of a set of interacting particles is a problem particularly amenable to specialized com-puter architecture because i) the algorithms are relatively

---

* Such increases in specialized computer power are in progress in other areas as well (1). Examples include the Parallel Ele-ment Processing Ensemble (PEPE) for missile tracking being con-structed for the Army Advanced Ballistic Missile Defense Agency which is designed (4) to run many times faster than any existing general purpose processor as well as the special aerodynamic com-puter (40) being considered by NASA which would be two orders of magnitude faster than existing general purpose machines.

simple and highly repetitive and ii) the computation can be split into parallel streams which need communicate only once (or perhaps a few times with more complex integration schemes) for each integration time step. Thus, instead of an array processor we can consider arrays of processors or even arrays of array processors (1).

When one considers such computational systems composed of so many active elements, several similarities between computer architecture and molecular architecture become evident (39). The basic determinant of structure becomes not the logical elements (atoms) themselves, but rather their interconnections (bonds) and these now become the focus of design (39) as shown in Table II.

Table II. Evolution of emphasis of computer architecture from logical elements to interconnections (39).

Characteristics	Past	Future
large, slow, expensive	logical elements	interconnections
small, fast, cheap	interconnections	logical elements

Because computer architecture can now be constructed containing so many elements and interconnections, the same problems in human conceptualization arise as in systems composed of many atoms and bonds, that no one person can possibly understand all the relationships among the individual detailed parts of the system. In response, the same approach of emphasizing the symmetry of the situation becomes useful.

For example, one obvious way of interconnecting processors in parallel is a single bus, as shown in Figure 10. To a chemist this is a linear polymer and shares its symmetry. If one branches the bus, it's a branched polymer, or one can make cyclic systems, etc.

A very appealing solution for a problem such as molecular dynamics which is to be solved in terms of Cartesian space is to map the 3D problem space onto a 3D space of an array of processors (39), an example of which is shown in Figure 11. Two ways of carrying out such a mapping for our case are as follows. First, one could map each atom onto a processor and then "dynamically reallocate processors" so as to maintain near neighbor relationships as atoms move about on their trajectories. A key question to investigate is whether there is a local reallocation algorithm which will efficiently maintain a satisfactory mapping by querying only other processors in the vicinity, and then exchanging assignments of processors to atoms. A second

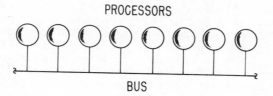

Figure 10. *The symmetry of an array of processors connected by a bus, or equivalently the symmetry of a linear polymer*

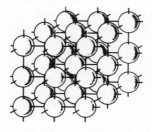

Figure 11. *The symmetry of a simple cubic 3D array of processors, or equivalently of a 3D simple cubic crystal lattice*

approach is to map regions of 3D coordinate space onto specific
processors; in other words, to divide all the space in which the
atoms move into volumes such that each processor takes care of
all atoms which happen to be in that volume. When an atom
crosses the boundary of that volume, it would be reassigned to the
processor handling the adjacent volume.

In considering such a scheme, it is important to note that
the force on any given real atom is only a function of the positions of other atoms within some finite volume about that atom
(1) and thus that each processor only need communicate with a
localized set of other processors. Thus in the limit of a very
large number N of atoms, the number of arithmetic operations required, if done properly, to solve the molecular dynamics increases only proportionally to N, in contrast to widely held
opinion (shared until recently by the author) that it must rise
faster than N. This is true both in force calculation from a
realistic potential surface in classical mechanics, in that in
reality all interatomic forces in dense systems are damped out at
some distance by intervening movable and polarizable atoms as
well as in quantum mechanics in that integrals among orbitals
sufficiently separated can be ignored.

If we consider 3D arrays of processors, we chemists already
know all the possible different symmetries of how to build the
processor array (39), the "crystal computer" (41). The possible
symmetries within each unit composing the array are just the
symmetries of crystal unit cells and the symmetries with which
the units can be stacked or interconnected into 3D arrays are
just the lattice symmetries, the 14 Bravais lattices, the grand
total of all combined unit cell and lattice symmetry possibilities being the 230 space groups (42). If we restrict ourselves
to building from symmetric, identical units which stack into a
space-filling 3D array, the possibilities are even more limited
and in fact we can refer back to the Greeks for the solid tessel-
lations. Out of the regular and Archimedean polyhedra there are
only 5 which are space filling: the cube, triangular prism, hex-
agonal prism, rhombic dodecahedron and truncated octahedron (43).

C. Other Instruments for Theory. One can imagine other
instruments for other theories. Instead of a NEWTON for classical mechanics, one could consider building a machine for quantum
calculations, a SCHRODINGER or a HEISENBERG. One can again map
3D configuration space onto a 3D array of processors, either or-
bital(s) or atom(s) to processor or volume of space to processor.
And again, as the number N of atoms grows large enough, one region of space will no longer directly affect another and the
arithmetic operations involved in the calculation will scale, in
the limit of quite large N, proportionally as N.

Lastly, one might want to build a SEMI, a semiclassical instrument for solving quantum mechanically (either ab initio or
semiempirically) for the electronic wavefunction and using this

wavefunction to analytically derive (44-46, 8, 15) on the fly a
force function for the nuclei whose trajectories are being integrated classically. For a system of very large N it is no longer
feasible to calculate and store a potential function
$V(r_1, ..., r_N)$ in advance on a 3N - 6 dimensional mesh. For
semiclassical dynamics, all one needs anyway are the forces at
those relatively few points actually sampled by the sequence of
nuclear coordinate sets generated by the classical numerical
integration of the nuclear trajectories.

It should be noted that all of the instruments for theory
described above could be implemented as the same 3D array of
stored-program processors.

V.   Summary

While we chemists have long built specialized instruments
for experimental studies, we are now discovering that we can
also build specialized instruments for theory, computational
apparatus designed to efficiently solve particular classes of
chemical problems. An example is NEWTON, an instrument we have
constructed to study the detailed mechanism, i.e. the molecular
dynamics, of many-atom chemical reactions, particularly in solution. NEWTON allows the chemist to control the state of a
simulated system of interacting molecules: selection of the particular molecules, initial conditions of position and velocity,
parameters of the potential surface, temperature and pressure.
In response, atomic trajectories are classically integrated on
the interatomic potential surface in a very fast processor. The
chemist can watch the evolving molecular dynamics on a 3D display
and interact with the molecules through knobs, keyboard and
touch interface. Applications in progress include dynamic
studies of vibrational spectra in solution and the dynamics of
the solvation process.

With increased computer speed, much of biochemistry might
become accessible; the relation among structure, dynamics and
function for example in enzymic action, active transport and
biomolecular self-assembly. Hope for such speed increases lies
in two directions: more power per computational unit and the
adaptation of over-all computer architecture to match the structure of the problem to be solved. A particularly appealing
route is the mapping of calculations in three dimensional configuration space onto a three dimensional array of parallel
processors, a route which can be applied equally to classical,
semi-classical and quantum calculations, all of which can be
shown to scale only proportionally to the number N of atoms in
the limit of very large N.

Acknowledgement

The vibrational spectra and dynamics of solvation are by

Peter Berens. Thanks to John Cornelius and the staff of the
Chemistry Department Computer Facility for their help, to Sylvia
Francl for aid on vibrational spectra, and to the Division of
Computer Research of the National Science Foundation and to the
Division of Research Resources, National Institutes of Health
(RR-00757) whose support has made this work possible.

Literature Cited

1.   Wilson, K. R. in "Computer Networking and Chemistry," Lykos,
      P., ed., American Chemical Society, Washington, D. C., 1975,
      p. 17.
2.   Murtha, J. C., Adv. Computers (1966) $\underline{7}$, 1.
3.   Lorin, H., "Parallelism in Hardware and Software," Prentice-
      Hall, Inc., Englewood Cliffs, New Jersey, 1972.
4.   Comptre Corporation, Enslow, Philip H., Jr., ed., "Multi-
      processors and Parallel Processing," John Wiley & Sons,
      New York, 1974.
5.   Berne, B. J., ed., "Statistical Mechanics, Part B: Time-
      Dependent Processes," Vol. 6 of "Modern Theoretical
      Chemistry," Plenum Publishing, New York, 1977.
6.   Levine, R. D., and Bernstein, R. B., "Molecular Reaction
      Dynamics," Oxford University Press, New York, 1974.
7.   Miller, W. H., ed., "Dynamics of Molecular Collisions, Parts
      A & B," Vols. 1 & 2 of "Modern Theoretical Chemistry,"
      Plenum Publishing, New York, 1976.
8.   Califano, S., "Vibrational States," John Wiley, London,
      1976.
9.   Williams, J. D., Stand, P. J., and Schleyer, P.v.R., Ann.
      Rev. Phys. Chem. (1968) $\underline{19}$, 531.
10.   Kitaigorodsky, A. I., "Molecular Crystals and Molecules,"
      Academic Press, New York, 1973.
11.   Hopfinger, A. J., "Conformational Properties of Macromole-
      cules," Academic Press, New York, 1973.
12.   Shipman, L. L., Burgess, W., and Sheraga, H. A., Proc. Nat.
      Acad. Sci. USA (1975) $\underline{72}$, 543.
13.   Blout, E. R., Bovey, F. A., Goodman, M., and Lotan, N., eds.,
      "Peptides, Polypeptides and Proteins," John Wiley & Sons,
      New York, 1974.
14.   Momany, F. A., McGuire, R. F., Burgess, A. W., and Sheraga,
      H. A., J. Phys. Chem. (1975) $\underline{79}$, 2361.
15.   Warshel, A. in "Semiempirical Methods of Electronic Struc-
      ture Calculation, Part A: Techniques," Segal, G. A., ed.,
      Vol. 7 of "Modern Theoretical Chemistry," Plenum Pub-
      lishing, New York, 1977.
16.   Bunker, D. L., "Theory of Elementary Gas Reaction Rates,"
      Pergamon Press, Oxford, 1966, Sections 2.2 and 3.2.
17.   Bennett, C. H., in "Diffusion in Solids: Recent Develop-
      ments," Burton, J. J., and Nowich, A. S., eds., Academic
      Press, New York, 1975.

18. Valleau, J. P., and Whittington, S. G., in "Statistical Mechanics, Part A: Equilibrium Techniques," Berne, B. J., ed., Vol. 5 of "Modern Theoretical Chemistry," Plenum Publishing, New York, 1977.

19. Weeks, J. D., Chandler, D., and Andersen, H. C., J. Chem. Phys. (1971) $\underline{54}$, 5237.

20. Atkinson, W. D., Bond, K. E., Tribble, G. L. III, and Wilson, K. R., Comput. & Graphics (1977) $\underline{2}$, 97.

21. Sutherland, G., Lawrence Livermore Laboratories, Livermore, California, private communication.

22. Park, T. C., Loma Linda University, Loma Linda, California, private communication.

23. Wilson, E. B. Jr., Decius, J. C., and Cross, P. C., "Molecular Vibrations," McGraw-Hill, New York, 1955.

24. Kettering, C. F., Shutts, L. W., and Andrews, D. H., Phys. Rev. (1930) $\underline{36}$, 531.

25. Herzberg, G. H., "Molecular Spectra and Molecular Structure II. Infrared and Raman Spectra of Polyatomic Molecules," D. Van Nostrand, Princeton, New Jersey, 1945.

26. Kubo, R. in "Lectures in Theoretical Physics Vol. 1," Brittin, W. F., and Dunham, L. G., eds., Interscience Publishers, New York, 1959.

27. Kadanoff, L. P., and Martin, P. C., Ann. Phys. (1963) 24, 419.

28. Felderhof, B. U., and Oppenheim, I., Physica (1965) $\underline{31}$, 1441.

29. Gordon, R. G., Advan. Magn. Resonance (1968) $\underline{3}$, 1.

30. Berne, B. J., in "Physical Chemistry, An Advanced Treatise, Vol. VIIIB, Liquid State," Henderson, D., ed., Academic Press, New York, 1971.

31. Kampen, N. G. van, Physica Norvegica (1971) $\underline{5}$, 10.

32. Lemberg, H. L., and Stillinger, F. H., J. Chem. Phys. (1975) $\underline{62}$, 1677.

33. Andrews, D. H., and Murray, J. W., J. Chem. Phys. (1934) $\underline{2}$, 634.

34. Warshel, A., University of Southern California, Los Angeles, California, private communication.

35. Warshel, A., and Levitt, M., J. Mol. Biol. (1976) $\underline{103}$, 227.

36. Warshel, A., Nature (1976) $\underline{260}$, 679.

37. Karplus, M., and Rossky, P. J., "Abstracts of Papers," Chemical Institute of Canada and American Chemical Society, Montreal, 1977, phys. 66.

38. Levitt, M., MRC Laboratory of Molecular Biology, Cambridge, U. K., private communication.

39. Sutherland, I. E., California Institute of Technology, Pasadena, California, private communication.

40. Datamation (March, 1977) $\underline{23}$, 150.

41. O'Leary, G., Floating Point Systems, Portland, Oregon, private communication.

42. Henry, N. F. M., and Lonsdale, K., eds., "International
     Tables for X-Ray Crystallography Vol. 1," Kynoch Press,
     Birmingham, England, 1952.
43. Cundy, H. M., and Rollett, A. P., "Mathematical Models,"
     Oxford University Press, London, 1961.
44. Gerratt, J., and Mills, I. M., J. Chem. Phys. (1968) 49,
     1719.
45. Pulay, P., Molec. Phys. (1969) 17, 197.
46. Pulay, P., and Török, F., Molec. Phys. (1973) 25, 1153.

Theoretical Chemistry via Minicomputer[*]

PETER K. PEARSON,[**] ROBERT R. LUCCHESE,[***]
WILLIAM H. MILLER, and HENRY F. SCHAEFER III

Department of Chemistry, University of California, Berkeley, CA 94720

Certainly one of the most important and far-reaching developments in chemistry over the past decade has been the emergence of theory as a predictive tool of semi-quantitative reliability. This statement is no way meant to detract from the pre-1960 theoretical chemistry that provided, through the work of men such as Linus Pauling, Robert Mulliken, and Henry Eyring, the modern foundations of valence theory and chemical kinetics. Contemporary theoretical research is obviously built upon the achievements of these pioneers. However the distinguishing feature of modern theoretical chemistry is the ability not only to correlate existing experimental data (and make rough qualitative predictions), but also to provide an a priori description of chemical phenomena that allows precise predictions to be tested by experiment.

The most striking example of this new age of theory is the understanding that the single-configuration self-consistent-field (SCF) approximation for electronic wave functions provides equilibrium geometries in very close agreement with available experimental data ($\underline{1}$). If one defines chemistry as the union of structure, energetics, and dynamics on the molecular level, then it seems fair to say that theory has a firm grasp on at least one third of this branch of science. Furthermore, since SCF theory may now be applied fairly routinely ($\underline{2}$) to systems as large as TCNQ-TTF (Figure 1) the range of applicability is clearly rather broad.

A second major insight gleaned over the past decade is the realization that the detailed dynamics of chemical reactions are well described by ordinary classical mechanics, i.e., by classical trajectory studies ($\underline{3}$). Although most theoretical studies to date have dealt with the canonical A + BC → AB + C reaction (for which the most detailed experimental data is available) ($\underline{4}$), systems as large as the methyl isocyanide reaction

$$CH_3NC \rightarrow CH_3CN$$

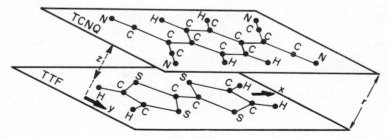

Figure 1

are readily accessible (5). In fact it is reasonable to assume
that much of the future research in this area will be directed
toward a theoretical understanding of model organic reactions.

The link between the above two branches of theory is clear:
electronic structure theory has as a principle aim the eluci-
dation of the potential energy surface(s); while the theory of
dynamics or collision processes begins with the same potential
energy surface(s). The present research project had its genesis
in collaborative studies between WHM (dynamics) and HFS (electronic
structure).

Here we have assembled a "final" (only in the sense of a
rapidly approaching deadline) report on our use of a minicomputer
for research in modern theoretical chemistry. At the outset we
should state that we have already written many words on this
subject, and repetition of these would not appear to serve a
purpose. A modified version of the original proposal has been
published in Computers and Chemistry. That proposal goes into
the justification and economic motivation for this pilot project.
Secondly, Appendix I contains four interim reports describing in
detail our experiences with the new machine. We strongly
encourage the reader to go over these documents carefully.
Finally we note that the proposal for a National Resource for
Computation in Chemistry (NRCC) has brought squarely to the
attention of the chemical community the need for improved
computational facilities. We therefore also urge the reader to
give serious consideration to the reports of Wiberg (6) and
Bigeleisen (7) committees.

The Economic Argument

The minicomputer chosen was the Datacraft 6024/4, which was
fully assembled at Berkeley on March 13, 1974. Thus our experience spans a period of roughly three years. Although the same

machine is still in production (ours is machine #3 of about 200 produced to date), several company changes have occurred and our minicomputer is now called the Harris Corporation Slash Four.

The cost of the machine was essentially $130,000, including California state sales tax. No overhead on the purchase price was required. Assuming amortization over a four year period, this amounts to $2708 per month. The other large cost is that of maintaining the service contract, currently $1715/month ($1280 to the Harris Corporation and $435 to the UC Berkeley overhead). On this basis the total cost is $4423/month or $7.30 per hour if we assume 20 hours of usage per day, as shown to be realistic in Appendix I.

As noted by one of the reviewers, this cost might be further reduced in a chemistry department where there is already a technical staff member with extensive digital hardware expertise. Of course the insurance aspects of the maintenance contract would be lost in this case.

Extensive timing comparisons (Appendix I) have shown the minicomputer to be 25-30 times slower than the Control Data Corporation (CDC) 7600. Thus the minicomputer generates the equivalent of 1 hour of 7600 central processor (cpu) time per $200. For comparison, we cite the charge structure of the Lawrence Berkeley Laboratory (LBL) CDC 7600. This machine is generally available to NSF grantees and offers 7600 machine time at prices roughly five times less expensive than commercial rates. Nevertheless the LBL rates range from roughly $350 to $900 per hour of cpu time. The former figure refers to weekend deferred priority time. On this basis, then, one concludes that the mini-computer is $\sim$ 2-4 times more economical than the 7600.

However, as we discuss in detail in the original proposal and in Appendix I, the above figures include input-output charges (especially disk accesses) for the Harris machine, but these are additional charges (often rather severe) on the CDC 7600. Thus as is seen in Appendix I, the cost effectiveness of the mini-computer sometimes exceeds that of the 7600 by a factor of six or seven.

In all fairness, the minicomputer does not provide the quality of service of the LBL CDC 7600, a smoothly functioning professionally operated computer center. Much of the savings made is simply a consequence of the fact that our operation involves no paid employees other than graduate students and postdoctorals.

Research Accomplishments

The ultimate test of the present proposal is undoubtedly whether the chemistry research completed justifies the NSF funds expended. Since this document is intended for perusal by academic and industrial research chemists, we leave this judgment to you. Available upon request is a list of seventy publications based on

research carried out using the Harris Slash Four minicomputer.
In several cases the research was carried out in collaboration
with theorists from other institutions. When such studies made
use of machines in addition to the minicomputer, an asterisk is
indicated. Papers in the course of publication will be provided
on request.

     Not wishing to be entirely impartial, we add the opinion that
the minicomputer has allowed us to make a number of important
contributions both to theory and to chemistry. With this machine,
our choice of problems has been primarily based on chemical
intuition and scientific inclination, rather than the pressing
economic circumstances many theoretical chemists regrettably
face.

Developmental Work in Progress

     As mentioned in the introduction, we are just now beginning
to take full advantage of the Harris machine. Bruce Garrett, a
student of Professor Miller's is continuing work on the development of a quantum mechanical transition state theory. Cliff
Dykstra has developed (8) and is continuing to work on a Theory
of Self Consistent Electron Pairs (TSCEP), a fundamentally new
approach to the correlation problem (9). Also in Professor
Schaefer's group, Robert Lucchese, Jim Meadows, Bill Swope, and
Bernie Brooks are working together to develop a new system of
programs for large scale configuration interaction (CI) studies of
electron correlation in molecules. The latter programs are
described in some detail elsewhere (10). Thus, although this
report is officially labeled "final", there is much work yet to
be done in the development of new theoretical methods and computational techniques. It is in such cases, where original programs
have been written specifically for the minicomputer, that its
advantages become most clearly apparent. In this regard it is
noteworthy that most students who have taken the time (perhaps
one month) to familiarize themselves with the mini actually
prefer it to the CDC 7600.

Qualms

     A balanced view requires us to admit that all is not sweetness
and light. We have already noted that there is no convenient
computer center staff to operate the machine. When problems
occur we not only must call the customer engineer, but also point
him rather carefully in the direction of the problem. As one of
the reviewers has pointed out, this is at least in part a result
of the fact that the support services of the Harris Corporation
are substantially less than those of IBM or CDC. An absolute
necessity is the presence of one very bright, knowledgeable, and
responsible computer expert in the group. The Lord has blessed
us with two such individuals, Dr. Peter Pearson (who went on to

greater things in September of 1974) and more recently Mr. Robert Lucchese. This sort of individual is required to make system changes and updates, determine whether the machine is really sick or just out of shape, and show the customer engineer exactly which machine instruction is failing when a definite problem is located.

Also, debugging a large program is much more difficult than on the CDC 7600. Programmers always blame most of their mistakes on the computer and this can be especially true when a mini is involved. Occasionally one finds a student who is simply unwilling to go through the exhaustive checking that is necessary to debug a large scale program on a machine such as the Harris Slash Four.

Successful utilization of the machine requires the physical presence of one student at any given time. For some individuals the idea of spending the night with a computer is not a pleasant one. We have found that the only satisfactory solution to this problem is to have a sufficient number of students (at least 10) using the machine that they simply cannot afford to risk the possibility of being absent in the event of a machine halt.

Two additional weaknesses of the mini relative to a large machine such as the 7600 are (a) the smaller memory and (b) the large amounts of elapsed time required to complete a given job. The former limitation restricts us, for example, to using about 80 contracted gaussian functions in electronic structure calculations. Although Cliff Dykstra has developed a method of increasing this limit to 120 contracted functions, such a computation might run into trouble on the second point. That is, about 24 hours is the practical limit for a single job. In general, the other users become quite hostile if a job requires even this long. In addition, 24 hours is about the mean time interval between machine failures if the machine is running a single job. It should be noted that this time restriction (to about 1 hour of 7600 time per job) would be a serious barrier in accomplishing some of the goals set out for the NRCC (6, 7).

Interfacing with Experiments

A question we are frequently asked is "Could you handle three or four on-line experiments at the same time?" The answer to this question, at least for the Harris Slash Four, is an unequivocal no. The cost effectiveness of machines such as ours is in part a result of its somewhat restricted capabilities. If one wants the flexibility of an IBM 370 system, tied in to 43 teletypes, one should probably be willing to pay ten times more to carry out a particular task in computational chemistry. Our system is ideally suited to batch operations, where only one job runs at a time. In fact if a particular job is long and not restartable (many of our programs are now restartable) it is better not even to read in another job during execution. Thus the possibility of on-line experiments is definitely slim.

However, there are all kinds of experimental chemists who rely
on computers for number crunching jobs designed to aid in the
analysis of their data. Such jobs are well suited to a machine
such as the Slash Four and could very well provide a major part
of the justification for a proposal to the NSF.

In light of several reviewers comments, we feel compelled to
note that the newer Harris machines (especially the Slash Seven)
now have virtual memory, which allows genuine time-sharing.
Having observed the Slash Seven at the International Engineering
Company in San Francisco we must conclude that the simultaneous
processing of three or four users is now a reality on the Slash
Seven. Although virtual memory is an additional expense (perhaps
$20,000) it would certainly be worthwhile in situations where
on-line data acquisition is a primary task.

Environmental Impact

Until quite recently, the primary medium for the dissemination of the results of this minicomputer experiment has been
personal contact. After the original proposal was submitted,
copies were mailed to $\sim$ 25 prominent theoretical chemists. The
interim reports have been distributed on request, of which we have
had $\sim$ 50 from research chemists. Another $\sim$ 50 visitors, including
an NSF review team, have toured the Berkeley facility.

A slightly modified version of the original proposal was
published (Volume 1, pages 85-90) in the new journal Computers and
Chemistry. Professor Schaefer presented an invited paper "Are
Minicomputers Suitable for Large Scale Scientific Computation" in
September 1975 at the Eleventh Annual IEEE Computer Society
Conference in Washington, D.C. The same lecture was given earlier
at the IBM Research Laboratory, San Jose. The trade journal
Computerworld published a popular description of the experiment in
its March 8, 1976 issue.

A number of recent papers have mentioned the Berkeley mini
experiments. Most recent and perhaps the most interesting is that
of Isaiah Shavitt, (11) entitled "Computers and Quantum Chemistry."
Finally, the American Chemical Society's Division of Computers in
Chemistry, under the direction of Professor Peter Lykos, has
organized the present symposium (June, 1977 in Montreal) on
"Minicomputers and Large Scale Computations".

Several research groups (perhaps 20) have expressed serious
interest in acquiring their own minicomputer for purposes comparable
to our own. However, to our knowledge the only group to actually
do so is that of the late Professor Don L. Bunker of the University
of California at Irvine. Although the Hewlett-Packard machine
purchased by Professor Bunker with NSF support was much less
expensive (and proportionally slower) than the Harris Slash Four,
he found it to be adequate for his research in dynamics and a vast
improvement over his former dependence on an incompetent campus
computer center.

Since the draft version of this final report was prepared, two groups of theoretical chemists have ordered Harris Slash Sevens. These are the groups headed by Professor Phillip Certain at the University of Wisconsin and by Drs. John Tully and Frank Stillinger at Bell Telephone Laboratories. These and other implications of our research have been noted in recent semi-popular reviews in <u>Science</u> (12) and <u>Nature</u> (13).

The Future

The controversy concerning the relative merits of mini-computers and large machines is likely to continue for some time. At present both the Slash Four and CDC 7600 appear to be relatively economical alternatives. The real losers in such comparisons are the machines between these two extremes (<u>11</u>). For example, several universities and research institutes (e.g. the University of California, the University of Washington, Colorado State University, and Battelle, Columbus) are currently using the CDC 6400. Although the 6400 is only about 1.5 times faster than the Harris Slash Four, the cost of using this machine can be as high (at Berkeley) as \$420/hour. This is clearly an absurd state of affairs, and we would encourage the abused supporters of such machines to consider their alternatives.

Since our original proposal, several developments have occurred in the minicomputer area. At that time the Harris Slash Four was by far the fastest machine available in our price range. Since then at least four machines of nearly comparable speed have appeared: the Data General Eclipse, the Varian V75, the System Engineering Laboratories (SEL) 32/55, and the Interdata 8/32. We have been especially interested in the SEL 32 since it is a true 32 bit machine and might be significantly faster than the Harris Slash Four if a powerful 64 bit floating point processor were available. In fact, such a fast floating point processor appears to be a real possibility for SEL in the near future. In addition the new Harris Slash Seven is about 30% faster than our Slash Four machine.

Another encouraging development is the fact that memory prices have now come down by nearly a factor of two relative to our purchase price for the 64K of Datacraft 24 bit core memory. Thus it seems quite reasonable that future mini purchasers will not be required to restrict themselves to small memory machines.

Certainly the most spectacular technological achievement of the last three years is the introduction by Floating Point Systems (Portland, Oregon) of their high speed array processor. At a cost of $\sim$ \$40,000, this device is able to carry out 38 bit floating point operations at essentially the speed of the 7600. Professor Kent Wilson of UC San Diego has already purchased the FPS array processor for use in simulating the classical dynamics of biological systems (<u>14</u>).

We have studied this device carefully and while very en-thusiastic about it, have some reservations. First the 38 bit

word, corresponding to 8 plus significant figures, is not quite
adequate for our type of theoretical computations. As we have
emphasized on many occasions, the 48 bit word of the Harris
machine is ideal for our purposes. Secondly, interfacing the FPS
device to a standard mini is going to be quite a challenge, and
hand coding must be done whenever the array processor is to be
used. Since the array processor is so much faster than the host
mini, the FPS must be used very judiciously to avoid its
degradation.

In short we do not feel that the FPS array processor is suitable at present for general large scale computations. The use
of such a specialized device would tend to "freeze" one into a
particular theoretical approach, with future options severely
limited. However, the mere fact that FPS can manufacture a device
of this speed for only $40,000 is certainly a remarkable achieve-
ment. We look forward to the further development of this concept.

Finally it must be noted that a very important development
has also occurred in the large scale machine area. This is the
introduction of the CRAY machine, which is at least a factor of
five faster than the 7600 and will be sold at essentially the
same price ($\sim$ $10 million). At present CDC has legally succeeded
in stalling the official delivery of the first CRAY, but this
should not be allowed to continue indefinitely. Our personal
opinion is that by the time the CRAY machine becomes commercially
available, both Harris and SEL will have introduced machines about
five times the speed of the Harris Slash Four. Thus it seems
likely that the present relative economic comparisons will be valid
for perhaps another five years.

After completion of our draft report, we learned of the
introduction of the PDP 11T55 machine by the Digital Equipment
Corporation. Although timing and pricing information is still
incomplete, this new DEC mini claims to exceed the speed of the
Harris Slash Four. We are skeptical that a corporation as large
and "respectable" as DEC will be competitive with Harris or SEL,
but this announcement is certainly welcome. At the very least it
will force Harris and SEL to accelerate the development and
release of their new faster machines.

Recommendations

The greatest challenge presently before the NSF (and ERDA)
with respect to computation in chemistry is the above mentioned
NRCC. We strongly recommend that these bodies agree as quickly
as possible on a procedure for implementing the NRCC (hopefully
for Fiscal 1978). One conclusion drawn from our investigations
is that the ultimate goal of the NRCC should not be the
acquisition of its own 7600, but rather of the much more powerful
and economical CRAY machine. Although initial implementation
will probably involve some fraction of a 7600, the CRAY alternative
should be kept in the forefront of consideration.

At the same time the NSF should continue to carefully monitor new developments in the minicomputer area. A reasonable procedure would involve the funding of two such minis per year for the next five years. Our Harris Slash Four has remained fortuitiously current during the four plus years since the submission of our proposal. However, as discussed in the previous section, the winds of change are now beginning to blow. Personally we intend to submit a new proposal to NSF as soon as a reliable manufacturer meets the following specification: for less than $200,000 complete (including California sales tax) a machine four times the speed of the Slash Four. Our current opinion is that innovations of a less comprehensive nature are not worth the tribulations (see Appendix) inherent in breaking in a new machine. Since the Harris Slash Four will still be a very desirable machine (especially with its resident programs, including POLYATOM, GAUSSIAN 70, SCEP, and BERKELEY), we would leave it to the discretion of the NSF to find a suitable new owner.

Appendix I

Interim Reports on the Berkeley Minicomputer Project.

Quarterly Report No. 1, December 14, 1973

Notice was received on June 15, 1973 that the proposal "Large Scale Scientific Computation via Minicomputer" had been funded to the extent of $129,600 by the National Science Foundation. At this point final negotiations with the Datacraft Corporation was entered into. The University of California was represented by Mr. R. J. Brilliant of the Purchasing Office, while Datacraft was represented by Mr. Don Faltings, of their Walnut Creek office. A final agreement was reached on October 5, 1973. The primary change relative to the proposed system was the substitution of a 56,000,000 byte disk for the original 28,000,000 byte disk.

In a parallel development, we received a letter on June 28, 1973 from Professor D. R. Willis, Assistant to the Chancellor-Computing. On behalf of the Campus Advisory Committee on Computing, Professor Willis requested that we advise him on how progress reports could best be made, on a regular and continuing basis. On August 30, 1973, we agreed to file quarterly reports, one or two typewritten pages long, to the Berkeley Campus Computing Committee. These quarterly reports will also be sent to Dr. W. H. Cramer, Program Director for Quantum Chemistry, National Science Foundation.

The majority of the 6024/4 system was delivered at Berkeley on November 14, 1973. As discussed with Datacraft, the scientific arithmetic unit (floating point hardware) and 56 megabyte disk did not appear. These items are scheduled at be delivered in early January, 1974. In the meantine, a temporary 11 megabyte disk was supplied by Datacraft.

The Datacraft engineer, Mr. Mike Crumbliss, arrived in Berkeley on November 19 and proceeded to connect the system. Several early problems were cleared up during the first week. For example, an inability to plug in the final 8,000 words of memory was traced to a misadjustment in the power supply. Within the first week the machine was able to diagonalize a 50 x 50 matrix in single precision (six significant figures). This calculation was done using the benchmark program HDIAG discussed in our NSF proposal. However, the machine was unable to properly diagonalize the same 50 x 50 matrix in double precision. This error, which as of today still occurs, was traced back to trouble in the square root routine, which in turn fails due to an error in the floating point divide operation. The specific problem is that the quantity $(1.0 - 2^{-38})/1.0$ is computed to give $1.0 - 2^{-38} - 2^{-7}$. The Datacraft engineers are working on this problem now and indicate that it should be resolved shortly.

Despite the peculiar divide problem outlined above, Professor Miller's classical trajectory programs appear to execute properly in both single and double precision. The complex-valued trajectories run only in single precision, since the floating point hardware is required for double precision complex operations. The first electronic structure program we are attempting to set up is HETINT, Professor Schaefer's diatomic molecular integrals program. The program has been rearranged to fit in memory without overlaying, but does not yet execute properly due to the divide error discussed above. In general we have found the double precision software to execute 150-200 times slower than the CDC 7600. This is about as expected, and a factor of 3-4 from the floating point hardware will put us in the speed range discussed in the proposal.

In our research groups, the individual most knowledgeable about computers and computing is Mr. Peter K. Pearson, and he has taken over responsibility for the care of the system and dissemination of necessary information to the other research students. At least four other students have a good grasp of the system. In that most of us know a great deal more about computers than we did one month ago, it appears that our minicomputer experiment has had considerable educational value already.

On March 29, 1974 our installation will be visited by a special National Science Foundation committee, tentatively composed of Drs. W. H. Cramer (NSF), O. W. Adams (NSF), J. C. Browne (University of Texas), and P. G. Lykos (Illinois Institute of Technology).

Quarterly Report No. 2, March 27, 1974

Our first quarterly report documented the arrival of most of the Datacraft 6024/4 system, described in our NSF proposal. This proposal has now been modified slighly so as to be suitable for publication, and will appear in the new journal "Computers and Chemistry".

At the time of our first report, the 6024/4 had been unable to successfully complete our 50 x 50 matrix diagonalization benchmark in double precision, due to an error in the floating point divide subroutine. Shortly thereafter this error was further traced by Peter Pearson to a machine instruction, the AMD instruction, Add Memory Double. We should point out here that the Datacraft engineers (or those of any other data processing manufacturer) can usually solve a problem only after it has been traced to a specific machine instruction failure. In the present case, the AMD instruction did function properly when one of the central processor byte slice boards was put on an extender board. This being the case, the error was eliminated by positioning a piece of copper foil between the two offending cpu byte slice boards. The matrix diagonalization then executed properly at a speed 166 times slower than the CDC 7600. With the floating point hardware, however, we expect (see original proposal) the benchmark to execute at a speed 49 times slower than the 7600.

With the AMD instruction corrected, we return to the problem of implementing HETINT, Professor Schaefer's diatomic molecular integrals program. Although the program did execute, incorrect answers were obtained. Peter Pearson eventually traced this difficulty to improper treatment of exponents by the system's arithmetic routines in underflow cases. In fact, he had to modify the floating point subroutines for double precision add, subtract, and multiply. This was a particularly difficult job, since at that time we did not have the source program listings for the software floating point subroutines. With these corrections made, HETINT executed properly on December 19, 1973. This program executes at a speed roughly 105 times slower than the CDC 7600.

The next major program to be implemented was the Ohio State-Cal Tech-Berkeley version of POLYATOM, a general molecular program for the computation of multiconfiguration SCF wave functions (the original version of POLYATOM was developed by Jules Moskowitz and co-workers at NYU). To this end, Dean Liskow began an intensive effort on the first of the year. One of the most serious difficulties was the setup of the overlay structure, consisting of three levels with seven segments. Success was achieved on January 11 when a proper self-consistent-field wave function for the water molecule was obtained. Comparison with the 7600 results showed an accuracy of between 9 and 10 significant figures for the total energy.

Toward the end of January, we began to run POLYATOM on a production basis. One of the first problems tackled was the possible existence of two isomers of the NO_2^- ion. A (9s 5p/5s 3p) gaussian basis was centered on each atom, and the three geometrical parameters optimized for the nonsymmetric $N \overset{O}{\diagup} \overset{O}{\diagdown}$ form. A complete calculation at a single geometry required between four and six hours of elapsed time. This is about a factor of 85

times slower than the CDC 7600. During the same period Gretchen
Schwenzer used the 6024/4 for a thorough preliminary study of
H_2S and the two hypothetical hypervalent molecules SH_4 and SH_6.
Similar 7600 timing comparison were obtained.

Due to the floating point software's inability to perform
complex operations in double precision (11 significant figures),
we have thus far been unable to implement Professor Miller's
semiclassical programs involving complex-valued trajectories
(i.e., generalized tunneling). Several real-valued trajectory
programs (rotational excitation of He + H_2 and trajectory
"surface-hopping" calculations for $O(^1D) + N_2 \rightarrow O(^3P) + N_2^\ddagger$) initially ran successfully but numerical irreproducibilities began
occuring. This was a source of much frustration, and was perhaps
due to crosstalk between several additional byte slice boards.
To correct this problem several additional sheets of copper foil
were positioned in the central processor one week ago.

The large disk (56 megabyte) and scientific arithmetic unit
(SAU) arrived at Berkeley on March 13, 1974. This was two
months after the promised delivery date and a source of considerable frustration. It is important to note here that none of the
time comparisons made heretofore utilized the SAU (floating point
hardware). The individual hardware floating point add, subtract,
multiply, and divide instructions execute at speeds 6-14 times
faster than the software subroutines. Realistically, however, we
expect the SAU to result in an overall increase in speed of a
factor of 2 to 3. This would put us within our original estimate
of being a factor of 64 slower than the 7600.

As of the time of writing of this report, neither the large
disk nor SAU are yet fully operational. The Datacraft engineers
are hopeful, however, that the complete system will be functional
within a week.

Quarterly Report No. 3, June 17, 1974

A well-respected book describing the first twelve months of
infancy makes a statement to the effect that the third month of
your child's life makes the first two seem bearable in retrospect.
In a remarkably analogous manner, the frustrations of the first
two quarters with our Datacraft 6024/4 minicomputer were more
than compensated by the successes of the third quarter, just
completed.

Our second quarterly report left off with the machine in-
operative due to the recent arrival of the 56 megabyte disk and
floating point processor [referred to by Datacraft as the
scientific arithmetic unit (SAU)]. Since the NSF visitation
committee (Drs. W. H. Cramer, O. W. Adams, J. C. Browne and P. G.
Lykos) was to arrive on March 29, one might describe the
situation on March 27 as being on the verge of panic. From Fort
Lauderdale Datacraft flew out Mr. Russell Patton, director of
field service. Working through the night, he and Mr. Ron Platz

installed a separate power supply for the SAU and located and corrected a problem with the disk automatic block controller.

With these modifications implemented, Peter Pearson was able to execute the 50 x 50 matrix diagonalization benchmark program. In the last quarterly report, we noted that, without the floating point hardware, (SAU), this program executes at a speed 166 times slower than the CDC 7600. With the SAU and the standard Datacraft 6024 compiler a ratio of 59 was found. Using the "optimizing" compiler (actually still a rather crude compiler), the diagonalization executed at a speed 43 times slower than the 7600. This result is consistent with the factor of 49 predicted in the original proposal, a modified version of which has now been accepted for publication in the new journal Computers and Chemistry.

The NSF visitation provided the framework for a thorough discussion of the machine's progress through March 29. Bill Cramer and Bill Adams stressed the importance of keeping an accurate record of machine utilization, a key factor in the economic analysis central to this experiment. Peter Lykos suggested we calibrate the 6024/4 using the MFLOPS (measure of floating point operations per second) benchmark. A copy of MFLOPS has been obtained and an analysis will be presented in the next quarterly report. Jim Brown gave us many useful insights from his experience at the University of Texas as both chemist and computer scientist. Don Faltings of Datacraft was on hand to answer a number of questions from the committee and briefly discuss some new features (including virtual memory) of the Datacraft line. Finally, it was agreed that a second visitation would be advisable, after the machine is fully operational and its characteristics thoroughly documented.

Steady progress was made during the first 10 days of April. That is, a number of programs were modified to run on the complete system, including SAU and large disk. However, several nagging problems persisted, one being that 5.4 volts, 0.4 above the recommended level, were required to sustain the central processor. When this minimum functioning voltage increased to 5.5 volts, Datacraft advised us to turn the machine off. After a week of investigation, this surprisingly subtle problem was located and quickly eliminated on April 22 by replacement of an integrated circuit on the memory timing and control board. As it turned out, this small machine defect had been responsible for many of the problems encountered during the first five months of operation. Not only did the machine run properly at 5.0 volts, but it was also possible to remove the pieces of copper foil previously necessary (see Quarterly Reports 1 and 2) to shield the different boards from each other.

Since April 22, the 6024/4 has been running quite smoothly. Some occasional parity errors were put to rest by replacement of a memory board chip on May 16. A current problem with the add memory to double (AMD) instruction has been temporarily relieved

by a sheet of copper foil between byte slice boards 2 and 3.
However, these are minor problems, and overall we have been very
pleased with the operation of the machine during this quarter.

     With technical problems pushed into the background, we were
able to turn to the central goal of the experiment, the evaluation
of the performance of the 6024/4 relative to the CDC 7600. For
this purpose we report the results of two direct comparisons, one
involving electronic structure theory and the other molecular
collision theory. It is to be emphasized that the programs used
are by no means optimally efficient. However, of primary
interest here are the relative speeds of the two machines, and
for this purpose our comparisons should be valid.

     The first test case arose in Dean Liskow's study of the
chemisorption of hydrogen by clusters of beryllium atoms. For
the Be_5H system, a double zeta basis set was adopted: Be(4s 2p),
H(2s 1p). The modified POLYATOM program was used to compute self-
consistent-field wave functions for this open shell doublet. The
results are summarized below:

	Times (seconds)		
	6024/4	7600	Ratio
Generate list of unique nonzero integrals	3091	174	17.8
Compute unique integrals (total of 476,000)	2506	119	21.5
SCF (time per iteration)	1548	36	43.5

This comparison indicates that the SCF iterations show the 6024/4
in the worst light. We intend to correct this weakness by recod-
ing this section of POLYATOM in machine language. However, all
our direct comparisons with the 7600 must of necessity employ the
same FORTRAM programs. The complete calculation, including 17
SCF iterations, required 0.25 cpu hours on the 7600 and cost
$243. The identical calculation required a total of 8.86 hours
of 6024/4 time, or an overall factor of 35 longer than the 7600.

     The second test case arose from George Zahr's study of the
quenching of $O(^1D)$ by N_2. Assuming a simple analytical potential
energy surface, classical trajectories were performed within the
surface-hopping model of Preston and Tully. 330 such trajectories
required 480 minutes on the 6024/4 and 18.2 minutes on the 7600.
The 7600 cost was $193. The Datacraft machine is seen to be a
factor of 26 slower. Note that this computation involves
virtually no input/output operations.

     Both of the above comparisons show the Datacraft minicomputer
to be significantly faster than the factor of 64 predicted in our
original proposal. There we concluded that the total monthly cost
(including amortization over four years) of the 6024/4 would be
$4156. Experience has shown this figure, which we now round to

$4200, to be realistic. Yet to be firmly established is the average number of hours of computing attained per day at our installation. We will discuss this point in detail in our next quarterly report. However, if we take the pessimistic view that only 12 hours of computing per day are achieved, 360 hours per month translates into a cost of $11.67/hour. Thus the Be_5H job cited above costs $103, as opposed to $243 for the 7600. The $O(^1D) + N_2$ job by the same criterion cost $93, as opposed to $193 for the 7600. Again it is only fair to remark that the cited 7600 costs at the Lawrence Berkeley Laboratory include only operational expenses and completely neglect the initial purchase price of the machine.

Added in proof: A surprisingly simple reordering of the POLYATOM file structure (no changes in the FORTRAN program) by Peter Pearson has resulted in nearly a factor of two increase in the SCF speed cited above.

Report No. 4, March 30, 1975

By the time of writing of our last report, it had become clear that the Datacraft 6024/4 minicomputer was meeting or exceeding the goals that had been set for it. The past nine months have served to substantially strengthen that conclusion.

A particularly crucial test has been passed in that it is now apparent that relatively little maintenance of the machine is required. Typically, it is necessary to call the computer engineer once or twice per month, and repair "down time" for a typical month is roughly one day. In fact, the service contract is necessary primarily as an insurance policy, since we would otherwise be unprotected against disasters, e.g., if for some mysterious reason the entire memory were burned out. In this regard it should be noted that the Datacraft Corporation was swallowed up by the Harris Corporating during this period. Thus our minicomputer is now marketed as the Harris Slash Four. The only effect (on us) of this takeover was the increased cost of the service contract, for which Harris proposed a price of $1500/month. This suggestion was particularly distressing to us since (a) it represented a large increase over the $1155/month we had budgeted for and (b) the University of California has during the past year changed its policy and we now pay 34% overhead on the service contract. After some delicate negotiations Harris lowered the service contract price to $1280/month and we accepted it.

Before leaving the subject of maintenance, it should be mentioned that most of our problems requiring service involve the teletype and line printer. It turns out that neither of these devices was intended for the sort of full time usage they are receiving. Incidentally, the teletype is not covered under the new service contract, but is instead serviced by University of California personnel.

In one respect, the minicomputer has proved less expensive to operate than we had predicted. In the original proposal, $300/month was allocated for "electricity, cards, paper, etc." As it turns out, although we do pay the above-mentioned overhead of $437/month on the service contract, the University pays our electrical bill, and the cost of cards, paper, etc., is less than $50/month. Thus this savings of $250/month partially cancels the high cost of the service contract.

During this period we have from time to time run programs to gather statistics on the utilization of the minicomputer. These data suggest that the machine is busy for about 90% of the time it is not being serviced. Thus the overall (including repair down time) utilization is in excess of 85%, a figure considered quite acceptable for large scale machines. This utilization rate is also remarkably close to the 20 hours/day estimated in our original proposal. It is necessary, however, to point out that such a rate could not be achieved (without a paid operator) without an aggressive and hard working group of eleven active users (students and postdoctorals). Since each user zealously guards his $\sim$ 13 hours/week, he/she is quite likely to be on hand should any temporary machine problem interrupt his/her job. Due to machine demand, it should be noted that jobs rarely run longer than 13 hours; and the thought (raised in our original proposal) of jobs running consecutively for one month has been long since abandoned. A typical job now runs for about two hours.

Scheduling the computer turned out to be more of a problem than we initially anticipated. It was clear in July, 1974 that the machine had become sufficiently popular that "good will" would not be a sufficient deterrent to squabbles. The system that has now been settled upon involves giving each active user 13 hours of machine time per week. In addition four hours (10 AM - 2 PM) per weekday are available on a first come-first serve basis for debug jobs, with a time limit of ten minutes. The time is signed up for on Thursday afternoons for the week beginning Saturday. The order of sign-up is a regular one, with the user having first choice one week being demoted to last choice the following week. A final restriction is that the block to time between 2 AM and 8 AM cannot be subdivided. That is, a single user takes the entire block. Although this scheduling system will probably be slightly revised on occasion, it seems to be working reasonably well at present.

Two major program conversion efforts were undertaken since the third report. The first, involving the Gaussian 70 programs of Hehre, Lathan, Ditchfield, Newton, and Pople, is now completed. The second, involving the polyatomic configuration interaction (CI) program of Charles F. Bender, began very recently and has been implemented thus far only in a restricted version. The Gaussian 70 conversion was deemed especially important since it now appears that this program will become significantly more widely distributed than any previous ab initio progarm for single determinant SCF studies. Thus the times we report with this program may serve as a basis for comparison with many other types of computers. The major difficulty in the implementation of Gaussian 70 was the relatively complicated (for the 6024/4) overlay structure.

One of the earliest studies undertaken using Gaussian 70 involved the $C_6H_6-C\ell_2$ molecular complex. Using the standard STO-3G basis set (162 primitive gaussians, 54 contracted functions), a complete calculation at one geometry, including 8 SCF iterations, required 64 minutes of 6024/4 elapsed time. Thus it is clear that the study of reasonably complicated organic systems using minimum basis sets is quite feasible with the minicomputer. Using analogous minimum basis sets, computations have been carried out on $(CH_3O)_2PO_2Ca$ $C\ell$ (67 contracted functions; 59 minutes for integrals plus 86 minutes for 13 SCF iterations) and the Be_{13} cluster (65 contracted functions; 80 minutes for integrals, 250 minutes for 20 SCF iterations).

We continue to investigate a large number of systems using the Berkeley-Cal Tech-Ohio State version of POLYATOM. Advantages of this program are that it yields exact spin eigenfunctions for open-shell systems and can perform limited MCSCF computations. One of the larger systems studied was the $NH_3-C\ell F$ charge transfer complex. A basis set of size $C\ell(12s\ 9p\ 1d/6s\ 4p\ 1d)$, $N,F(9s\ 5p\ 1d/4s\ 2p\ 1d)$, $H(4s/2s)$ was used, totaling 62 contracted functions. A list of non zero-unique integrals is generated in 40 minutes (this process need be done only once for the entire potential curve), integral computation required 130 minutes, and 11 SCF iterations consumed 50 minutes. A study of trimethylene methane which we had earlier found exceedingly difficult to finish on the 7600 (due to cost considerations) has now been completed on the 6024/4. Using a double zeta basis set (120 primitive functions contracted to 52), 74 minutes were required for integral generation. Twenty SCF iterations on the $^3A_2$ ground state (two SCF hamiltonians) devoured 220 minutes of elapsed time.

During the past nine months, a series of production runs was made on the glyoxal molecule $(HCO)_2$ using a standard double zeta basis set. Since, a number of runs were also made on the 7600, a comparison of the costs for the entire project is possible. The POLYATOM timing comparisons are seen in Table I.

The ratio of elapsed 6024/4 time to 7600 CPU time is 25.0, a very encouraging figure. Since the cost of machine time on the mini is about $8/hour (including amortization of the purchase price over four years), the total minicomputer cost of the project was less than $3500.

An interesting development has been the increasing use of the mini in an interactive mode. This is especially helpful in SCF calculations. The total energy is printed on the teletype after each SCF interaction and the user has four options: a) continue; b) go to a weighted averaging of orbitals; c) go to an extrapolation scheme; d) stop. Use of this interactive feature can remarkably improve the rate of convergence for certain types of molecular systems.

Table I.   POLYATOM timing comparisons for glyoxal.

| Job | 7600 | | 6024/4 |
	CPU-Seconds	Cost	Minutes Elapsed Time
Lister	35	8	9
Integrals (cis/trans)	215	34	46
Integrals (gauche)	240	61	86
SCF - ground state per iteration	6	2.75	2.5
SCF - excited states per iteration	17	7.70	7
Glyoxal Project:			
3 listers	105	24	27
70 cis/trans integrals	8050	2380	3220
60 gauche integrals	14400	3660	5160
130 SCF ground state[a]	7020	3250	3510
40 SCF - excited states[b] vertical	13600	6160	5800
60 SCF - exicted states geometry search[c]	7140	3245	3240
	50,315 = 14.0 hours	$18,719[d]	20,957 = 349.3 hours

a) Based on nine SCF iterations for convergence.
b) Based on twenty SCF iterations for convergence.
c) Based on seven SCF iterations for convergence.
d) If run exclusively on weekends and holidays, cost reduced to
    $9360. If in addition run at deferred priority, cost falls
    to $7488.

    Much of WHM's current research involves numerically computed
classical trajectories. In "classical S-matrix" calculations,
for example, classical trajectories, and the action integral along
them, are used to construct quantum mechanical S-matrix elements
for specific collision processes. Also, a newly formulated
quantum mechanical version of transition state theory, which
correctly incorporates non-separability of the transition state,
uses trajectories--periodic trajectories in imaginary time--to
determine the net rate constant for reaction. Although the
calculation of classical trajectories themselves is fairly standard
nowadays, these novel kinds of theory usually involve search

procedures, i.e., they require <u>particular</u> classical trajectories rather than a Monte Carlo average over them all. The ability to operate the minicomputer "hands on" has greatly facilitated the application of these new kinds of theoretical models. Also, this type of work requires a great deal of new program debugging, and the 6024/4 has proved quite adequate in this regard, even though the diagnostics are not as comprehensive as those produced by the LBL 7600.

Our final fairly typical timing comparison concerns a three-dimensional phase space integral calculation. To obtain the rate constant for D + H_2 at 200°K, 237 classical trajectories (both real and imaginary) were computed. The minicomputer required 60 minutes for this job, while the 7600 used 2.42 minutes of CPU time. Thus the 7600 was a factor of 25 quicker than the 6024/4. The cost of the 7600 job was $20.57. This comparison puts the large machine in a relatively favorable light since there are essentially <u>no</u> 7600 input/output charges associated with trajectory-oriented jobs of this type. In closing we note that this factor of 25 is characteristic of trajectory studies, which involve the numerical integration of ordinary differential equations.

Acknowledgments

We wish to sincerely thank Drs. W. H. Cramer and O. W. Adams of NSF for their support of this project, especially during its early and more controversial stages. We also thank Professors Jim Brown, Edward Hayes, Maurice Schwartz, Don Secrest, Stanley Hagstrom, and Peter Lykos for their thoughtful comments on the draft version of this report.

* Supported by the National Science Foundation, Grant GP-39317.

** Present address: Lawrence Livermore Laboratory, University of California, Livermore, California 94550.

*** Address after September 15, 1977: Arthur Amos Noyes Laboratory of Chemical Physics, California Institute of Technology, Pasadena, California 91125

Literature Cited

1. Pople, J. A., "Modern Theoretical Chemistry", Vol. IV, ed., H. F. Schaefer, Plenum, New York, 1977.
2. Cavallone, F., and Clementi, E., J. Chem. Phys. (1975), <u>63</u>, 4304.
3. Miller, W. H., Advances in Chemical Physics (1974), <u>25</u>, 69.
4. Herschbach, D. R., Faraday Discussion Chem. Soc. (1973), <u>55</u>, 233.

5. Bunker, D. L., Accounts of Chemical Research (1974), 7, 195.

6. Wiberg, K. B., "A Study of a National Center for Computation in Chemistry", National Academy of Sciences, Washington, D.C., March, 1974.

7. Bigeleisen, J., "The Proposed National Resource for Computation in Chemistry: A User-Oriented Facility", National Academy of Sciences, Washington, D.C., June, 1975.

8. Dykstra, C. E., Schaefer, H. F., and Meyer, W., J. Chem. Phys. (1976), 65, 2740, 5141.

9. Schaefer, H. F., "The Electronic Structure of Atoms and Molecules: A Survey of Quantum Mechanical Results", Addison-Wesley, Reading, Massachusetts, 1972.

10. Lucchese, R. R., Brooks, B. R., Meadows, J. H., Swope, W. C., and Schaefer, H. F., J. Computational Phys., in press.

11. Shavitt, I., paper presented at the Third ICASE Conference on Scientific Computing, Williamsburg, Virginia, April 1-2, 1976.

12. Robinson, A. L., Science (1976), 193, 470.

13. Richards, G., Nature (1977), 266, 5597, 18.

14. Wilson, K. R., "Multiprocessor Molecular Mechanics", in Computer Networking and Chemistry, Peter Lykos, editor (American Chemical Society, Washington, D.C., August, 1975.

Large Scale Computations on a Virtual Memory Minicomputer

JOSEPH M. NORBECK and PHILLIP R. CERTAIN

Theoretical Chemistry Institute and Department of Chemistry,
University of Wisconsin, Madison, WI 53706

In October, 1976, the Chemistry Department at the University of Wisconsin-Madison installed a Harris SLASH 7 computer system. The SLASH 7 is a virtual memory minicomputer and is equipped with 64K of high speed, 24 bit, memory; an 80 Mbyte disc storage module; a 9 track tape drive; and a high speed paper tape punch and reader. Other peripherals include two interactive graphics terminals, a 36" CALCOMP plotter, a 3'×4' data digitizing tablet, remote accessing capability for terminals and other departmental minicomputers and remote job entry (RJE) capability to the campus UNIVAC 1110.

The SLASH 7 is a departmental resource for the faculty, staff and graduate students as an aid in their research. The computational and data processing needs of the department can be grouped into four main categories:

(1) Real time data acquisition
(2) Data reformatting and media conversion
(3) Interactive data processing and simulation
(4) Batch computing, including large scale number crunching.

In this paper we discuss the performance of the Harris computer to date and the role it plays with respect to the categories mentioned above. The information provided is based on less than six months of operation, with much of this time used for program conversion and user education. Consequently we focus most of our attention on category (4) (batch computing and large scale number crunching), since it is in this area that cost analyses and performance criteria with respect to larger machines have been concentrated. It is also the easiest area to assess in a short period of time.

Although we concentrate on the number crunching capabilities of the computer in this paper, we first briefly discuss the role of the computer in the other categories. There are presently 16 minicomputers in the department associated with either departmental facilities or instruments dedicated to the research groups of individual staff members. These minis are generally adequate only for control of instrumentation and data acquisition, while the

necessary processing of data in the past has been carried out at
the university computing center. Nearly all of these minis are
equipped with paper tape I/O, with five having magnetic tape units.
In the future, we expect that much of processing of data will be
carried out on the SLASH 7. In addition, the SLASH 7 is equipped
with a direct memory access device which is capable of providing
a direct link between the other departmental minis and the SLASH 7.
At the present time, three minis are being hardwired to the SLASH 7
throgh RS232C interfaces and will be capable of data transfer of
up to 9600 baud. Although direct control of experimental instruments by the departmental computer is not contemplated, these
direct links to the SLASH 7 will provide fast turn-around for the
processing of experimental data.

A large number of instruments in the department produce
graphic output. This includes a variety of spectrometers,
electrochemical instrumentation, chromatographs and custom devices.
Since most do not provide digital output, the Harris computer is
equipped with a large data digitizing tablet, which is tied to a
high quality plotter through an interactive graphics terminal.
These peripherals facilitate the processing of graphic data via
curve fitting, integration, and so on.

Turning now to number crunching, after a brief description
of the computer hardware and the virtual memory structure, benchmarks and stand-alone run times are reported for several programs
currently in use in the department. One of the most important
items of information obtained to date is the extent to which
"paging" of the virtual memory degrades job through-put. This has
been evaluated by investigating the CPU time to Wall Clock (WC)
time ratio under different operating conditions. The CPU/WC
time ratios are given for jobs alone in the computer and mixed
with others. Stand-alone benchmarks correspond to the optimum
conditions for each job and give the most favorable CPU/WC time
ratio. This provides a bound with respect to CPU time, which is
used in a cost analysis with respect to larger, "hard cash" computer facilities. We discuss this point in more detail later in
the paper.

Virtual Memory and Paging

The Harris SLASH 7 Virtual Memory System (VMS) involves both
hardware and software to control the transfer of user programs and
data in 1K word (K=1024) segments--called "pages"--between main
memory and an external mass storage device, which in our case is
the 80 MB disk. This operation, termed "paging", allows a
program's memory area to be noncontiguous and even nonresident,
and provides a maximum utilization of available memory. This
permits the computer (1) to run programs larger than the physical
memory (the SLASH 7 has an 18 bit effective memory address that
selects one of 256 pages, thus allowing for a maximum individual
program size of 262,144 words) and (2) to "page" to disc a low

priority task (e.g. a long running number cruncher) to provide faster turn around for shorter, high priority jobs.

The paging feature is obviously a great advantage in a multi-user environment. For the individual user, the virtual memory system allows programs to directly address up to 256K words, thus avoiding the necessity of explicit overlaying.

The disadvantages of the virtual memory system are that (1) the operating system occupies approximately 27K of high speed memory at all times, (2) even small programs that do not page incur a paging "overhead", and (3) it is possible to create a "thrashing" situation if the demand for paging becomes greater than a critical value. The mean seek time for a disc read is 30 milliseconds, so that more than about 30 paging operations per second will stall the system.

Our present SLASH 7 has approximately 37 user pages available for programs and data storage. Since many jobs which are executed on our system require significantly more storage area than this, we have paid particular attention to how paging effects program run-times, and to programming techniques that minimize paging.

To give an example of a thrashing situation, we present in Table I the CPU and WC times required to calculate all eigenvalues of various real, symmetric matrices. These programs were executed in double precision on our SLASH 7 with the subroutine GIVENS, distributed by the Quantum Chemistry Program Exchange. Note that as long as the matrix can be stored in 37K (the number of user pages available) the program is CPU bound. For larger matrices (dimension greater than 200×200) the CPU/WC time ratio drops significantly due to thrashing.

The reason thrashing occurs in the present example is because the matrix is stored in upper triangular form by columns, while the program code processes the matrix by rows. Consequently, depending on the row being processed, it is possible to require a new page be brought into memory with each new matrix element which is referenced.

To eliminate thrashing in the present example, it is necessary to modify the code to process the matrix in the same order in which it is stored. The run times with the modified code are given in Table I by the entries marked with an asterisk. With the modified program, the CPU/WC time ratio still decreases as the dimension of the matrix increases, but at a more acceptible rate.

In the course of converting programs to execute on the SLASH 7, we have found it necessary to modify several codes to minimize paging. In all cases encountered thus far, the changes were straightforward and required little program reorganization. Thrashing would be difficult to eliminate in a program that required rapid and random access of a large data set, but we have not encountered this problem.

TABLE I. BENCHMARK RESULTS FOR GIVENS.

Matrix Dimension	Program Size (Words)	CPU Time	Wall Clock Time	CPU/WC Time Ratio
50	2.5K	3 sec.	12 sec.	.25
75	5.7K	8 sec.	19 sec.	.42
100	10.1K	18 sec.	36 sec.	.50
125	15.8K	35 sec.	51 sec.	.69
150	22.6K	59 sec.	1 min. 18 sec.	.76
175	30.8K	1 min. 32 sec.	1 min. 57 sec.	.79
200	40.2K	1 min. 56 sec.	90 min. 53 sec.	.02
200*	40.2K	2 min. 24 sec.	3 min. 41 sec.	.65
290*	84.4K	7 min. 11 sec.	15 min. 57 sec.	.45
400*	160.4K	18 min. 31 sec.	47 min. 24 sec.	.39

* Modified GIVENS routine, see text.

Benchmarks

In this section we present results of programs which were run alone on our SLASH 7.   Where available we also present the run times for other machines and, in particular, the UNIVAC 1110 which is the computer at the Madison Academic Computing Center.

The following is a short description of each job, the purpose of running the particular task, and the results.

(1) CRUNCHER. This program is a small CPU bound job which includes four arithmetic operations plus exponentiation. The main purpose of running this program is to establish the expected accuracy of the Harris 48-bit double precision word (39 bit mantissa) and to compare machine speeds.

In Figure 1 we give the Fortran code for this program and in Table II, the results of CRUNCHER are compared with runs obtained on an IBM 370/195 and the UNIVAC 1110. Each computer has a different word length and the precision of the final result is as expected. The "correct" answer is 2.0. For this particular benchmark the SLASH 7 is approximately 15 times slower than the IBM 370/195 and about one-half the speed of the UNIVAC 1110.

```
      IMPLICIT DOUBLE PRECISION (A-H,O-Z)
      ROOT=DSQRT(2.0DO)
      SUM=0.DOO
      DO 5 I=1,1 000 000
    5 SUM=SUM+ROOT*ROOT/ROOT -0.DOO
      SUM=(SUM/1 000 000.0DO)**2
      WRITE(6,9)SUM
    9 FORMAT(5H TWO=,E30.20)
      STOP
```

Figure 1. FORTRAN listing of benchmark·
CRUNCHER

TABLE II. BENCHMARK RESULTS FOR CRUNCHER

	Harris/7	IBM 370/195	UNIVAC 1110	UNIVAC 1110
Word Size	48 Bits	64 Bits	36 Bits	72 Bits
Answer (Exact=2.0)	1.999 992 774 8		1.993 870 154 0	
		1.999 999 999 8		1.999 999 999 98
CPU Time	27.2 sec.	1.75 sec.	12.8 sec.	15.5 sec.

TABLE III. BENCHMARK RESULTS FOR MATMUL

	Harris/7	UNIVAC 1110
CPU Time	5 min. 14 sec.	2 min. 18 sec.

TABLE IV. BENCHMARK RESULTS FOR SCFPGM

	Harris/7	UNIVAC 1110
CPU Time	36 min. 3 sec.	26 min. 46 sec.
Wall Clock Time	54 min. 26 sec.	N/A
CPU/WC Time Ratio	.66	N/A

(2) MATMUL. In this program two 60×60 matrices are
multiplied together 50 times. In Table III the results are given
for the Harris computer and the UNIVAC 1110. Both runs are in
double precision.

(3) SCFPGM. This program package calculates the one- and
two-electron molecular integrals needed for an ab initio
electronic structure calculation and subsequently performs a
restricted self-consistent-field (SCF) calculation using the
integrals. The benchmark calculation involved a gaussian lobe
basis set of 39 contracted functions appropriate to the carbon
monoxide molecule. In this particular run more than 5×10^6
gaussian integrals were calculated and the SCF program ran for
20 iterations. In Table IV we present the results of the benchmark. This program is CPU bound, with a 66% CPU/WC time
efficiency.

(4) LEAST SQUARES. This program, which was provided by
Dr. J. C. Calabrese of our department, does a least-squares
analysis of x-ray crystallographic data and is one part of a large
x-ray data analysis package. Such calculations are responsible
for a substantial portion of the CPU utilization of our computer.
In Table V the times for a typical LEAST SQUARES run are given for
both the Harris/7 and the UNIVAC 1110. This program is also CPU
bound.

TABLE V. BENCHMARK RESULTS FOR LEAST SQUARES.

	Harris/7	UNIVAC 1110
CPU Time	26 min. 22 sec.	15 min. 9 sec.
Wall Clock Time	36 min. 39 sec.	N/A
CPU/WC Time Ratio	.72	

(5) TPROB. This program, which was provided by Professor
C. F. Curtiss and Mr. R. R. Woods of our department, calculates
atom-diatom rotational excitation cross sections. This program
was selected as a benchmark because (1) it requires 193K words of
core which is considerably larger than our 37K physical memory.
(The program's paging rate is approximately 10 page requests/sec);
(2) the program does a considerable amount of mixed-mode and complex arithmetic so these functions of the Harris Fortran compiler
could be tested; (3) for each set of input parameters the program
requires approximately 7 hours of CPU time. In normal operation,
this program runs at the lowest priority to soak up unused CPU
cycles.

The CPU and Wall Clock times for this run on the Harris/7 are
given in Table VI. Although this program requires more than 5
times the available core, the program received a 57% CPU/WC time ratio.

TABLE VI.   BENCHMARK RESULTS FOR TPROB.

CPU Time	448 min.
Wall Clock Time	942 min.
CPU/WC Time Ratio	.57

Batch-Run Benchmarks

In this section we report the results of mixing the programs described in the previous section in order to determine the extent to which the virtual memory system can handle several jobs running simultaneously. For each run in Table VII, the total size for all programs greatly exceeds the 36 user pages of physical memory. The results in Table VII are representative of a larger set of statistics for numerous job mixes run at various priorities. These jobs are typical for our department.

For each run in Table VII, the final job was aborted when the penultimate job was complete.

Based on our experience to date, we make the following observations:

(1) For most jobs mixes (e.g. example 1 in Table VII) the total CPU/WC time ratio is close to the combined result obtained when the jobs were run alone. In fact, for some mixes (e.g. example 2) there is an overall improvement in through-put.

(2) Two or more large jobs running at the same priority results in a decrease in through-put (e.g. example 3). This occurs because in this situation the operating system time-slices the available CPU cycles by alternating between the two programs. The result is more paging and less CPU utilization.

(3) If two moderately paging jobs are mixed at the same priority, it is possible to generate a thrashing situation. For example, if two unmodified GIVENS jobs for 175×175 matrices are run alone or at different priorities, they are CPU bound. If they are run at the same priority they thrash. To correct the problem, it is necessary to suspend one job until the other is finished.

(4) Programs execute faster if the paging feature of the operating system rather than explicit disk I/O commands, is used to reference data sets. This is not possible if the total code and data is greater than 256K.

(5) For large data sets, where it is necessary to use explicit disk I/O commands, it is inefficient to read into memory in a single command more pages of data than there are available user pages in the physical memory. For example, if there are 4 user pages available and 6 user pages are read from disk, the first two pages will be read, but then might be paged back to disk in order to generate space for the last two pages. A subsequent program reference to the first two pages results in additional swapping.

TABLE VII. BENCHMARK RESULTS FOR BATCH RUNS.

Job	Priority	CPU Time	Wall Clock Time	CPU/WC Time Ratio
1. SCFPGM	6	27 min. 8 sec.		
GIVENS (400)	4	18 min. 44 sec.		
TPROB	0	11 min. 22 sec.		
TOTAL (Size=396K)		57 min. 14 sec.	95 min. 18 sec.	.60
2. TPROB	4	36 min. 54 sec.*		
GIVENS (400)	0	20 min. 2 sec.		
TOTAL (Size=359K)		56 min. 56 sec.	100 min. 25 sec.	.57
3. GIVENS (400)	0	18 min. 42 sec.		
SCFPGM	0	13 min. 37 sec.*		
TOTAL (Size=205K)		32 min. 19 sec.	71 min. 55 sec.	.45

* Aborted before completion, see text.

Cost-Effectiveness

We enter a discussion of this topic with reluctance, since the real cost of operating either our departmental computer or the central university computer is difficult to establish with precision. For the present, we restrict consideration to estimating the dollar cost to the Chemistry Department of computations performed on the SLASH 7, compared to the cost of using the central computing center (MACC).

Based on our records of actual charges, the effective cost at MACC is approximately $380 per hour at normal rates. This is a composite charge which includes CPU and memory utilization, I/O operations, and data and program storage. Most of the number-crunching calculations are run at a variety of reduced rates (overnight or weekend), so we adopt an average cost of $210/hour.

We next estimate the number of UNIVAC 1110 hours that we can generate on the SLASH 7. Based on our experience thus far, we expect to be able to achieve a maximum of 12 to 14 hours of SLASH 7 CPU time per day. This includes the estimated paging time and maintenance time. (The paging overhead could be reduced by adding more core.) Thus, at saturation we expect approximately 350 hours per month; this is a conservative estimate. The equivalent UNIVAC 1110 time is 175 hours per month, at a total cost of $450,000 per year.

In the three months since the SLASH 7 has been in full operation, we have obtained an average of approximately 150 CPU hours per month, or approximately 40% of saturation. This corresponds to an annual cost at MACC of $180,000 per year. Interestingly, this is close to the purchase price of our SLASH 7 ($152,000).

The direct costs to the Chemistry Department for operating the SLASH 7 are approximately $40,000 per year, which includes the salary of the systems manager, the on call/complete service contract ($1160 per month), and supplies. If the system cost is amortized to zero value over a five-year period ($30,400 per year), the total cost of the SLASH 7 is approximately $71,000 per year, irrespective of the degree of utilization of the computer. Thus, at the present rate of usage, the cost effectiveness of the SLASH 7 is approximately 5:2, while at saturation it will be approximately 6:1. We emphasize that we consider this to be a conservative estimate of the effectiveness of the SLASH 7.

Discussion

After less than six months of full operation, we feel that the SLASH 7 has been an effective departmental resource for research-oriented computing. Departmental users have had little trouble in converting programs to the new machine. At present, a complete set of ab initio electronic structure programs (including configuration interaction), a complete x-ray data analysis package, the MINITAB statistical package, MINDO3, CNDO, Xα and other semiempirical programs, an NMR spectra-simulation package, and other chemistry codes are operating on the SLASH 7. For most applications the 48-bit double precision word-length has provided sufficient accuracy. After an initial shake-down period of about four months, the hardware has proved reliable. All standard programming languages are included in the operating system, with FORTRAN and BASIC receiving the most use.

A significant by-product of the departmental computer has been greatly increased interaction among experimental and theoretical research groups. With more than ten groups actively using the computer, a stimulating research environment has been created in which expertise and ideas are shared across the boundaries of specialization and field. This perhaps will be the most significant and long-lasting benefit of our departmental computer.

Acknowledgements

Total funding for our SLASH 7 was provided by the University of Wisconsin-Madison. Professors Richard F. Fenske and John C. Schrag, together with the Departmental Computer Committee, were instrumental in the acquisition of the computer.

15

Computation in Quantum Chemistry on a Multi-Experiment Control and Data-Acquisition Sigma 5 Minicomputer

A. F. WAGNER, P. DAY, and R. VANBUSKIRK

Chemistry Division, Argonne National Laboratory, Argonne, IL 60439

ARNOLD C. WAHL

Science Applications, Inc., Rolling Meadows, IL 60008

There has been considerable effort in the past few years to lower the cost of performing quantum chemistry computations. An alternative that we have examined is the utilization of a computer system whose primary task is the provision of real-time support for the experimentalist in the laboratory. There are several reasons why such a system is bound to have resources available for execution of a program on an 'as-time-is-available' basis. The usage of system resources required by many on-line experiments is usually not constant. The system is usually scaled to provide service for worst case conditions. Effective response to real-time events requires that the sum of the 'event-driven' tasks should be less than 100 percent of the system's capacity. This incidental 'free' time may then be used for doing useful work, such as quantum chemistry computations. In a way our facility provides a service to the computationally oriented user in the same way that a mini provides the service when connected to a network where some of the mini's are involved with instrument control and other mini's support the computational operations. The difference being that we perform all the tasks on a single computer of somewhat larger capability than a mini-computer. For those installations interested in both greater experimental automation and quantum chemistry computing at nominal cost, our experience suggests that bootlegging batch computations on a computer dedicated to experimental control is an attractive and feasible alternative to a collection of dedicated mini-computers.

System Overview

Our chemistry division of about 120 research scientists is involved in basic research, requiring highly flexible instrument automation, experiment control and experiment analysis. In addition, there is a strong program of ab initio calculations, performed mostly on Argonne's central IBM 370/195. Frequent instrument replacement and enhancements require rapid and efficient modifications to the associated computer programs and services.

In 1967, before the proliferation of low-cost minis, a careful study of our diverse laboratory automation needs led us to the conclusion that a central computer could support all of the real-time needs of the current and projected instruments and, on the average, have enough left-over resources to support a useful amount of theoretical computation [1]. A suitable hardware configuration would require an operating system to provide effective protection, fast real-time response and efficient data transfer. An SDS Sigma 5 computer satisfied all our hardware criteria. However it was necessary to design and write our own operating system [2]. Services include program generation, experiment control, real-time analysis, interactive graphics, batch processing and long-term computation (hundreds of hours).

Our system is currently providing real-time support for 26 concurrently running experiments (see Fig. 1), including an automated neutron diffractometer, a pulsed NMR spectrometer, ENDOR and ESR spectrometers, infrared spectraphotometers and nuclear multi-particle detection systems [3]. It guarantees the protection of each user's interests and dynamically assigns core memory, disk space and 9-track magnetic tape usage. Multiplexor hardware capability allows the transfer of data between a user's device and assigned core area at rates of up to 100,000 bytes/sec. Real-time histogram generation for a user can proceed at rates of 50,000 points/sec. The facility has been self-running (without computer operator) for seven years with a mean time between failure of 11 days and an uptime of 99% of a weekly schedule of 160 hours.

Foreground Tasks. Serving the foreground tasks is the highest priority function of the system. These tasks consist of the execution of programs associated with each of the on-line instruments. A software priority is associated with each program controlling an interfaced instrument. Upon receipt of a request for execution (e.g., a data buffer is full), the user's real-time program will commence execution within about 160 microseconds if it is the highest priority "ready-to-run" job; otherwise it will commence running when all higher priority tasks are completed. Since foreground service cycles typically complete in less than 100 milliseconds (maximum allowed is one second), the lowest priority foreground task seldom remains in the "ready-to-run" state for more than a fraction of a second.

Non-Resident Program Execution. Real-time computational requirements vary over a wide range. The pulsed NMR spectrometer may require scan averaging a 16K word histogram every 300 milliseconds, taking about 100 milliseconds per update. Other experiments may require the execution of a 25K word histogram transformation program (correlated nuclear fission particles) every minute, taking about 10 seconds. Still other users require this type of execution every 10 minutes with execution times ranging

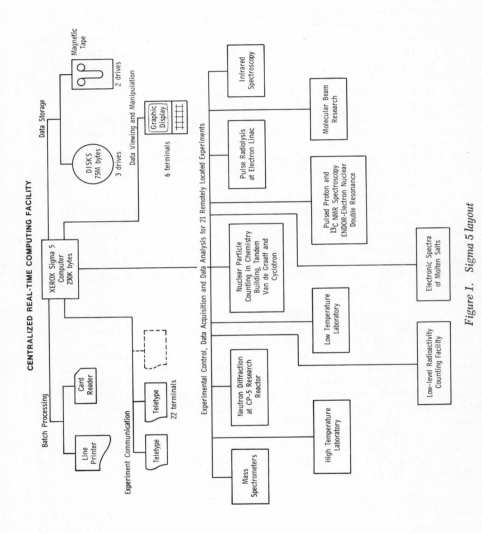

Figure 1. Sigma 5 layout

from a few seconds to 30 seconds.

To satisfy this variety of demand without requiring an inordinate amount of core memory, the operating system provides for the time-shared execution of non-resident programs (not always resident in core) in the background core area (where batch and long-term are executed). These programs are disk-resident core-images of relatively large programs required infrequently and without severe time constraints. Two queues for this type of service are provided: one with a 1 and the other with a 32 second time limit. These programs are usually written in FORTRAN by the individual users.

Batch Processing. An open-shop batch-processing capability is supported by the system. Queuing jobs through the card reader provides the casual user with immediate feedback for the rapid debugging of programs. Although the on-line user has the option of performing extensive analysis of an experiment from a remote terminal, the batch level is often used where large amounts of output are required or for the transferring of file data between magnetic tape and disk file storage. The batch level is also used extensively to generate and debug code for the control of on-line experiments and for performing most of the computations described in this paper.

The batch level may use all CPU cycles not used by higher priority processes: foreground execution, non-resident execution, system loading functions. Under normal daytime loading, the foreground usage requires about 10 percent of the CPU cycles and the non-resident execution about another 40 percent. Thus, it appears to the batch user that his program is executing on a computer with about half the speed of a Sigma 5 computer dedicated to batch-processing.

Long Term Computation. Utilization of the CPU seldon exceeds 40 percent in a 24 hour period, even with considerable batch usage. The remaining CPU cycles are made available for executing very long (hours to weeks) batch-type computations running at a priority level below batch processing. These jobs differ from batch jobs in that they only have access to disk files, not the batch peripherals. Once initiated (from the card reader), the job is read into batch core memory from the disk anytime there is sufficient space and higher priority usage permits. The daily saving of disk files on magnetic tape also copies the current core image of the long term job along with its files. Automatic file (and long-term) restoration at system boot-in supports execution extending over long periods. Table 1 indicates the distribution of long-term jobs that might be performed during a busy week.

LENGTH (HOURS)	JOBS PER WEEK
<1	15
1–2	4
10–15	2
>100	0.3

Table I.   Long-Term Job Length Distribution

Queuing Low Priority Tasks. As the system is required to
provide real-time support, the batch processing suffers. Since
many of the batch jobs are I/O bound, consideration is being given
to spooling all batch I/O. This would overlap the I/O with foreground and non-resident executions and thus speed up the apparent
execution speed of the batch job. As a further enhancement to
batch execution, consideration is also being given to including
batch in the non-resident execution queue. This would further
enhance batch processing speed and at the same eliminate the priority advantage of the time-share user.

As implemented, the long-term queue consists of starting the
next job from the card reader after the previous long-term job is
completed. A queue is going to be set up to execute jobs in a
cyclic manner, with more execution time being given to the shorter
jobs.

Quantum Chemistry Computations

The usefulness of the Sigma 5 system for the quantum chemist
depends on the scale of the calculations. Broadly speaking, we
may distinguish large scale calculations, requiring tens of minutes on the equivalent of a fourth generation computer, and small
scale calculations requiring less resources. Large scale work
generally involves the ab initio calculation of wavefunctions for
either the bound motion of electrons and nuclei in structure studies or for the unbound motion of particles on potential energy
surfaces in dynamic studies. Such calculations are most conveniently performed by either a large computer (e.g., fourth generation) or a dedicated minicomputer. The Sigma 5 system is neither
sufficiently powerful or sufficiently dedicated to be conveniently
used for large scale calculations.

Small scale calculations are varied and not readily catego-
rized. They include the rigorous calculation of relatively simple
wavefunctions (e.g., for diatomic nuclear motion or for atom–atom
elastic scattering), the approximate calculation of wavefunctions
or their informational equivalent (e.g., Huckel theory or semiclassical trajectory studies), the reduction of the wavefunction
to observable quantities (e.g., equilibrium dipole moments or differential cross sections), the curve or surface fitting of wavefunction information at discrete system geometries (e.g., the
dipole moment curve or the potential energy surface), and the

graphics display of the results of all the above calculations.
Such calculations require a flexible but only moderately powerful
computer such as the Sigma 5. In what follows we will describe
several general features of FORTRAN programming for the Sigma 5
system in the batch and long term mode. Then we will review several small scale quantum chemistry programs now in operation.

FORTRAN Programming. A FORTRAN program can be written in
two ways: a deck of cards can be keypunched or card images can be
entered on an interactive display terminal. The latter alternative makes use of a page editing system TEXTEDIT which permits
the rapid typing, and editing of card images followed by trans-
mittal to a disk file. The file can be accessed with a batch job
and the card images listed and punched. Three types of terminals
are available: Lear-Seigler 7700, Tektronix 4023, and Tektronix
4010. TEXTEDIT also can be used with a teletype.

There are several system routines which allow the FORTRAN
programmer the use of exceptionally useful I/O instructions. For
reading data from cards, the system routine READ causes the FOR-
TRAN statement

CALL READ(A,B,C,...)

to instruct the computer to read in a format free mode A, B, C,
etc., on a single card provided at least one blank space separates
each member of the argument list. For reading from or writing on
the disk, no JCL is required. A program may have up to two files
open at one time (file pointers are core resident). A file may be
private, in which case it is defined by the statement

CALL DEFDSK(NAME,NSEC)

where NAME is the address of a 20 character EBCDIC file name and
NSEC is the number of sectors (256 words) in the file. Up to 120
private files may be defined by each user. A scratch file is also
available, and it can be accessed by the statement

CALL OPNSCR.

Disk I/O can involve reading, writing, or write-reading fixed or
variable records. The write-read option allows one logical record
to be written on the disk and the next logical record to be read
into the same core occupied by the first record, thereby saving
one disk revolution period (25 ms.). As an example of a FORTRAN
call for disk I/O, a variable record read occurs with the execution of the statement

CALL DISKR(ARRAY,N,ISEC,IOVER)

where ARRAY is the name of the first element in the record, N is
the number of words per logical record, ISEC is the disk sector
number, and IOVER is a file overflow indicator. For magnetic tape
I/O, labeled and unlabeled tape may be directly referenced by the
standard FORTRAN I/O statements READ (U,F) and WRITE (U,F) where U
is the unit number of one of two tape drives and F is the format
statement number. Prior to execution, the relevant magnetic tapes
must be reserved and mounted. A tape drive can be reserved by a
single JCL assign card, for example,

!ASSIGN   111=LMT TAPELABEL

where a labeled tape (LMT) with the label TAPELABEL is reserved
for drive 111.

The JCL for executing a batch or long term job is particularly simple. This is illustrated by the examples given in Fig. 2.
In example A, a subroutine or complete program is stored as an object module in a private library under the name of the program.
Card 1 in the example is the job card which is the first card in
every batch or long term submission. It gives the user's ID num-
ber(XXX) and name. The last card in the example is the end-of-
data card which ends every batch submission. In example B, the
main program START is to be executed. Any unresolved external
references in START lead to a single pass search through subsequent entries in the private library. Then the public library is
searched for the referenced utility programs (e.g., DSQRT, ABS,
etc.). In this way individual subroutines stored as members of
the private or public library are selected and linked together to
form an executable module. In example C, the program stored in
the private library under the entry MIDDLE will be executed in the
long term mode. LT on card 2 identifies the mode and NNN is the
estimated CPU time required in minutes. All input and output for
a long term job must be via disk I/O, so there can be no data
deck. Preceeding and following batch jobs read in any input and
print, punch, tape or plot any output. System routines permit
identification of any long term job current in the computer. The
examples given in Fig. 2 all deal with executing jobs via a private subroutine library. Many other ways of running jobs are possible and all have a JCL as simple as the examples in Fig. 2.

The various FORTRAN programming features we have just described have all been used to assemble a library of operational
small scale quantum chemistry programs. Several members of this
library we will now discuss under the loose catagories of structure studies, dynamic studies, and graphics. Several of these
programs have been run on an IBM 360/195. While precise comparisons are not available, our experience indicates that the Sigma 5
is roughly 30 times slower than the IBM 360/195 for jobs that are
not I/O bound.

Structure Studies. The program POTFIT will least squares
fit Morse and Hulbert-Hirschfelder potential functions to a set
of diatomic potential energies as a function of vibrational
stretch. The nonlinear least squares code used in the fit is an
adaptation of STEPIT(QCPE program #66) [4]. The method involves
a pattern search for the nearest minima in the least square expression, starting from an initial guess of parameter values. The
input to POTFIT consists of the option for a Morse or Hulbert-
Hirschfelder fit, the masses of the atoms, the initial guess of
the parameter values, and the set of data to be fit. All input
is format free. The output consists of a listing of the input,
the final parameter values, the accuracy of the fit, the spectro-

Example A.

```
!JOB       XXX MYNAME
!ST ROM    PROGRAM
!FORTRAN   LS
(FORTRAN DECK)
!EOD
```

Example B.

```
!JOB       XXX MYNAME
!LOAD      START
(DATA DECK)
!EOD
```

Example C.

```
!JOB       XXX MYNAME
!LOAD      MIDDLE      LT   NNN
!EOD
```

Figure 2.   JCL examples described in text

scopic constants derived from the parameter values, and the resulting vibrational levels. Figure 3 reproduces the last two pages of output for a Morse fit to a set of ab initio calculated potential energies for H_2. POTFIT runs in 25K bytes and typical execution times are about two minutes.

The program CR360 is another nonlinear least squares fitting routine. CR360 will fit a supplied functional form to a set of functional values for one, two, or three independent variable, i.e., CR360 will produce curves, surfaces, or hypersurfaces. The method used in fitting is to distinguish linear from nonlinear parameters, to solve the linear least squares problem for a supplied grid of nonlinear values, and to display maps of the sum of the squares of the errors on the grid. There is no automatic search for the nearest minima to the initial guess. The user, through examination of the maps, must select the next set of nonlinear parameter values to search through. The program was designed for problems where there is the possibility of many minima and the location and display of all the minima are important. Prior to execution of CR360, the user must insert into the private library a subroutine that, for any given set of fitting parameters and constants, will calculate the functional form for any combination of independent variables in the data set. At execution, the input for CR360 consists of the number of independent variables, any bias and scaling to be applied to the data, the data and the weight that is to be attached to each data point, the grid of nonlinear parameter values, and the map resolutions for the maps of the sum of the square of the errors over the grid. The output consists of the listing of the input data and the data biased and scaled, a listing of the final parameter values and the fitting errors, and the display of up to ten maps of different resolutions for the residuals over the grid. The program runs in 120K bytes and its execution time is strongly dependent on the amount of data and the number of fitting parameters. For 150 data points, 30 linear fitting parameters, and 200 nonlinear parameter grid points, CR360 takes between 5 to 10 minutes.

A rather specialized program used in conjunction with large scale ab initio wavefunction calculations is STVTWC, a program modified from one by Hagstrom (QCPE program #9) [5]. This program calculates selected diatomic one-electron integrals for a given basis set of atom-centered Slater type orbitals (STO). The integrals that can be requested are the overlap, the kinetic energy, the nuclear attraction, and the z-moment. For a given basis set of STO's, the selected integral for every pair of orbitals is computed to give a matrix of results. The integration is performed by expanding the STO's in elliptical orbitals followed by analytic integration. The input is format free and consists of the internuclear distance, the charge on the two nuclei, the selection flag for the integral desired, the number of STO's, and the quantum numbers and zeta value for each STO. The printed output consists of a list of the input followed by a listing of the calculated

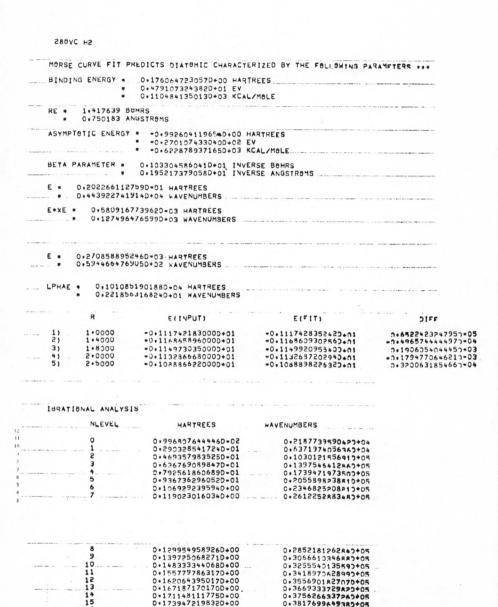

Figure 3.   The last two pages of printed output from a typical run of POTFIT

integral matrix. The program runs in 25K bytes and takes on the
order of 3 minutes to execute a typical job.

A final program that relates to structure studies is FCF, a
routine to calculate the Franck-Condon factors connecting the vibrational states of two different Morse potentials. The calculation consists of the numerical determination of the Morse vibrational wavefunctions followed by Simpson integration of the product. The input consists of the reduced mass followed by the identification title, the Morse parameters, and the maximum vibrational level of each electronic state. The integration range and grid
size complete the input. At most 1000 grid points and 15 vibrational states in each electronic state are allowed. The output
consists of a listing of the input and the calculated Franck-
Condon factor matrix. There is an option to punch the matrix if
desired. The program runs in 30K bytes and requires about five
minutes for a typical case.

Dynamic Studies. The program PHASE will calculate the elastic cross section and differential cross section as a function of
collision energy for an atom-atom collision system. This is done
by calculating the quantum phase shift for an input interaction
potential for each angular momentum quantum number of importance
at the given collision energy. The phase shift calculation can be
done either rigorously by finite difference solution of the
Schroedinger equation or approximately by a JWKB solution involving special quadrature formulas to handle the classical turning
point singularity in the JWKB integrand. Once all the phase
shifts are obtained at a given energy, the cross section and differential cross section are obtained by standard formulas. Before
the program can be executed, the private subroutine library must
contain the appropriate routine to read and display the parameters
of the desired interaction potential and to calculate the potential and its derivative at any point in space. Routines already
available include those for Lenard-Jones and EXP-6 potentials as
well as a spline potential for a numerically calculated set of
potential points. Given the potential routine in the library, the
input to phase consists of the reduced mass, the energy (or
velocity) spectrum, the potential parameters, and parameters
governing the finite difference or quadrature solution. The output consists of a listing of the input followed by a list, for
each energy, of the phase shift as a function of orbital angular
momentum. Along with each phase shift, the program also lists the
potential at the turning point, the centrifugal potential at the
turning point, the contribution of the phase shift to the cross
section, and the accumulated cross section from all the preceeding phase shifts. At the end of the phase shift list, the total
cross section and its log are printed and punched if desired. Optional printout consists of a listing of the differential cross
section over an input range of scattering angle, a listing of the
extrema in the differential cross section, and a line printer plot

of the log of the differential cross section versus scattering angle. Figure 4 reproduces such a plot from a study of the Ar-H elastic scattering. The program runs in 100K bytes. Execution times per energy vary with the energy, the collision system, and the solution method (rigorous or JWKB). Rigorous calculations take longer and vary from 20 seconds to ten minutes, with a typical time on the order of two minutes.

Another operational dynamics program is TRAJ3D, a three dimensional classical trajectory routine. The program is an adaptation of Muckerman's routine in QCPE (program #229) [6]. Given the potential energy surface, any three atom collision system can be studied. For a given energy, the standard semiclassical initial conditions are used for each trajectory and the calculated final conditions are analyzed according to the bin method. After calculating the desired number of trajectories, the program analyzes the bins for the nonreactive, reactive, dissociative cross sections and differential cross sections. The method of calculation is a combination of a Runga-Kutta and an 11th order predictor-corrector solution to Hamilton's equations. Before the program can be executed, the private library must contain a package of routines to read and display the potential energy surface parameters and to calculate the potential energy and its derivative at any point in space. Given this package, the input consists of the reduced mass, the collision energy, the initial state of the diatomic molecule, the range of impact parameters to be studied, the initial separation of the reactants, the number of trajectories, parameters relating to the method of calculation, and parameters relating to the analysis and display of the results. The output consists of the above mentioned cross sections and differential cross sections as well as the translational energy loss as a function of scattering angle and the correlation of rotational and vibrational energy gain or loss. TRAJ3D runs in 100K bytes. For a given energy, the execution time varies with the energy and the collision system. A typical time per trajectory is about 1 minute.

TRAJ3D is not a good program to run in the batch mode as the usual trajectory study would involve up to a few thousand trajectories, i.e., a number of hours of CPU time. However, the long term mode is ideal for trajectory studies. Under ordinary circumstances the initial and final conditions of each trajectory would be saved for any additional analysis desired later. Thus TRAJ3D can be readily decomposed into an input program that places all input on the disk, a central program that reads the input, calculates the trajectories, and stores the information for each trajectory on the disk, and finally an analysis program that reduces the trajectory information to measureable quantities. The central program is run on long term and in this way several thousand trajectories can typically be run overnight between two work days.

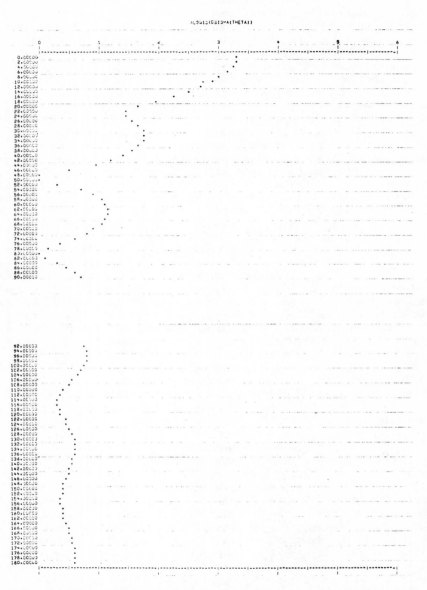

Figure 4.   Line printer display of a differential cross section produced by PHASE

Graphics. The program WSPLOT fits cubic spline polynomials to sets of data and plots the resulting curves in page six (8 1/2 x 11) figures. There is an option to make the X or Y axis 8 inches long with the other axis 6 inches long. Tick marks automatically occur every inch on both axes. The input consists of the limits of the X and Y axes, the figure title, the axes titles, and the input for each set of data. This data input consists of first a selection of a solid or dashed line with or without symbols marking the data points or no line at all with the data marked by diamonds. Then the actual data can be submitted in two ways: one format free data card for each abcissa-ordinate pair or under the control of a subroutine placed in the private library prior to execution of WSPLOT. Options allow for the internal biasing and scaling of both the ordinate and the abcissa. The data points must be arranged in order of increasing abcissas. Up to two hundred data points can be accomodated in a single set. Each set of data produces one curve on the figure. The printed output consists of a listing of all the input, a listing of the biased and scaled data, and a listing of the spline fit to the data points to test for any numerical errors in the spline fit. The plot output is on the plot disk file. In a separate job, a system routine will direct the Calcomp plotter to plot what is on the file; this separate job requires only the job card (see Fig. 2) followed by a plot card:

```
!LOAD        PLOT
```

As many figures and as many curves on each figure can be run in a single job as desired. The program runs in 25K bytes and takes about 30 secs to process a typical curve.

Another graphics program that displays surfaces instead of curves is KPLOT which makes a contour plot of any function of the polar coordinates (R, theta). The titling in KPLOT assumes what is being plotted is the potential energy surface of an atom approaching a diatom frozen at a fixed vibrational stretch. However the contour plot itself can be for any surface. Prior to the execution of KPLOT, a surface subroutine must be stored in the private library. This routine must handle all information regarding the surface to be plotted, i.e., it must read and display all surface parameters and calculate the surface at any arbitrary point. KPLOT then searches for contour values along given radial vectors. When a desired contour value is discovered, it is numerically traced and the resulting curve is stored in the plot file. If the trace is lost due to kinks in the surface that are missed, an error message is given. The input to KPLOT consists first of title cards for the figure, for the radial scale insert in the figure and for the chemical symbols of the AB+C potential energy surface assumed in the titling. Then comes the maximum and minimum radial values within which the contours will be plotted and the dimensions of the figure. Next is given the angles for which radial vector searches for contour values are to be performed. The

second to last piece of information is the number of positive contours, the largest contour, the fraction relating adjacent contours, and the percent fit of the computed contour trace to the
actual contour. Both positive and negative contours are searched
for and traced. Finally any surface parameters are submitted
under the control of the subroutine discussed above. The printed
output consists of a listing of the input and a digest of the
trace information for each contour. The plot output consist of
the figure and, as an option, to the right side of the figure, a
summary of the contours found and where they were found. As
always the plot information is placed in a plot disk file to be
accessed in a second batch job by the system routine PLOT. Figure 5 reproduces a figure produced by KPLOT; the plotted surface
is the potential energy surface for $Li + H_2$ with H_2 frozen at
1.4 bohrs. The program runs in 30K bytes and takes about 3 minutes to execute the plot in Fig. 5.

Assessment for Quantum Chemists

The major advantages of the Sigma 5 system is its power,
flexibility, simplicity of operation, and nominal cost. Most FOR-
TRAN programs for small scale quantum chemistry calculations require little reworking to become operational on the system. The
JCL, as illustrated by Fig. 2, is exceedingly simple and direct.
The system is open shop and thus each person directly runs his
own job without the delay of working through an intermediate staff
of computer operators. The nominal cost of the batch and long
term computations is due to the fact that these calculations use
extra capability unavoidable in achieving the primary mission of
direct experimental control.

The disadvantages of the system for the quantum chemist come
in two forms: foreground interference and peer pressure. Foreground interference of background batch and long term jobs occurs
whenever the foreground tasks and non-resident program executions
for experimental control assert their priority in the use of the
CPU. On the average, this interference ties up the CPU 50% of the
time during regular working hours (8 AM to 5 PM) Monday through
Friday). It is also highly variable, ranging from no interference
to as much as 55 minutes of interference per hour during regular
hours. After regular hours, foreground interference is not a substantial problem. As described earlier, spooling, to permit I/O
during foreground interference, and time sharing batch with certain foreground jobs will alleviate some of the pressure of foreground interference. However, foreground interference is a fundamental feature of the system.

Peer pressure constrains batch or long term usage because, in
the open shop system, the length of time one user can tie up the
batch or long term facilities is inversely proportional to the
number of people in line waiting for the same facilities. Since
there are 120 research scientists in the division, this is a sub-

15HF LI + H2: RH2 = 1.4

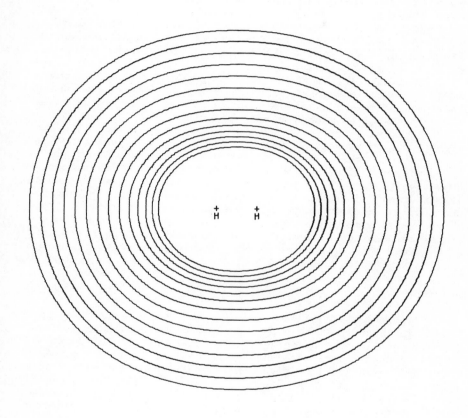

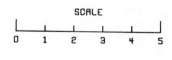

RH2 = 1.4

Figure 5.   A plot produced by KPLOT

stantial problem. During regular working hours, the number of
batch users per hour ranges from 1 to 20 with an average of 12.
In practice, a job requiring more than 5 or 10 minutes generally
attracts a crowd of users waiting to run jobs of less duration.
After regular working hours, this is much less of a problem. For
the long term mode of operation, a week's usage has been given in
Table I. In practice, a long term job in the system for longer
than 24 hours during the work week would cause others with shorter
long term jobs to complain. As described earlier, the establish-
ment of a queue would loosen the constraints of peer pressure by
allowing very long long term jobs to run with reduced priority
relative to shorter long term jobs.

    Foreground interference and peer pressure make it inconve-
nient at best and impossible at worst to run large scale quantum
chemistry calculations on the Sigma 5 system. Such large scale
computing requires access to either a standard large computer or
a dedicated minicomputer. However as our examples indicate, the
Sigma 5 system is very well suited for small scale quantum chemistry calculations. It has a power, flexibility, and simplicity
of operation, all at nominal cost, that would be difficult and
expensive to match with dedicated minicomputers. Thus for those
laboratories interested in both greater experimental automation
and a wide range of small scale quantum chemistry computations,
our experience suggests that bootlegging batch and long term computing on a system dedicated to experimental control is a feasible
alternative to a collection of mini-computers.

Abstract

    Computation in quantum chemistry and dynamics is being per-
formed in batch and long term mode on a Sigma 5 computer whose
primary task is to provide real-time instrument control, data-
acquisition and final analysis for 26 on-line experiments. A
brief discussion will be given of the multi-programming operating
system which provides, in order of priority, real-time interaction
with a large number of concurrently running instruments, interactive graphics, time-sharing, batch and long term computation.
The efficacy of this facility in three areas of computational
chemistry will be reviewed. First, the analysis of wavefunctions
and associated energies will be considered with several examples
involving property calculations, analysis of potential curves, and
least-squares fitting routines for potential energy surfaces. Next,
dynamics programs for quantum elastic scattering and three body
trajectory studies will be examined. Last, graphics (Calcomp
Plots) programs will be discussed in regard to the display of
potential energy curves and surfaces. The use of both batch and
long term modes will be illustrated and several typical calculations discussed.

Acknowledgements

The primary programmer for POTFIT, STVTWC, WSPLOT, and KPOT was Dr. Walter J. Stevens, now of the National Bureau of Standards in Boulder, Colorado. The program FCF was a minor adaptation of a program written by Dr. Patricia Dehmer of the Physics Division at Argonne National Laboratory.

Literature Cited

[1] Day, P. and Ktejci, H., Proc. AFIPS FJCC (1968) 33, 1187-1196.
[2] Day, P. and Hines, J., Operating Systems Review (1973) 7 (4) 28-37.
[3] Day, P., Computer Networking and Chemistry, ACS Symposium Series 19, Peter Lykos, ed., (1975) 85-107.
[4] Chandler, J. P., Program #66 in QCPE Catalogue and Procedures (1974), X, 29.
[5] Hagstrom, Stanley, Program #9 in QCPE Catalogue and Procedures (1974), X, 19.
[6] Muckerman, J. T., Program #229 in QCPE Catalogue and Procedures (1974), X, 85.

16

An Effective Mix of Minicomputer Power and Large Scale Computers for Complex Fluid Mechanics Calculations

R. J. FREULER* and S. L. PETRIE**

The Aeronautical and Astronautical Research Laboratory,
Ohio State University, 2300 West Case Road, Columbus, OH 43220

A "hybrid" computer system employing minicomputers
linked to various large scale computers has been implemented to perform varied, complex calculations in fluid
mechanics. The requirement for and application of such
a system is not unique to the area of fluid mechanics.
Similar motivation exists in theoretical chemistry and
advanced physics. Basically, the increased power of
computing equipment, the exponential rise in costs
associated with experimental analyses, and the greater
versatility of numerical experimentation has led researchers to turn to various computing techniques to
examine physical phenomena. Although costs are also
rising in many areas of the computer industry, the fact
that computational speed has been increasing much
faster than computational cost explains the trend of
increased use of computers for research based on theoretical computations. The purpose of the present paper
is to describe a unique "hybrid" computing system which
has been assembled at the Aeronautical and Astronautical Research Laboratory (AARL) of The Ohio State University to perform numerical experimentation with fluid
flows.

System Description and Background

The computing system is configured with two minicomputer mainframes: a Harris Corporation SLASH 5 and a
Harris SLASH 4 connected in a non-redundant dual processor arrangement. Synchronous communication devices
are utilized to link the SLASH computers with the desired large scale machine. AARL typically employs

---

*Senior Computer Specialist, Member AIAA.
**Professor, Associate Director, AARL.

dial-up Remote Job Entry (RJE) to an IBM System/370
Model 168, although other types of mainframes such as
those from Control Data Corporation (CDC) or Sperry-
Univac may be called upon as needed. The communication
is accomplished with conventional dial-up modems so
that the optimum connection of the minicomputers to a
large scale machine can be obtained for the particular
problem at hand. A detailed description of the two
SLASH computers system of AARL is included as Appendix
A to this paper.
    It should be noted that the description in
Appendix A makes reference to a Harris SLASH 6, not a
SLASH 4. The SLASH 4 was made available to AARL until
the SLASH 6 delivery could be effected. As a result,
the work reported here deals mainly with observations
about and comparisons between the Harris SLASH 4 and
the previously mentioned IBM System/370 Model 168. Some
direct comparisons between the SLASH 4 and the SLASH 6
have been made however and will be reviewed later. It
is notable that the Harris SLASH 4 has been selected by
others for use in large scale computations (1), particularly in theoretical chemistry (2).
    In 1973, AARL established its Digital Computer and
Data Acquisition System after an extensive survey and
benchmarks by Petrie (3). The original intent of the
computer system was to provide an on-line real-time
data acquisition and reduction facility utilizing a
digital computer based system, replacing an analog computer of limited capability and questionable maintain-
ability. This digital system, which is used to ac-
quire and reduce experimental data from the varied wind
tunnel testing facilities at AARL (4), is based on the
Harris SLASH 5 and was installed for approximately
$130,000 (in 1973), including the analog signal condi-
tioning equipment and real-time peripheral gear. As is
so often the case when the first digital computer is
installed at a site, the routine use of the computer
system was expanded into new areas at AARL. Soon, the
real need for the availability of extensive computer
power in support of theoretical fluid mechanics and
other large scale numerical calculations was recognized. This need is being satisfied by the addition of a
Harris SLASH 6 processor configured in the dual processor arrangement with the SLASH 5. The addition of
the SLASH 6 including an 80 Mbyte disc drive, another
9 track magnetic tape drive, a 36 inch drum plotter, and
several other peripherals amounts to approximately
$180,000. Thus the entire system represents invest-
ments totaling $310,000 in two phases.

SLASH 4 vs. IBM System/370 Model 168

As related to large scale computations, the AARL
SLASH computers are currently employed to examine the
performance of aerodynamic surfaces, usually airfoil
sections or wings, under varying fluid mechanical conditions. These analyses are accomplished with a library of some two dozen or more computer programs, each
one of which can perform specific types of calculations.
All of these programs are coded in the FORTRAN language.
Some are derivatives and modifications of earlier versions and undoubtedly contain portions of inefficient
and dead code. Most, including those used for comparisons to be made here, are more or less typical of
FORTRAN based large scale computational codes written
by researchers first and computer programmers second.
The codes are typified by moderate to large memory requirements due to heavy usage of arrays, and they require substantial floating point processing power. The
input/output (I/O) requirements are moderate in most
cases, usually consisting of a few card images input
and a couple of thousand lines printed output.
Since the programs vary greatly in their memory
requirements, numerical stability, and run times, no
one machine can be expected to perform in an optimum
way for all programs which might be used in the analysis of an airfoil or wing section. The SLASH 4 however,
with its 48 bit floating point word with a 39 bit mantissa providing 10+ digit accuracy is well suited to
most fluid mechanics calculations. On the other hand,
the IBM System/370 single precision floating point word
length of 32 bits with 24 bit mantissa is often not
long enough, requiring use of double precision (64 bit
floating point word length with 56 bit mantissa) with
an accompanying increase in memory needs and run times.
Maximum use of the SLASH computers is employed since
the cost per run is generally less than that for the
larger computer, even though the run times are longer
with the SLASH 4.
A representative list of execution time comparisons between the SLASH 4 and the IBM 370/168 for
several cases of four different airfoil analysis codes
is presented in Table I. Each code is identified by a
unique letter and each case executed by the code is
summarized. The execution times indicated are for case
execution only; compile and link-edit or catalog time
is not included. As mentioned earlier, all the codes
listed are written in FORTRAN and draw on a manufacturer supplied library of FORTRAN arithmetic support
routines (SIN, COS, ALOG, etc.). All programs

TABLE I

HARRIS SLASH 4 AND IBM SYSTEM/370 MODEL 168 COMPARISONS

Program Code	Case Number	Execution Time in CPU sec. IBM 370/168	SLASH 4	Percent Slower*
C**	I	114.30	728.20	537.1%
C**	II	82.19	498.26	506.2%
C	III	149.84	1912.55	1176.4%
E	I	18.89	157.28	732.6%
E	II	18.78	172.86	820.5%
E	III	26.49	296.26	1018.4%
E	IV	45.47	427.05	839.2%
K	I	136.28	1807.26	785.9%
K	II	69.12	732.79	960.2%
N	I	123.53	1031.71	735.2%
Totals/Average		784.86	7164.22	812.8%

*SLASH 4 is slower than IBM 370/168 by X%, based on IBM 370/168.
**Compiler used on IBM for this case was FORTRAN G1. All other
cases used FORTRAN H Extended on IBM with the maximum optimization level.

executing on the IBM machine were run in IBM single
precision. On the SLASH 4, although simple arithmetic
operations are always performed with a 39 bit mantissa,
the arithmetic support library offers either single
precision routines with a 24 bit mantissa accuracy, or
double precision routines with the full 39 bit mantissa
accuracy. It was determined that results produced by
Programs C and K would be improved by using 39 bit mantissa accuracy for all calculations. On the SLASH 4,
the change from single precision to double precision
arithmetic routines is a simple matter of selecting a
compile option, and so this was done. Since the floating point word on a Harris SLASH computer is always 48
bits, the resultant increase in memory requirements as
a result of selecting this double precision compile-

time option is very small and is caused by the slightly longer double precision arithmetic routines. The mechanism here is that the 24 bit mantissa accuracy in the single precision library routines is extended to the full 39 bit accuracy of the normal Harris SLASH series floating point word.

The programs were run in an overlay structure on the SLASH 4 because of their memory requirements. No overlay structure was used on the IBM machine. No attempt has been made to adjust execution times to account for non-overlaying on the IBM 370/168 and overlaying on the SLASH 4. Overlaying on the SLASH 4 is the difference between being able to obtain results or not being able to run at all for these programs. A fairer comparison of what is required in terms of CPU seconds for each of the computers results from not adjusting for such factors as non-overlay vs. overlay. It would be expected that overlay structures usually require more disc I/O operations and longer wall clock execution times, but have only a slight affect on actual CPU seconds.

Referring to Table I, it can be seen that the SLASH 4 runs only about 8 times slower than the IBM System/370 Model 168 on the average for the cases presented. Since the same FORTRAN Compiler was used for all cases on the SLASH 4, it is notable that the SLASH 4 runs only about 5 times slower than the IBM 370/168 when the FORTRAN G1 Compiler is used on the IBM machine. Alternatively, it would appear that the G1 Compiler generates much less efficient machine code than the H Extended Compiler. Worst case comparison points out that the difference between the SLASH 4 and IBM 370/168 is only a factor of 12.

The Effective Mix

Because the SLASH 4 compares favorably with the IBM 370/168, maximum use of the SLASH computer is employed since the cost per run is generally less than for the IBM machine, even though the run-times are longer by an average factor of 8 with the SLASH 4. Program development and initial checkout are conducted with the SLASH computers with a resultant lowering of program development. The Harris interactive alphanumeric editing package combined with the FORTRAN IV extended compiler running under control of the Harris Disc Monitor System (DMS) provide an excellent means for program development including program source editing and updating, program compiling for syntactical error correcting, and program execution for debugging and checkout purposes. Because the computer

utilization charging rates are considerably lower for
the smaller AARL computing system than most large mainframes, program development costs have been reduced
appreciably.

   While much of the calculations can be conducted
with the SLASH computers system, there are still a few
of the programs within the fluid mechanics library
which have excessive memory requirements and/or very
long run times. In these cases, each program is
optimized for which ever large mainframes produces the
best cost-performance. Usually, this requires minor
re-writing of the program code to provide the best
tradeoffs between execution speed and storage requirements. This involves taking advantage of hardware or
software features of the particular computer system on
which the program is being run. It has been found that
programs which do not suffer from numerical significance problems will show marked improvement in performance when fine-tuned for use on an IBM System/370
Model 168 as compared to a version for use on the
available CDC Cyber 73 machine and will result in a
lowered cost per run. These results stem directly from
the differences in word size employed for single precision arithmetic between the IBM 370/168 and the CDC
Cyber 73, and also from the performance differences
between the two mainframes.

   The large mainframe fine-tuning or optimization
process is most often applied to versions of programs
running on the IBM 370/168. The major optimization is
performed automatically by using the IBM FORTRAN H
Extended Compiler. The comparison cases reviewed
earlier demonstrated a significant performance increase
obtained by using H Extended instead of Gl. The extra
time and cost required for an H Extended compile step is
repaid, sometimes several times over, by the savings
obtained in the resultant execution. The H Extended
Compiler is routinely used for "production" versions of
programs and is even helpful during final stages of
program checkout by offering good diagnostics and a
cross reference capability. Minor rewriting of the
code is also performed to allow the compiler optimization process to be carried to the fullest possible extent. Increased execution efficiency results when
input/output operations are performed on variables
stored in contiguous storage locations, such as a
COMMON block. The number of separate COMMON blocks is
kept as small as possible and the variables ordered
such that the largest arrays occur last in the block.
This allows fewer base registers and less frequent base
register loads, improving performance. In general,

references to higher-dimensional arrays are slower than
references to lower-dimensional arrays. Thus use of
several one-dimensional arrays is more efficient than a
single two-dimensional array if the two-dimensional
array can logically be treated as a set of one-
dimensional arrays. The use of EQUIVALENCE statements
is avoided where possible since equivalenced variables
weaken the optimization processes. Finally, on IBM
machines, a logical IF statement will generate equivalent or better machine code than the corresponding
arithmetic IF statement for simple comparisons. These
considerations then form the basis for fine-tuning programs for an IBM machine.
     A philosophy has been developed and is being re-
fined for the routine use of interactive graphic display devices for the viewing of the numerical results.
The results of, say, a pressure distribution calculation
over a complex aerodynamic surface can be viewed more
effectively with graphic displays rather than in conventional tabular forms. Such review of the data
usually mandates that a minicomputer system be available; the general paucity of interactive graphics capability and the high cost of such graphic operations in
large central systems is well known to central system
users. The SLASH computers system outlined here includes a large drum plotter, a high speed storage type
CRT display with graphic capability, and several interactive terminals of either the teletype or alphanumeric
CRT variety. AARL is in the process of fully implementing a software system which can access data returning
from either a remote host site or from the in-house
SLASH computers. The mechanism here is that a dynamically created disc file on the SLASH computers system
is used to save the data, regardless of which machine
was used to generate the results. This file can then
be accessed by a post-processing program operating in
the minicomputer system for the purposes of previewing
the results, usually displayed in a plotted form, prior
to committing the data to hardcopy on the drum plotter.
This allows the researcher to have a closer interaction
with his program, which usually operates in a batch
environment because of its memory and/or run time requirements. If the previewed results indicate that perhaps the program input specifications should be modified, this can be done by editing the input parameters
at the interactive terminal and then resubmitting the
job to which ever machine (i.e., locally to the SLASH 4
or via RJE to the large mainframe) is being used for
the calculations. The operating system of the SLASH
computers allows any interactive terminal to submit jobs

to the local batch stream or to the RJE queue. By this "interactive batch" technique, the results from large scale computations can be stored, saved, previewed, and optionally committed to hard copy at a significant cost savings over that incurred by using only the capabilities of a large cenral system mainframe.

The SLASH Family and a SLASH 6 vs. SLASH 4 Comparison

The Harris family of computers began with the Datacraft 6024/1 processor announced in 1968. (Datacraft Corporation became a division of the Harris Corporation in 1974). The 6024/1 was a 600 nanosecond machine, an excellent processor for large scale computations. The 6024/3 (1 μsec.) followed in 1970, with the SLASH 5 (950 nsec.) coming in 1971, the SLASH 4 (750 nsec.) with virtual memory in 1973, and the SLASH 7 (400 nsec.) in 1975. Each new machine basically offered a central processor architecture similar to its predecessor while incorporating some available new technology and adding new features. The SLASH 6, announced in June 1976, is based on a completely different processor architecture, utilizing a microprogrammed asynchrounous CPU with a 48 bit central system bus structure. Addition SLASH 6 information appears in the Appendix A.

The earliest information about the Harris SLASH 6 processor indicated that perhaps it might be as much as 20% faster than the SLASH 4. As shown by Table II,

TABLE II

Harris SLASH 4 and Harris SLASH 6 Comparisons

Job Stream Identification	Job Time(sec) SLASH 4	Job Time(sec) SLASH 6	Percent Slower+
Job 1	80.591	85.008	5.481%
Job 2	15.450	16.157*	4.576%
Job 3	19.360	20.983	8.383%
Job 4	1174.862	1210.234	3.011%
Job 5	4.676	4.981	6.523%
Job 6	5.337	5.714	7.064%
Totals	1300.276	1343.077	3.292**

NOTE: All comparisons are for FORTRAN Compiler Version 24 except as indicated below.
  *Version 26 Compiler.
**Reflects mostly time of Job 4.
 +SLASH 6 is slower than SLASH 4 by X%, based on SLASH 4

this is clearly not the case as the SLASH 6 runs
slightly but consistently slower for all the jobs
listed in the table. The times shown are for the total
job time for identical jobs on the two SLASH computers.
The versions of the FORTRAN Compiler, Assembler, Cataloger, and support library were the same on the SLASH 6
as on the SLASH 4 with one exception as noted, and
compiler options were identical. The jobs reflected a
range from simple compile and catalog (JOB5, JOB6) to a
compile, catalog and execution of one of the airfoil
analysis codes (JOB4) requiring heavy floating point
operations.
       AARL has tested a single program on several com-
puters and the results are given in Table III. This

TABLE III

Comparisons of Several Computers for a Single Program

Computer Tested	Hardware Floating Pt. Available/Used	Word Size (Bits)	Execution Time (Seconds)
IBM 370/165	Yes/Yes	32	13.24
IBM 370/168	Yes/Yes	32	11.39
CDC 6400	Yes/Yes	60	68.43
CDC Cyber 73	Yes/Yes	60	52.28
DEC PDP-15	Yes/Yes	18	340*
GA SPC-16/65	No/No	16	970*
SLASH 1	Yes/No	24	146.65
SLASH 3	Yes/Yes	24	90**
SLASH 3	Yes/No	24	244**
SLASH 5	No/No	24	244.29
SLASH 4	Yes/Yes	24	60.11
SLASH 4	Yes/No	24	183.22
SLASH 6	Yes/Yes	24	64.75

NOTE: Time determined by timing subroutine unique for each
        machine, except as indicated below.

   *Timing mechanism unknown.
  **Timing determined by stop watch.

"benchmark" program was used in evaluating the candidate
computer systems for the first phase of the AARL Digital Computer and Data Acquisition System in 1973. More
recently, it has been run on the SLASH 4, the SLASH 6,
an IBM 370/168, and a CDC Cyber 73. While there is
always a question as to what any given single benchmark program actually tests, the speed of execution

indicates the efficiency of the instruction set and how well the compiler optimizes the coding. This FORTRAN program was constructed with no particular machine in mind, and it should not be used as an overall recommendation nor condemnation for any specific computer. The execution times listed are for the case solution time only, no compile time or link-edit time is included. The program has no required inputs and produces little printed output; it is therefore compute bound and the results reflect mostly compiler generated code efficiency and central processor speed differences.

Maintenance and Operating Costs

Both software and hardware maintenance on the dual SLASH processor system are done in-house. A computer technician devotes approximately 80% of full time to corrective and preventative maintenance and to the design of new device interfaces. A single system analyst spends approximately 50% of full time on software maintenance and development related to the overall system (i.e., cannot be related to a single research project). These efforts plus nominal cost of expendable supplies result in an average monthly maintenance and operating cost of approximately $1800. This cost appears to be relatively independent of the system size. That is, our operating costs did not change appreciably when the SLASH 4 processor subsystem was added.

The computer facility was financed by The Ohio State University. The capital equipment and implementation costs are being recovered with connect rate charges to all users. Since the system is used for data acquisition as well as straight numerical computations, wall-clock time accounting cannot be used. Instead, the concept of connect time is employed where users are charged if they are connected to the system. For example, a user who is connected to an A/D converter must be charged for use of the system, even though data acquisition is not in progress since his connection precludes use of that portion of the system by others.

The charging scheme is designed to recover the installation costs over a five year period. For the original SLASH 5 system this required an average recovery of $2000 per month at a connection rate charge of $45/hour. For the dual processor configuration, a recovery of $5200 per month is required with a connection rate charge of $76/hour. Over the last year, we have had little difficulty in meeting the scheduled cost recovery.

Conclusions

The AARL approach to complex numerical experimentation allows great flexibility in the choice of computer to conduct a set of specific calculations. The dial-up capability to other computing systems, combined with the in-house computing power available, has provided significant advantages over more conventional arrangements which employ either a large, single mainframe computer or a dedicated minicomputer system. In the dial-up mode of operation utilizing modems operating over standard telephone lines, the AARL computing system can interact with any host computing site which can support communications from a remote terminal. The SLASH computers used at AARL offer a cost-effective alternative to large scale machines for a large majority of the fluid mechanics calculations performed at AARL. The Harris SLASH 4 or the Harris SLASH 6 are well suited for the varied tasks of program development, "production" running, and Remote Job Entry communications with the large machines. While the approach described has been used for numerical experiments in fluid mechanics, it can be applied to any discipline requiring extensive numerical calculations.

Appendix A. The Digital Computer and Data Acquisition System.

The AARL Digital Computer and Data Acquisition System is an example of state-of-the-art techniques in the computer and electronics fields applied to experimentally and theoretically oriented research. The major components of the data acquisition and reduction portion of the system and the inter-relationships among the devices and the central processing units are shown schematically in Figure App-1 below. The system can be broken into four groups of components for descriptive purposes: (1) the analog front end consisting of various analog and signal conditioning devices; (2) the central processing units (CPU); (3) the various input and output peripheral devices (I/O devices) to handle assorted I/O functions associated with more typical computer systems; and (4) the Remote Job Entry (RJE) subsystem which enables communication with any remote host computer in a dial-up mode of operation.

The analog fron end serves to interface continuous analog signals to the data acquisition central processing unit in digital (discrete) form. Analog signals enter the central patch panel where they may be routed

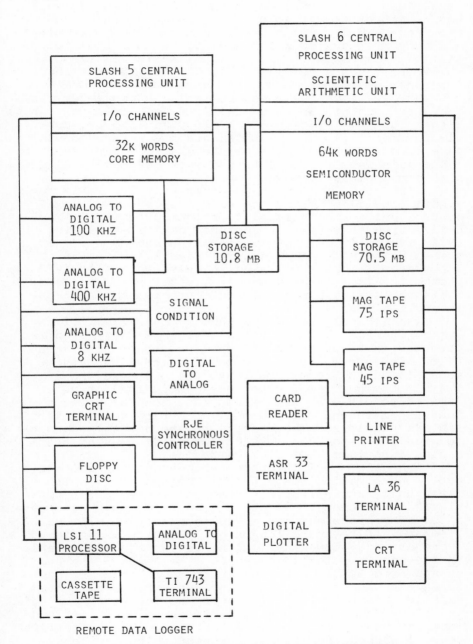

Figure 1. The AARL digital computer and data acquisition system

as desired to the various signal conditioning devices
and/or converters. Two analog-to-digital (A/D) converter systems are available: (1) a high speed multiplexed
A/D converter system which accepts up to 128 differential high-level inputs with a full scale voltage of
$\pm$ 10V, provides a resolution of 10 bits, has an input
impedance of 100 megohms, and has a throughput rate of
100 kHz; (2) a medium speed multiplexed converter system which accepts up to 64 differential low-level inputs
with a full scale voltage of $\pm$ 1000 millivolts, provides a resolution of 12 bits, and has a throughput
rate of 8 kHz. The latter system has 8 program-control-
lable gain ranges and is transformer coupled to allow
high common mode voltages.

Eight pre-amplifiers are currently available for
signal conditioning and ten bridge balance and span
control units are included to accommodate strain gage
bridge type sensors. A 5 channel digital-to-analog
(D/A) system is also available which can be used for
transmission of various control signals. Part of the
D/A system is presently used to drive an analog X-Y
plotter. Also included are 16 digital relay outputs,
8 discrete input switches, and a programmable 10 kHz
interval timing unit.

The AARL Digital Computer and Data Acquisition
System utilizes two central processing units which are
operated in a non-redundant dual processor configuration. One processor is assigned the on-line data
acquisition and reduction tasks while the second generally is assigned most other task including but not
limited to off-line data reduction, program development and maintenance, and heavy floating point scientific calculations. The processors are directly connected via a CPU-to-CPU link and in addition, they share
a disc cartridge mass storage device.

The data acquisition central processing unit is a
Harris Corporation SLASH 5 and consists of an arithmetic unit, control unit, interface elements for the
planar core memory, and the input-output channel interface. The processor has a 950 nanoseconds full cycle
time and a fixed word length of 24 bits plus parity.
There are over 120 generic instruction types available
at the assembly language level. The SLASH 5 operates
on and from 24 bit data and instruction words. The
SLASH 5 employs a multi-access bus structure, fully
parallel binary arithmetic, fully buffered I/0 channels,
and single address capability direct to 96 Kbytes and
indirect and/or indexed to 192 Kbytes. There are five
general purpose registers, three of which may be used
for indexing which is performed without a speed pen-

alty. Memory may be accessed at the word, double word, and byte levels. Memory size in this processor is 32,768 words (32K) and is expandable to 64K words.

The second central processing unit is a Harris Corporation SLASH 6, the newest member of the Harris SLASH Series family. The SLASH 6 offers total software compatibility with the SLASH 5 but offers a micro-programmed architecture asynchronous CPU with a central system bus structure. Other state-of-the-art SLASH 6 features include MOS memory with error correction, bi-polar microprocessor Arithmetic-Logic Unit (ALU), and microcode execution PROMS. The ALU is comprised of six high-speed microprocessor chips - each representing a 4 bit logic slice. The auxiliary PROMS are utilized for instruction decoding and subsequent microcode exe-cution - resulting in program and feature compatibility with the Harris SLASH 5 processor. Memory size in this processor is 65,536 words (64K) and is expandable to 256K words via a demand paging virtual memory option.

The input-output system, exclusive of the devices which comprise the analog front end, consists of the following peripheral devices: (1) a removable pack disc system with 70.5 megabytes formatted capacity and a 342.7 kHz transfer rate; (2) a cartridge disc system including one fixed disc platter and one removable disc cartridge each with a 5.4 megabytes formatted capacity and a 89.5 kHz transfer rate; (3) a dual density 800/1600 bits/inch 9 track industry compatible magnetic tape drive with a nominal tape speed of 75 inches/second and vacuum column tape handling; (4) an 800 bits/inch 9 track magnetic tape drive with a nominal tape speed of 45 inches/second; (5) a 300 cards/minute card reader; (6) a 135 characters/line, 400 lines/minute line printer; (7) an ASR-33 standard teletype with paper tape facilities; (8) a Tektronix 4010 cath-ode ray tube (CRT) operating over an asynchronous in-terface at a 9600 baud rate providing graphic as well as alphanumeric display capabilities; and (9) a four pen 36 inch drum type plotter offering 0.0025 inch re-solution and drawing speeds of up to 8 inches/second on a major axis.

The Remote Job Entry (RJE) subsystem, which is shown schematically in Figure App-2, supports communi-cation with a remote host computer. Such communica-tions are carried out concurrently with other computer tasks including real-time data acquisition and reduc-tion. Included in the RJE subsystem are: (1) a syn-chronous controller with baud rate to 9600 bits/second; (2) a Bell system compatible modem with dial-up tele-phone dataset; and (3) a CRT display device providing 24 lines with 80 characters/line of display.

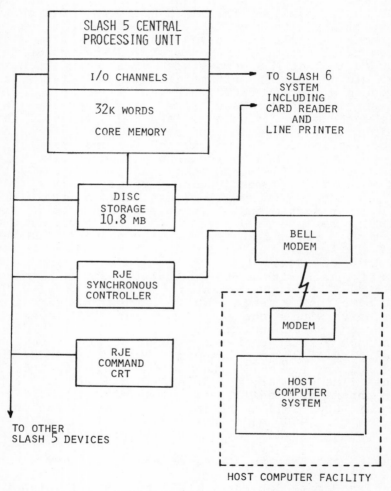

Figure 2. Remote job entry subsystem of AARL digital computer and data acquisition system

The CRT is used for RJE operator communications but may be utilized in an interactive fashion when RJE is not in progress. The card reader and line printer are used to support RJE activities as needed. The RJE subsystem can operate under three disciplines:
* CDC UT-200 for the 6000/7000 series
* IBM 2780/3780 for the System 360/370 series
* UNIVAC 1004 for the 1100 series

Each processor in the AARL Digital Computer and Data Acquisition System is under the control of the Harris Series 6000 Disc Monitor System (DMS). DMS is a real-time operating system that provides foreground multiprogramming concurrent with sequential batch processing in the background. The foreground is designed for application-related programs which could control a wind tunnel, process real-time data from an acoustic experiment, or interact with multiple terminal users in either a local or remote fashion. These programs receive highest priority and their requirements are met first. Batch processing is conducted in the background and is never time-critical so that background is serviced when processor time and memory space are available. Salient features of the DMS are:
* Dynamic loading of foreground programs
* Dynamic memory allocation services
* Dynamic spooled I/O for any list output device
* Optional spooled job stream input from any input device
* Full file security for every user including read, write and delete protection modes with optional password
* Re-entrant foreground program capabilities
* Program priority structure that governs the allocation of memory, disc files, and processor time; 255 priority levels
* Time slicing among programs executing at the same priority
* Program communications via a special Common area, initiation parameter passing, or a program switch word
* Timer scheduling of periodic foreground programs
* Automatic checkpointing and reloading of the background memory area as required by activation of non-resident foreground programs
* Re-entrant editor package for terminal users
* Complete memory protection of all inactive programs from currently active programs
* Concise job control language for batch processing

* Complete operator control over the system environment via the console typewriter or CRT
* System file manager that maintains program and data files in source and object formats
* FORTRAN IV interface routines for foreground services
* Sequential, indexed sequential, and direct random access methods for data files on disc
* Optional automatic disc file compression and blocking
* Overlay Link Cataloger that prepares and stores programs on disc in a format designed for rapid loading and relocation
* RJE subsystem protocol interpreter which performs most of the normal operator functions automatically but does not require a dedicated terminal

The computer system is operated in an "open-shop" mode. All users have full access at both the hardware and software levels to the majority of the features of the system. The computer system is used extensively in on-line, real-time, interactive data acquisition and reduction.

Literature Cited

1. Robinson, A. L.: "Computational Chemistry: Getting More from a Minicomputer", Science, (1976), 193, pp. 470-472.
2. Schaeffer, H. F.: "Are Minicomputers Suitable for Large Scale Scientific Computation?", paper presented to 11th Annual IEEE Computer Society Conference, Washington, D. C., September 1975.
3. Petrie, S. L.: "Design of a Digital Data Acquisition System", paper presented to the 39th Semi-Annual Meeting of the Supersonic Tunnel Association, Bethesda, Maryland, March 1973. (Referenced by author's permission).
4. Freuler, R. J.: "State of the Art Data Acquisition and Reduction Techniques for Transonic Airfoil Testing", paper presented to 6th International Congress on Instrumentation in Aerodynamic Simulation Facilities (ICIASF), Ottawa, September 1975.

INDEX

INDEX

237